HAN

People of the River

HAN

People of the River

Hän Hwëch'in

An Ethnography and Ethnohistory

Craig Mishler and William E. Simeone

University of Alaska Press, Fairbanks

© 2004 Native Village of Eagle and Tr'ondëk Hwëch'in First Nation

University of Alaska Press
PO Box 756240
Fairbanks, AK 99775-6240
888.252.6657
fypress@uaf.edu
www.uaf.edu/uapress

paperback ISBN 1-889963-41-0
hardback ISBN 1-889963-40-2

Library of Congress Cataloging-in-Publication Data

Mishler, Craig.
Han, people of the river : Han Hwech'in : an ethnography and ethnohistory/
Craig Mishler and William E. Simeone.
p. cm.
ISBN 1-889963-40-2 (cloth: alk. paper) – ISBN 1-889963-41-0 (pbk.: alk. paper)
1. Han Indians–History. 2. Han Indians–Folklore. 3. Han
Indians–Social life and customs. 4. Yukon Territory–History. 5.
Yukon Territory–Social life and customs. I. Simeone, William E. II. Title.

E99.H26 M57 2004
971.91004'972–dc21
2003003862

Cover and text design by
Hal Gage, Gage Photo Graphics
Anchorage, Alaska

This paper meets the requirements of ANSI/NISO Z39.48-1992 (Permanence of Paper).

Printed in the United States

Contents

Contents

Contents

Illustrations

Maps

Table

Plates

Illustrations

Figures

Illustrations

Dedication

We want to dedicate this book to all of those who are memorialized in its pages, especially our elders. Because of it, we feel more open to reviving our traditions and culture, and we are very happy that these stories will now be passed on to future generations. We are especially grateful to Craig, Bill and the Department of Fish and Game for working with us to write this book and to Cyd Martin and the National Park Service for supporting it. Please excuse any names that may have been misspelled or left out.

Joanne Beck, Chief
Eagle Village

Preface

It was still dark when all hands were awakened, the stars were shining brightly, the white aurora flashed feebly in the northern sky, the black domes of the village were dimly outlined against the snow and the black wall of spruce, and a few sparks and thin smoke were rising from the early fires. —Tappan Adney (1900)

THE UPPER Yukon River basin is one of the wildest and most beautiful places on earth. It is also one of the coldest. The Han Indians who have traveled this country as hunters and gatherers for hundreds and perhaps thousands of years have developed survival skills that exemplify their intelligence and toughness. Today they continue to form an integral part of the northern boreal forest, which topographically is mountainous and riparian, with just a few small lakes. The Han try to live, as their ancestors did, off the country, eating hares, ducks, moose, caribou, several species of fish, and berries. Once spread out over hundreds of miles along the Yukon and its tributaries, they are now largely consolidated into two communities: Eagle Village, Alaska, and Dawson City, Yukon.

The Han are not only an ethnic and linguistic group, but a community of individuals, and we have attempted to write about them as people who spoke to us and touched us in a special way. Our ethnography, then, is a patchwork quilt pieced together from past and present lives and a chorus of voices. Several elders who first taught us about the Han have left us now, but this book provides both a professional and a personal way of remembering them and what they lived through. Our research of historical particulars can never be complete but must eventually find an end, and we have been surprised at how many revisions this book has undergone as a result of the emergence of new sources. No matter how well we document, there is always some mystery left in history.

We have tried, as much as possible, not to repeat material found in Cornelius Osgood's seminal ethnography, *The Han Indians*, published in 1971, even though we cover many of the same topics and make numerous references to it. Osgood, who did his fieldwork among the Han in the summer of 1932, was able to supplement his observations and interviews with those of the anthropologist Richard Slobodin, who visited the Han in Dawson in 1962. As a young graduate student, Robert Jarvenpa spent the summer of 1970 working in Dawson and Eagle Village, but to our knowledge, no sustained focused ethnographic fieldwork has been done among the Han since then, except our own.

We have been lucky to find additional sources on the Han in Anglican and Episcopal missionary records that were not available to Osgood, allowing us to fill in many more details in Han history. We have also had access to a substantial number of oral interviews with Han elders done by ourselves and others in the 1970s, 1980s, and 1990s. Through archival research we have come across a wealth of old photographs, most of which have never before been published. Our research methodology is outlined in Appendix A.

Introduction

Purpose

THIS BOOK, envisioned as both an ethnography and an ethnohistory, was commissioned to the Alaska Department of Fish and Game by the National Park Service, Alaska Region, to recognize and honor the indigenous Han Indians of the upper Yukon River valley. The Charley River, Charley Creek, and Charley Village were all named after Chief Charley, and the Yukon-Charley Rivers National Preserve, created by the U.S. Congress through the Alaska National Interest Lands Conservation Act of 1980, was in turn named after the Charley River. Therefore, to help evaluate and interpret the preserve, it is essential to compile a short life history of Chief Charley and to know something of the many Han Indians who inhabited and used the land before it ever was a preserve. But since the Han homeland is much larger than the 2.5-million acre preserve and reaches well into the Yukon Territory, it makes good sense to write about all of it, rather than just a piece.

Language and Identity

The word Hän signifies "river" in the Hän language, and the dialect terms *Hän Hwëch'in*, *Hän Huch'in*, or *Hän Gwich'in* all translate into English as "River People." What fundamentally distinguishes the Han from neighboring groups of interior Native Athabaskans (Map 1) is their language and the Han homeland (Map 2), which is largely defined by the mountains, creeks, rivers, and lakes named by this language (see Plates 1–3). As in Europe and many other parts of the world, political boundaries are often synonymous with linguistic ones. A preliminary map of Han place names, which unfortunately could not be included here, has been developed by John Ritter of the Yukon Native Language Centre in Whitehorse.

Map 1
Northern Athabaskan Groups

The Hän language, which has fewer than a dozen fluent speakers left, is truly endangered, although there is a sincere effort underway in the Yukon to document and teach it. Hän is characterized by many sounds not normally found in English, such as glottal stops (shown as '), voiceless l's (written as ł), and vowels which may be short or long, nasalized or tonal.

Map 2
The Han Homeland

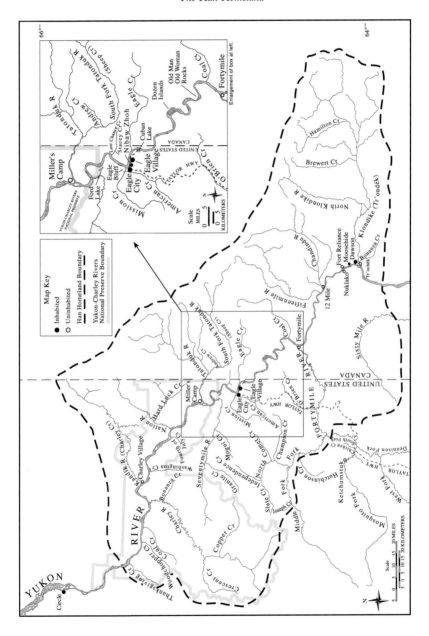

For example, Hän has one unmarked *a* which sounds like the *a* in the English word mad, and another *ä* which resembles the *a* in the English word father. It is our practice to write Hän when using or referring to the language and Han when referring to the people, but in both cases the pronunciation remains the same, conforming to the *a* in father.

Hän is a member of the Athabaskan or Na-Dene language family, which includes Eyak and Tlingit, and is partially intelligible to speakers of Gwich'in Athabaskan, but it is nevertheless a distinct language and not just a dialect. Hän phonology and the Hän writing system are briefly described by Michael Krauss in his introduction to Ruth Ridley's book, *Eagle Han Huch'inn Hòdök* (1983:7–8). Since that book was published, however, linguistic conventions for the orthography have been simplified, eliminating the need for double consonants. *Huch'inn*, for example, is now written as *Huch'in* in the Eagle Village dialect, and the name for the old village site of Nibaww Zhoo is now written as Nibaw Zhoo. Readers should be aware that some slight differences between the Dawson and Eagle Village dialects of Hän result in spelling variants.

Separation and Fragmentation

Almost 130 years ago, through historical accident and outsiders' indifference to Han needs and desires, the Han, like their Athabaskan neighbors the Gwich'in and the Upper Tanana, were divided in half as they became overpowered by Canada and the United States. Han chiefs were never consulted about this division.

The 141st meridian became the boundary line between British North America and Russian America in 1825, and this division was maintained when Russia sold Alaska to the United States in 1867. Following the sale, the Hudson's Bay Company was forced to relocate at Rampart House on the Porcupine River in Canada, and the Han, who for numerous reasons were averse to trading with the Americans, had to travel a greater distance overland to the Porcupine River to sell their fur and obtain trade goods.[1] This situation lasted for at least ten years, until the mid-1870s, when the Alaska Commercial Company built their trading post at Fort Reliance (see Chapters 1 and 4).

As a result of the gold rush that followed in the 1880s and 1890s, the international border was reaffirmed by boundary surveys in 1891 and again in 1911. Obstacles created by the border have gradually fractured the Han nation. In recent years, for example, the Canadian Han have enjoyed far better subsistence hunting and fishing rights than their Alaskan counterparts.

As one of the smallest of all the northern Dene tribal groups, the Han seem to have suffered far more from this international boundary separation than their neighbors, the Gwich'in and the Upper Tanana. Not only were the Han separated from one another by the border, they were also separated from their ancestral lands and villages by the influx of stampeders to the Fortymile River, the Klondike, and Alaska between 1886 and 1898. Today the celebrated name "Klondike" signifies and embodies the adventure and excitement of the gold rush, but as elder Percy Henry tells us, the river's English name was appropriated from the Han word *Tł'oondëk*, which simply means "grassy banks river" or "water flowing through grass."

Social Change

The history of the upper Yukon valley, from the earliest contact with the Han in the 1840s, until our own visits in the 1970s, 1980s, and 1990s, has been a time of continuous change, almost all of it initiated by outsiders. These changes began gradually, with encounters between Native people and fur traders interested in bartering guns, knives, clothing, beads, and other manufactured goods for furs. Dramatic, and often traumatic, change came with the discovery of gold in the late-nineteenth century. Mineral development brought an influx of people who had little or no interest in Native people but an intense interest in occupying, developing, and owning the land. Interspersed among the traders and prospectors were Christian missionaries from various denominations who attempted to the convert the Han and reform their lives to fit a pattern more acceptable to whites.

It is important to recognize that there are many different perspectives on history. The written history of the North is based on the accounts of English-speaking explorers, traders, missionaries, and travelers who were all strangers in a strange land. They viewed the upper Yukon valley as virgin territory, to be explored, mapped, and exploited for furs, gold, and souls. As a result, their accounts create a history essentially different from a Native history based on oral narratives told by people who were living at home. For Native people the upper Yukon valley, including every hill, mountain, creek, lake, and island, is a familiar land filled with ancestral memories.

The narrative we present here reflects our concern with arranging and reconstructing history in a chronological order based on a linear perspective of time. Native oral histories are less concerned with time than with place, and we have made a special effort to record and include some of these testimonies. Both Native and non-Native histories offer useful descriptions and interpretations of the past which help explain the present. Both are subject to revision based on changes in social circumstances and new evidence.

The gold rush was a complex, monumental event in Han history as well as in the history of Alaska and the Yukon Territory. In the popular imagination it exemplifies the taming of the wilderness, the wild, buoyant spirit of life on the last frontier, and the American dream of quick riches. Every few years it seems there is another excuse to display the gold rush and celebrate it, often for the sole economic purpose of attracting more tourists.

However, from the Han perspective and from the authors' perspective, the gold rush has been unduly romanticized. It created a socially stratified society with the Han at the bottom. As 30,000 stampeders ran roughshod over the ecologically fragile environment, decimating the timber and wild fish and game resources, the Han were forced to move out of their ancestral villages. In doing so they became dependent on the charity and protection of Anglican and Episcopal churches. Almost overnight, the Han became homeless in their own homeland.

And the scars on the land remain. Anyone visiting the Klondike River valley today will be appalled by the miles and miles of ugly dredge tailings, bulldozed gravel, and rusting machinery which border the river and its tributary creeks. Throughout these pages, we return again and again to the theme of dislocation of the Han and the stressful disruption of Han culture due to changes forced on them by Euro-Americans and Euro-Canadians. Herein lies the tale.

Viewed in the context of global history, what happened to the Han is not some anachronistic, isolated phenomenon. It is part of a well-established historical pattern. The Han experienced much of what the Calfornia Indians experienced after the gold rush of 1849 and what the Yanomamö Indians of Venezuela and Brazil are facing from gold miners of the present day, as many square miles of tropical rainforest wildlife habitat are being cut down to build roads and erect new mining camps. These same ruthless capitalist forces have been at work to subjugate and displace indigenous peoples for hundreds of years.

Nevertheless, to simply view the Han as helpless victims is to deprive them of a role in shaping their own history. When necessary the Han have acquiesced to the demands placed on them by the dominant society. But the Han have adapted and have survived tenaciously against all odds. They have sought to change their predicament through land claims agreements and have turned to reviving and reinventing many of their traditions. Starting in the 1990s, Han gatherings and culture camps have built a new social solidarity. The Han are relearning their songs and dances, are attempting to reinvigorate their language, and are actively documenting their own history. As anthropologists who believe that a healthy measure of Han identity and pride can be found in learning Han ethnohistory, we hope this book becomes a symbolic, supportive part of that revival.

Acknowledgments

We are especially grateful to the National Park Service for providing us with an opportunity to research and write this book. For hospitality we want to acknowledge the support of the Park Service staff, who supplied us with all the necessary things to stay clean, warm, and dry. It is not often that we find tent frames furnished with electricity and cook stoves. In Eagle City, Kevin Fox, Pat Sanders, and Linda Mott all did their best to make us feel comfortable. In Fairbanks, Cyd Martin of the National Park Service ably guided us over many administrative hurdles and helped negotiate the publication of this manuscript. She also gave up precious time to secure our many photo permissions and credits and often acted on our behalf in working with the University of Alaska Press. Without Cyd's advocacy, this book would never have happened.

There are a multitude of people who contributed cosmic energy to this book, including virtually the entire population of Eagle Village. On kinship and family trees we are especially indebted to Howard David, Edward David, Richard Silas, Ruth Ridley, Benny Juneby, Adeline Juneby Potts, Angela Harper, Silas Stevens, Bertha Ulvi, Oliver Lyman, Martha Malcolm, Joe Joseph, Joanne Beck, Ethel Beck, and Louise Paul. Adeline Juneby Potts also supplied us with the bilingual title to the book and capably translated her father Willie Juneby's legend of the Indian wars.

At Moosehide, Debbie Nagano fed us, made us feel welcome, and opened a lot of doors. In Dawson, Michael Mason generously shared with us his notes and photos of his family at Twelve Mile. Were it not for Michael, we might never have known about this important village.

For in-depth oral interviews, we wish to thank Silas Stevens, Joanne Beck, Ruth Ridley, Tim Malcolm, Martha Malcolm, Isaac Juneby, Max Beck, Bill Goebel, and Angela Harper on the Alaskan side, and Debbie Nagano, Angie Joseph-Rear, Percy Henry, and Martha Roberts Kates on the Yukon side. There is no substitute for face-to-face personal communication, for this is the way we make friends.

Our boat drivers gave us the greatest feeling for the wild beauty of the Han homeland. We thank Victor Henry, Tim Malcolm, and Scarlet Hall for showing us the smooth circling waters and majestic bluffs of the upper Yukon River valley.

For assistance in library and archival research we cannot say enough for the services provided by Linda Johnson, Peggy D'Orsay, and other staff at the Yukon Archives in Whitehorse; by Diane Brenner at the Anchorage Museum of History and Art; by India Spartz and her staff at the Alaska State Library, Alaska Historical Collections; by Jane Ward, curator of manuscripts at the Essex Peabody Museum in Salem, Massachusetts; by Tess Powter, Moriah Whitley, and John Richthammer, archivists at the Dawson City Museum; by Elva Scott at the Eagle Historical Society, and by the many volunteers at the Eagle Public Library.

The authors are also greatly indebted to Tom Alton of the Alaska Native Language Center for constructive copyedits and to Kenneth Frank of Arctic Village for assistance with Han family trees. Our computer cartographer, Carol Belenski at the U.S. Bureau of Land Management in Anchorage, merits special recognition for her patience and good cheer as we edited drafts of the fine maps she prepared. We also want to thank two photographers, Charles Backus and Dan Sidle, who supplied us with outstanding portraits of people in Eagle Village. Add a kindly tip of the hat to Robert Jarvenpa, who helped us on family trees, and to Jennifer Collier at the University of Alaska Press.

We extend our deepest appreciation to the unflagging support provided by the Alaska Department of Fish and Game, Division of Subsistence. Elizabeth Andrews contributed by locating photographs and reading early drafts of the manuscript. Terry Haynes was largely responsible for compiling the chronology and helping us see the entire timeline. James Fall also reviewed the manuscript and smoothed the way administratively for us to sequester ourselves and get the writing done.

We are also much obliged to other individuals who reviewed the manuscript and offered numerous constructive comments for its improvement. These were Joanne Beck, Georgette McLeod, Adeline Juneby Potts, Jody

Potts, Karma Ulvi, Isaac Juneby, Catharine McClellan, Judy Thompson, and Tim Cochrane.

Distinguished Elders

Although we have worked with many of the Han over the years, the following five elders provided us with a wealth of information in focused interviews that we have been able to draw upon frequently in the chapters that follow. They are pictured in Plates 4 through 9.

Silas Stevens

Born in 1926 and raised in Eagle Village and the surrounding area, Silas spent much of his adult life away at school in Eklutna, serving in the Army, and working for the Alaska Railroad and the Alaska Road Commission. Like his father before him, he is a veteran of the steamboat era, having worked during his youth as a mess boy on the steamboats *Yukon* and *Nenana*. He has five children from his late wife, Mary Ann Juneby, and was formerly married to Ethel Beck. Now residing in Fairbanks, Silas is an excellent and cheerful source of historical knowledge about the Han and still visits the village frequently. He serves on the Board of Directors of the Hungwitchin Corporation.

Percy Henry

Percy Henry, the eldest son of Joe and Annie Henry, originally came from the Blackstone River country but later moved to Moosehide with his parents in the mid-1930s. The Henrys moved to Moosehide so that their children could attend school there. By blood, Percy is *Teetl'it* and *Takudh Gwich'in*, but he grew up speaking the Hän language, which he learned from his childhood peers.

Born in 1927, Percy never spent much time in school. As he likes to say, "The land is my university." At age sixteen he set off into the Ogilvie Mountains with his father to become a trapper. Unfortunately, he lost his dog team and froze his lungs, so he decided to try a different profession. From 1940–1941 Percy helped run a fish trap near the old village site at Tr'ochëk, where the Klondike River flows into the Yukon River. He then worked in a sawmill in Mayo for nine years and crewed on the steamboat *Klondike* for three seasons during World War II. He married his wife Mabel in the late 1950s and together they have had seven children.

For twenty summers, between 1952 and 1972, Percy was the captain of a motorized riverboat called *The Brainstorm* which barged freight from Dawson to Old Crow. After that he captained the car ferry across the Yukon River at Dawson for sixteen years, retiring in 1988. At the same time he was working these jobs, he served as the soft-spoken chief of the Tr'ondëk Hwëch'in First Nation in Dawson, an elective office he held almost continuously from 1969 until 1984. During his tenure as chief, Percy was instrumental in pursuing First Nation land claims with the Canadian federal government.

In recent years Percy has received many awards. In October 1999, he was ordained Reverend Deacon Percy Henry by Bishop Terry Buckle of the Anglican Church. In March, 2000, Percy was given the Heritage Award for Lifetime Achievement by the Yukon Historical and Museum Association, recognizing his efforts to preserve the Hän language. And in December, 2001, Percy was the recipient of the first-ever Conservation Award presented by the Yukon Fish and Wildlife Management Board.

Percy's wife Mabel teaches Hän at the Robert Service School in Dawson, and the two together have produced a Hän language lesson booklet and cassette tape for the Yukon Native Language Centre. Percy also remains active as an elder with Council of Yukon First Nations.

Sarah Malcolm

With her wide high-waisted skirt, large cheekbones, and hair wrapped in a cloth or silk kerchief, Sarah Malcolm had a striking appearance. When we interviewed her in the summer of 1975, she spoke in a slow and distinctive nonstandard dialect of English, her second language. At this time she was living alone in Eagle Village but was visited daily by her children and grandchildren.

Born in 1905 to Phoebe and Caribou Steve (also known as Little Stephen), Sarah Stevens spent virtually all of her early life following a seasonal round of hunting, trapping, and fishing on Sheep Creek (the South Fork of the Tatonduk River), Shade Creek, and other tributaries of the Yukon River near Eagle. Then in 1920, at age fifteen, she married Edward Malcolm, a Gwich'in man from the Peel River, and had eleven children by him. Her exquisite spruce root and birchbark basketry, her beadwork, and her clothing are now showcased in several Alaskan museums. A woman of many talents, she was also well versed in traditional Han stories. Sarah died in 1991.

Introduction

Matthew Malcolm

The son of Sarah and Joe Malcolm, Matthew was born in 1926 and served in World War II. After the war he drove heavy equipment and helped build the Taylor Highway connecting Eagle with Anchorage and Fairbanks. Over the years he has undergone several surgeries on his eyes, but these have not prevented him from gradually losing all of his sight. Operating the only subsistence salmon set net in Eagle Village in 1997, Matthew provided us with a prime opportunity to witness subsistence fishing as a productive daily work activity. Matthew generously shared his time and his fish with us and let us take lots of photographs and videotape of his boat, setnet site, and fish camp. Matthew's hard work is an inspiration to everybody.

Willie Juneby

Willie spent much of his life as a trapper, freighter, catskinner, and miner. A fluent speaker of Hän, he was also a noted storyteller and a musician, one who introduced us to Han fiddle music and dance. Willie was born in Eagle Village on December 14, 1912, the youngest of five children born to Sarah Peter (see cover photo) and Big Jim Juneby. His parents previously lived at Fortymile and Charley Creek (the Kandik River). His mother first came to Eagle when the soldiers arrived at Fort Egbert in 1899.

Willie's father was appointed deputy U.S. Marshal for both the village and the city of Eagle and was also a layreader for the Episcopal Church, but died in 1915 when Willie was only three years old. Willie's mother's father, Old Peter, taught him to set snares for hare and ptarmigan.

At the age of fourteen, Willie had to leave school to hunt for his mother. A year later, in the summer of 1927, Willie was hired as a deckhand on the steamboat *Yukon*, where he worked with other Eagle Village men such as Arthur Stevens, Susie Paul, and Susie Paul's father, Porcupine Paul Josie, who were seasoned veterans.

In the winter of 1928–1929 he started trapping on Hard Luck Creek, a tributary of the Nation River, with his future father-in-law, Andrew Silas. The next winter he and Arthur Stevens went to Slate Creek to trap marten, and in 1933 he stayed and trapped at a cabin on Gold Run Creek, a tributary to Slate Creek, which runs into the North Fork of the Fortymile River. It was about this time that he began to play guitar and fiddle.

In 1935 he met and married Louise Silas of Moosehide, Yukon Territory. Later that year Louise bore him the first of their eleven children. The Junebys then moved to Miller's Camp, located at the mouth of Sheep Creek (the Tatonduk River) where Willie went to work for Heinie Miller, a contractor who supplied the Yukon River steamboats with firewood (see Chapter 3).

In 1938 Willie went to work on Ernest Patty's gold dredge on Coal Creek and stayed there with his family each summer through 1942. Then in the winter he would go back to hauling wood for Heinie Miller at Sheep Creek. Later on Willie moved his family to Woodchopper Creek, where there was another dredge operation.

The federal government closed down the dredges at Coal Creek and Woodchopper in 1942, declaring gold mining nonessential to the war, so Willie went to Fairbanks and worked in a sawmill. During the last part of World War II Willie again drove a Cat and helped build the Richardson Highway. After the war he went back to work for Dr. Patty at Coal Creek, putting in nearly thirty years of summer work there.

The Junebys moved back upriver in 1952 and in 1953 the Eagle Village school reopened. Willie built a new log cabin in Eagle Village in 1954, and he and Louise raised eight of their eleven children there. This was the same year that the last working steamboat on the upper Yukon River, the S.S. *Nenana*, was removed from service.

Willie worked on the construction of the Trans-Alaska oil pipeline from 1974–1977, but at the age of sixty-five he retired to his cabin in Eagle Village. Willie died in January 1981, three days after slipping on an icy road and injuring his head. He is best remembered for his warm hospitality to friends and strangers and his fine old-time fiddling. Louise, his wife of forty-six years, passed away at a Fairbanks nursing home in July 1985.

Louise Paul

Louise Paul was a special friend and elder who told us a lot of what we know about Han life in the early-twentieth century. She was one of the last of the traditional Han storytellers still fluent in her language, and she gave us everything she could.

Born on July 10, 1921, in Moosehide, Louise was the daughter of Joe and Eliza Malcolm, a Gwich'in couple originally from the upper Porcupine River and Peel River area. Her father worked on the steamboats, hauling freight and loading wood, and her mother Eliza (Figure

53) had the distinction of being one of the last speakers of Takudh Gwich'in, a dialect spoken on the upper Porcupine River. Louise had one full brother and one full sister, who both died young. She also had nine stepbrothers and stepsisters from her mother's first marriage. Her parents raised her in a tent on a trapline and brought her to Eagle Village for the first time to attend school during the late 1920s, but she only attended through the elementary grades. Since her mother Eliza could understand but not speak Hän, Louise apparently learned to speak Hän from her childhood peers.

Louise married at a very young age in the mid-1930s, very much against her parents' wishes, because she did not want to return to Canada. Her husband Susie Paul came from Canada to Eagle Village and met her there. Susie, who was thirteen years her senior, worked on the gold dredges at Coal Creek and Woodchopper Creek, and the couple raised most of their seven children there. Like many Athabaskan women, Louise was an avid moose hunter and did her share of providing meat to feed her large family. The Pauls first moved to Snare Creek, a tributary of Coal Creek, in 1944, and lived near the Juneby and David families.

Later on they also spent some time on Iron Creek, a tributary of Woodchopper Creek, where there was another dredge. It was at Woodchopper about 1951 that they had a very close call with a grizzly bear (*shar choh*) which tried to break into their cabin. One of Louise's longest stories, not included here, describes this scary experience. After returning to Eagle Village during the early 1950s, Louise spent many years working as the cook at the Eagle Village school. In later years her widowed mother came to stay with her in Eagle. During the 1980s Louise served as a board member of Denakkanaaga, Inc., the non-profit association of Athabaskan village elders.

Craig first met Louise and began to record her stories in Eagle Village in 1973. It was not until the current project started in the spring of 1997 that he resumed working with her while she was living in an apartment in Fairbanks. After a lengthy illness that spanned several years, Louise passed away during the last week of June 1997, while this book was being researched and written. One of her last wishes was to be brought back to Eagle Village to die, and right after that happened, a bright rainbow suddenly came across the Yukon River. The whole family, which had gathered around her, accepted this rainbow as God's way of calling her.

Notes

1. See William Ogilvie, *Exploratory Survey of the Part of the Lewes, Tat-on-duc, Porcupine, Bell, Trout, Peel, and Mackenzie Rivers, 1887–88.* Annual Report for the Dept. of Interior 1889, Part VIII, Section 3. (Ottawa: B. Chamberlin, 1890), 48; and Melody Webb, *The Last Frontier: A History of the Yukon Basin of Canada and Alaska.* (Albuquerque: University of New Mexico Press, 1985), 58. Of special interest is a statement from Constable Constantine of the Royal Canadian Mounted Police attributed to Chief Charley: "I am quite happy and contented and would like to see the English come and take care of the country. I like the English better than the Americans," in Kenneth Coates, *Best Left as Indians Best Left Indians: Native-White Relations in the Yukon Territory, 1840–1973* (Montreal & Kingston: McGill-Queen's University Press, 1991), 162.

Plate 1. Tthee Täwdlenn *(Eagle Bluff) and Yukon River, August 1973.*

Plate 2. Looking upriver towards Eagle Village from the Yukon River bluffs, December 25, 1973.

Plate 3. Yukon River bluffs looking across from Eagle Village, with Eagle Creek off in the distance, August 1973.

Plate 4. Silas Stevens, Fairbanks, April 1997.

Plate 5. Chief Percy Henry visiting Talkeetna, October 10, 1999.

Plate 6. Sarah Malcolm, near Eagle Village, early 1980s.

Plate 7. Matthew Malcolm, July 1997.

Plate 8. Willie Juneby playing his fiddle, December 1973.

Plate 9. Louise Paul, Fairbanks, March 1997.

HAN

People of the River

Hän Hwëch'in

Furs, Missionaries, Gold, and Disease

THE HISTORY of the nineteenth century and early twentieth century in the upper Yukon valley can be divided into three stages. At each stage the Han became progressively more involved in an economy that linked them to the outside world. Before 1840, the Han lived off the land and received only a trickle of European-manufactured goods, which arrived indirectly through an extensive network of aboriginal traders.

The second stage began with the building of forts and the opening the fur trade in the 1840s, when manufactured goods became more widely available, when direct contact with Euro-Canadians and Euro-Americans increased, and an era of rapid material acculturation began. Finally, during the third stage, the arrival of missionaries in the middle of the century and the influx of gold miners beginning in 1886 totally transformed the Han universe. Like the Indians of California after the gold rush of 1849, the Han faced a major crisis in trying to protect their culture, their religion, their language, their population, and their subsistence way of life.

The Early Fur Trade

One result of the Han's involvement in the fur trade was that by the end of the nineteenth century they had developed a delicate balance between dependence and autonomy. That is, the Han had become dependent on the fur trade to provide them with manufactured goods such as metal knives, pots and pans, guns, beads, and cloth, while at the same time they continued to live off the country, supporting themselves by hunting, fishing, and gathering. Throughout the first half of the twentieth century, commercial trapping continued to be an important part of the Han economy and culture. Today, with a declining market in furs, hardly any Han continue to trap.

Before the arrival of Euro-Canadians and Anglo-Americans, the Han traded with other Native people who lived in different ecological zones and had access to different kinds of resources. One end of the aboriginal exchange network originated with Chilkat Tlingit who bartered maritime products—such as rendered sea mammal fat, fish oils, and dentalium shells—with Tutchone Athabaskans who provided the Tlingit with inland products such as furs, tanned caribou skins, and copper. The Tutchone, in turn, bartered coastal products with their Han neighbors for furs and red ocher.[1] In addition, the Han traded with other Athabaskan groups living to their north, such as the Gwich'in, who had access to maritime products from Inuit living on the Arctic coastal plain and near the mouth of the MacKenzie River.[2]

In the late eighteenth century, European manufactured goods and tobacco were introduced into the aboriginal trade system when Russian and English trading companies began operating along shores of the Gulf of Alaska. These goods intensified the Native fur trade as Native people located nearest the source of European goods attempted to protect their advantage by keeping other Natives from making direct contact with the Europeans.[3] Beads and steel knives reached the Han through the Tutchone and other intermediaries such as the Upper Tanana Athabaskans who traded with the Ahtna on the Copper River. In turn the Han moved European goods north and west to the Gwich'in living on the upper Porcupine and middle Yukon rivers.

Thus the Han became intermediaries in a trade network that supplied them with European goods before they ever saw a European. As a result of this trade, the arrival of the Hudson's Bay Company on the upper Yukon was less significant than it might have been otherwise. Instead of being the single source of Anglo-European goods, the Hudson's Bay

Map 3
Nineteenth-Century Trading Stations and Communities

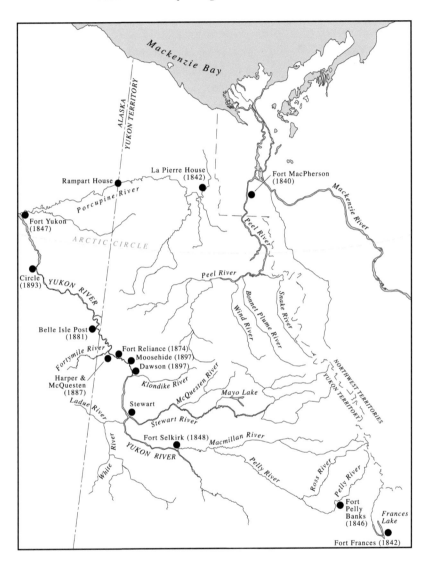

Company found itself in competition with a vibrant aboriginal trade and unable to direct that trade to its particular advantage.[4]

The arrival of the Hudson's Bay Company marks the beginning of Anglo-America's direct and sustained contact with the Han. The first recorded encounter of the Han with Company traders was on April 5, 1847, while Alexander Hunter Murray was at LaPierre's House on the upper Porcupine River. When the Han arrived, Murray was preparing for a trip later that summer when he and his men paddled downriver to establish a new trading post at Fort Yukon (see Map 3).

Murray wrote in a letter to Murdoch McPherson that a party of sixteen "*Gens du fou*" paid him a visit, after completing an exhausting twenty-five-day journey.[5] The young chief of the band, not identified by Murray, "appeared to have them all under complete subjection" and brought twenty marten skins expressly to trade for a gun. "Guns, kettles, Beads, tobacco, and amn [ammunition] are all the cry with these Indians," he wrote.[6]

Murray noted that the *Gens du fou* brought along a lot of "Geese-tongues—half dried meat—deer [i.e., caribou] skins & furs." Only three of them had ever seen a white man before. These same three men had traded earlier with Russians on the lower Yukon River around Nulato, but there are apparently no written records of that encounter. Unlike the Rat Indians in the vicinity of LaPierre's House, who saw Fort Yukon as a threat to their trade, the Han seemed glad that a new trading post would be built much closer to them.

Fort Yukon remained a company post until 1869, when the United States forced the company to move because it was on American soil. During this early period after direct contact, from 1847 to 1869, Fort Yukon was one of the principal sources of trade goods for the Han.

Wherever possible, the Hudson's Bay Company tapped into the Native trade system by using middlemen to barter furs from a wide area and funnel them to a centralized location, such as Fort Yukon. The currency of this early trade was the beaver, and the value of European-made trade items was measured in beaver skins. But the presence of the Hudson's Bay Company disrupted established aboriginal trading patterns and created tensions among groups who lost their trading advantage.[7]

In early August, 1847, the first large group of Han visited Fort Yukon. Local Gwich'in leaders had forewarned Murray that the Han were angry as one of the young Han chiefs had just died, and it was rumored his death was somehow connected to the presence of the English.[8] As Murray described it, the Han arrived in a fleet of twenty-five canoes and "glided down along the bank on account of the swell in the river, but there was no noise or singing as with the other [Athabaskan groups], they landed above our encampment assembled in silence on the bank."[9]

In Murray's view the Han presented a "very extraordinary and wild appearance" with their skin shirts covered with beads and brass decorations, and their long hair. They carried pipes made of tin or sheet iron traded from the Russians. At this meeting few came with anything to trade except for some bear skins, meat, and about one hundred geese they had killed with arrows on their way to the post.

While the Han acted friendly the first day, some of them threatened Murray on the second, telling him they had already killed some Russians and pillaged a Russian trading post because they were treated poorly. They were "troublesome" and "impertinent," "handling and asking for everything they saw" and "demanded guns, beads and axes on credit," which was refused.[10] Their chief attempted to persuade Murray that his people meant no harm and that they would return in the fall if the hunting was good; otherwise they would be back in the spring.[11]

In 1867 Russia sold Alaska to the United States. The subsequent arrival of American traders brought the fur trade directly to the Han when the Americans established several trading stations in Han territory. The first was Fort Reliance, built in 1874 by the Alaska Commercial Company six miles below the mouth of the Klondike River, across from the Han village of Nuklako. According to Francois Mercier, who was the impulse behind the creation of Fort Reliance, the station was opened at the insistence of the Han chief Catseah, a leader of the *Tr'ondëk Hwëch'in* (or Klondike) band of Han.[12]

In 1880 a second, competing trading station was opened by Moses Mercier of the Western Fur and Trading Company, the Alaska Commercial Company's rival. The post was located eighty miles downriver from Fort Reliance near David's Village, a Han community situated near the present site of Eagle, Alaska. A year later the post was abandoned as unprofitable. In 1882, Mercier, working for the Alaska Commercial Company, set up another post near David's Village, which he called Belle Isle. In retaliation, the Western Fur and Trading Company reopened the station it had abandoned and the two companies competed head to head, to the great advantage of the Han. This situation ended in 1883 when the Alaska Commercial Company bought out its rival, restricted credit, lowered the price paid for furs, and raised the price of goods.

The American traders' use of steamboats, such as the *Yukon* and *St. Michael*, increased the amount and variety of trade goods available to the Han. Fort Reliance stocked not only traditional items such as glass beads, but also bulk foods such as flour, repeating rifles (which the Hudson's Bay Company had never stocked), canvas for tents, and exotic items such as china teacups.

With direct access to a greater abundance of goods, the Han enhanced their position as middlemen to upper Tanana Athabaskans living in the hinterlands south of the Yukon River. A rare glimpse of this trade, as well as a view of Han culture just prior to the Klondike stampede of 1898, appears in the unpublished journal of the Anglican missionary Richard J. Bowen.

Bowen arrived on the upper Yukon River by steamboat in 1895, and that winter he accompanied the Han on a trip to Fort Reliance and on a trading expedition towards the Tanana River. In describing the Han, Bowen wrote that they relied on hunting and fishing to feed and clothe themselves but they measured their wealth in terms of Hudson's Bay blankets and decorated their clothing with trade beads. He wrote that the Han

> lived solely by the chase. . . . His food consisted of what the country afforded. Salmon which was caught in the summer, was dried and smoked for winter use. Cariboo [*sic*], moose, bear and mountain sheep, beaver and arctic hares were the chief sources of food. Should any of these fail, Lynx or wild cat, muskrat and other animals were eaten.[13]

He continued that the "wealth of a native consisted of and was designated by the number of four point Hudson's Bay Blankets he possessed." This wealth, along with the ability to provide for his wife's parents, was taken into consideration when a man wanted to marry.

Bowen was fascinated with the women's sewing ability:

> I witnessed a piece of hard dried sinew being bruised, with round stones, until it could be torn down the whole length of the sinew to the texture and thickness of thread. With this thread and bone needles I saw the hides tanned by the Indians, cut out and made into moccasins, shirts, trousers, coats, and a wonderful garment worn by the women, as an outer garment, in the coldest weather.... The beadwork on many of the articles made was artistic and neatly done.[14]

The trade in furs was critical, and the Han jealously guarded their position as intermediaries with the Natives living in the hinterland south of the Yukon River. On his second trip Bowen accompanied a Han trading party traveling from Fortymile into the hill country south of the Yukon River, beyond the village of Kechumstuk. Because of their direct access to trade goods, the Han had inserted themselves as middlemen into a trade network linking the Copper, Tanana, and Yukon rivers, and they had established a trading partnership with Tanacross-speaking people from Kechumstuk. Bowen wrote:

> A tribe of Indians, known as the Ketchem Stock [Kechumstuk] Indians also joined the Takudth [Han] Indians toward the head waters of the Fortymile Creek. These Indians were in touch with a tribe from beyond the Copper River area and made annual trips to their country for trading purposes. . . . The time arrived when the Takudth Indians decided it was time to for them to make their trip over the Alaska Border, to do their trading with natives less experienced than themselves.[15]

For this trip the Han had arranged to rendezvous with the Kechumstuk people and then venture further south to meet with an unnamed group of Natives, but at the final moment Bowen was prevented from meeting these "less enlightened" Natives, whom he refered to as "Indians of the Interior."

> The Indians of the Interior had seen me at the head of our dogs and sleighs and they went into the timber and would not come out again to trade. The Ketchem Stock [Kechumstuk] and Forty-Mile Indians [Han] had to go into the bush to a place decided upon before the Interior Indians would either trade or expose their furs.
>
> Only those who were deputed [sic] to trade went into the bush. The others, with myself and dogs remained in camp. I really believe I was refused this meeting through intervention of the Ketchum stock and Forty-mile Indians. It evidently was a preserve they did not wish to have interfered with either by missionary or white trader for fear the Interior Indians would be influenced to cease trading. The monopoly was worth something and must be held at all costs.[16]

Later in the day the party arrived at a Han hunting and trapping camp, which Bowen described as a "well selected spot with plenty of standing dry timber and a good creek from which to get water and ice. The skin tepees [sic] were erected so that the shoulders of the hills would protect them from heavy winter winds." Bowen estimated seventy people lived in the camp. The men were busy trapping marten, lynx, ermine, and fox, and hunting moose and caribou while the women tanned hides, which they used for moccasins and clothing. They had flour, baking powder, syrup, and raisins, along with plenty of dried caribou meat, roasted caribou heads, and tongues.[17]

Bowen's account shows the Han as an independent people able to provide for themselves by living off the land while maintaining a connection to the world economy. Up until the discovery of gold on the Klondike River in 1898, the Han were able to maintain a position of preeminence in the regional economy and assert some control over the extent and content of change within their own communities.[18] However, by developing a desire for exotic goods they did not make and could only obtain through the commercial harvest and trading of furs, the Han became enmeshed in an economic system over which they ultimately had no control. And when the focus of the regional economy shifted from furs to gold, their ability to control their relations with the non-Native world was substantially reduced.

Missionaries to the Han

As the Han became absorbed in the fur trade they also met another western "agent of change," the missionary. Missionaries often followed directly behind the traders and were sometimes supported by the trading companies. In 1861 the Church Missionary Society of London (CMS) sent the Anglican missionary William Kirkby to Fort Yukon. Kirkby did not remain long but was closely followed by other Anglican missionaries including Robert and Kenneth McDonald, William Bompas, and Vincent C. Sim. Bompas later recruited Richard J. Bowen, Frederick Flewelling, and Benjamin Totty (Figure 1).

Unlike the traders who came before them, the Protestant missionaries encountered by the Han sought to deliberately and fundamentally change Han culture. The CMS program rested on three points: to respect Native culture as much as possible, to rapidly appoint Native catechists, and to make the Bible more culturally relevant by translating it into Native languages.[19] While the CMS appears liberal in its attitude toward Native culture, the missionaries had a very fixed belief and value system that required the absolute acceptance of one truth. Declaring a theology that stressed a complete change of heart and allegiance, the Protestant missionaries saw the Indians as "sinners to be wrenched out of heathen darkness into the light of the gospel."[20] Furthermore, the missionaries linked their belief to a specific set of values about marriage (they were against polygamy), the status of women, patterns of work and leisure, sex, and gambling.

Initially the missionaries met Native people on their own ground, going to seasonal camps to provide religious instruction and to hold services. Over time, however, and especially after the discovery of gold in 1886, the missionaries stopped working in the field and instead set up missions for the Han in mining towns and eventually in the communities of Moosehide and Eagle Village.

Figure 1. Reverend Vincent Sim preaching to the Han at Fort Reliance, 1883.

Early on, the missionaries claimed varying success and sometimes displayed a startling impatience, considering the language and cultural differences between themselves and the Han. Vincent Sim, for example, became upset when, traveling up the Yukon in the summer of 1883, he saw a riverbank with some strange characters written on it and, asking what the characters were, was told they were to bring rain. Sim wrote: "I was so surprised to find such a practice still among them . . . but these Indians had only been visited once by a minister [Bompas] & only occasionally by Christian leaders" [i.e., Native catechists].[21]

Further upriver, Sim got upset again when the Natives at Fort Reliance had a "feast for the dead" or memorial potlatch. Sim wrote, "They knew I did not approve, but it is hard for them to get rid of their heathenism."[22] He also could not resist becoming involved in domestic disputes that violated his values. Again at Fort Reliance, the already married shaman named Enoch, or Ino, had taken another man's wife. Sim persuaded him not to bother the woman again.

Bowen also revealed the influence of the missionaries, describing how their teachings had begun to create a breach between different generations of Han as the elders were still swayed by the continuing influence of the shamans. Bowen was "surprised and delighted to see one of the men take from his wallet, the New Testament in the Takudth language, read from the scriptures, make a few remarks, then from his Takudth prayer book read some prayers."[23]

However, one morning the group observed four sun dogs and Bowen was startled by the older men's reaction as compared to those of the younger men who had attended the mission school at Fortymile:

> The Indians showed surprise and their ejaculations [i.e., exclamations] were most striking and according to their excitement. Roderick, my medicine friend expressed grave forbodings at such a phenomenon. It was surprising to see how the older members of the party were influenced by the weird story he told, but the younger men joked about it and pressed on. I really believe the older people were inclined to turn back as the incident seemed to presage some ill omen to their trading expedition, the success of which meant so much for the men who were making the trip.[24]

Robert McDonald and William Bompas may have been the most influential of the early missionaries. McDonald was an able linguist, and with the aid of his Gwich'in wife, Julia Kutug, translated the Bible, Anglican prayer book, and hymns into the Takudh dialect of the Gwich'in language. A number of Han learned to read Takudh and used McDonald's translations. McDonald's influence can be seen in this comment by the Canadian explorer William Ogilvie, who related with obvious admiration how members of Chief Charley's band integrated Christian worship into their life:

> Some years ago, when Archdeacon McDonald was situated at Fort McPherson, and afterwards at Rampart House, Charlie's band used to resort to those posts for their trade, and that gentleman taught them to read, and instructed them in the principles of the Christian religion. It is pleasant to be able to testify that they have profited by this instruction, and still retain a loving memory of those times. They hold every Sunday a service among themselves, reading from their books the prayers and lessons for the day, and singing in their own language to some old tune a simple hymn. They never go on a

journey of any length without their books, and always read a portion before they go to sleep.[25]

While McDonald attempted to impart the gospel through the use of Native language, Bompas wanted to "civilize" and "educate" Native people. His lack of faith in Native missionaries led him to enlist other English missionaries such as Bowen, Flewelling, and Totty. Bompas also held the view that only by removing the children from the influence of their "backward" home environment were they to be made useful members of society and "instruments of civilization." To this end he established boarding schools where he could control what the children learned. Early in his tenure Bompas had his headquarters at the town of Fortymile, near the Alaska-Canada border, where he opened a mission and school. In 1900 he moved from Fortymile to Carcross, in the southern Yukon, where he established a boarding school that formed the basis for the Carcross Residential School opened by the Anglican Church in 1911. It is the residential youth boarding school that many Han today view as the root cause of many current social problems.

Originally the Carcross school administration had hoped to attract the best and brightest students. Many parents, however, resisted sending their children away for a period as long as ten years, since neither the government nor the school would authorize summer vacations. When children did go, the separation often traumatized both parents and students. In 1928 Ellen Wood of Moosehide wrote a letter to Bishop Stringer, telling him,

> I am broken up you send my daughters little babies to Carcross, its too much for me-now-this you do. I no [sic] I am getting old, but I have two daughters, Magdaline and [Mary Simon] and besides I have Micah a boy now seventeen years old who will become a man and when those children come away from school, I wish them to come back to my family at Moosehide.[26]

As historian Kenneth Coates points out, the school failed in many ways. The teachers taught the students to despise their culture and disciplined them to speak English instead of their own language. As a result, the children often ended up not fitting into either Native or non-Native society.[27] Sarah-Jane Essau, a woman from Moosehide, observed that "[w]hen they are too long at school they won't have anything to do with us; they want to be with White people; they grow away from us."[28]

Diseases

There is no way to gauge the effect of early epidemics on the Han because most of the victims died out in the bush, alone or with their families, and away from the recorder's pen. Although the Han were among the last Northern Athabaskan people to come into direct contact with non-Natives, their isolation probably did not protect them since intertribal trade networks acted as conduits for contagious disease.

Disease probably killed the most vulnerable segments of the population, the young and the old; the loss of elders disrupted the transmission of cultural knowledge, which would be especially serious in a society based on oral communication. Infectious diseases may have also influenced fertility rates in two ways. If males in the prime of life died, there would be fewer couples of reproductive age, and if there were fewer hunters the production of food would decline. As a result, instead of obtaining moose and caribou and other sources of necessary proteins and fat, people would have been reduced to eating arctic hares and other less nutritious foods, which could affect pregnancies.

Evidence for early problems with disease comes from several sources. Anglican missionary T. H. Canham concluded, after long discussions with Native people in the Porcupine River area during the 1880s, that there had been "a great diminution during the past century in the number of Native inhabitants." He attributed this decline to smallpox "communicated from the southern Indians soon after the date of earliest exploration."[29] Alexander Hunter Murray noted a "great mortality" among Native women in the summer of 1846, and Hudson's Bay trader Robert Campbell described an epidemic killing large numbers of Native people in 1851.

In 1865–1866 Hudson's Bay Company boat crews brought scarlet fever into the region, and while no exact figures exist on the number of deaths, Company officers estimated that between 170 and 200 Gwich'in who lived in the vicinity of Fort Yukon died. Of Han deaths, Robert McDonald reported in June of 1866 that four Han arrived at Fort Yukon bringing news of twenty-two deaths from scarlet fever.[30]

This epidemic may have been the most severe, but it certainly was not the last, as a variety of diseases swept the region. In 1873, William Bompas reported that an epidemic (a sort of dysentery) had reached the Han. In 1883 Lieutenant Frederick Schwatka recorded an outbreak of what was apparently diphtheria on the Yukon River near the Canadian border and observed that the disease "completely desolated some families and was particularly fatal among the younger members."[31] Two years later Vincent Sim reported that while he was traveling on the Yukon River he met or heard of Gwich'in, Han, and Tanana River Athabaskans who had been stricken by an epidemic which he, like Schwatka, thought was diphtheria. Initially, Sim was inclined to dismiss the number of deaths reported by the Natives but on reflection thought "the report of the deaths among the Indians below was greatly exaggerated but still the mortality has been terrible."[32]

Ferdinand Schmitter, an army doctor stationed at Fort Egbert in Eagle City from 1906 to 1908, recorded the story of a smallpox epidemic that may have occurred in the 1880s: "About five hundred Indians encamped in skin houses about a mile up Mission Creek were taken with small pox and most of them died. The remnant of the band moved to Fortymile, where they were attacked in 1897 by an epidemic of coughing and bleeding from the lungs, and many of them died in from four to six days."[33] These may have been some of the thirty-nine deaths recorded by Bompas in the Dawson-Fort Selkirk region between 1895 and 1898.

These epidemics were devastating to the Han because in a small space of time entire families died. Hudson's Bay Company traders noted particularly the deaths among women and several of the most "influential men," which must have had an effect on leadership and the ability of families to hunt and feed themselves.

The Discovery of Gold

Beginning in 1885, a succession of gold strikes occurred on tributaries of the upper Yukon River, the first of which occurred in 1885 on the Stewart River at the southern limits of Han territory. A year later, in 1886, prospectors discovered gold on the Fortymile River, and the town of Fortymile, which soon had two saloons, was established in the very center of Han territory. Gold was discovered on the Seventymile River in 1888, on Birch Creek in 1893 (sparking the town of Circle in 1894), and then on American Creek in 1895 near what is now Eagle City. Then in August of 1896, Dawson Charlie, Skookum Jim, and George Carmack struck gold on Bonanza Creek, a tributary of the Klondike River, sparking a defining event in Han history, the Klondike stampede.

In general the discovery of gold and subsequent developments produced a great upheaval among the Han and forever changed the economy and society in the valley of the upper Yukon River. Cornelius

Osgood acutely observed that "the various early gold strikes, with a sizable population of miners rushing from one creek to another, building towns and then evacuating them, shooting and fishing where convenience demanded, must have been something like having alien warring groups moving back and forth over one's territory."[34]

More broadly, mineral development and the subsequent influx of people focused international attention on the region. The stampede set in motion the growth of an infrastructure composed of a legal, political, economic, and social apparatus that would have far-reaching effects on the Han and everyone living in the region.

The gold discoveries that preceded the Klondike stampede had a relatively small effect on the Han. The number of non-Natives attracted by the earlier gold strikes was insignificant compared to the deluge following the Klondike discovery. In 1896 the non-Native population in the upper Yukon was probably between 1,000 and 2,000 people.[35] There was little competition over resources, and even as gold became the economic linchpin of the regional economy, fur remained an important commodity and the Han continued to trap. In addition, with an economic boom fueled by gold, the Han found employment as river pilots, woodcutters, packers, stevedores, and provisioners, supplying an increasing demand in foodstuffs caused by a fast-growing population.

Under Canadian law, Natives were allowed to stake mining claims, but most of those who did sold them to whites. In the United States Natives were not recognized as citizens so they could not legally file claims. Placer mining technology was not labor intensive, in that it did not require large numbers of workers, so the Han were never recruited as a source of labor. Besides, in the eyes of most prospectors, the Han were too irresponsible to hold mining claims or even to work as laborers. Harold Goodrich, of the United States Geological Survey, who reported on the Yukon Gold District in 1897, stated the prevailing ethnocentric view: "Even when successful he [the Indian] has not the necessary ambition; and however willing he may be, as soon as he gets a little money he will stop work and spend his entire fortune with no thought of tomorrow."[36]

Largely excluded from working in the gold fields, the Han generally gravitated toward more casual and seasonal labor which enabled them to maintain a life on the land. This ability to tap into both worlds provided the Han with a certain amount of affluence. Bishop Bompas commented:

Nothing could be of greater contrast than the squalid poverty and want of all things in which the Indians here lived thirty years ago, and the lavish luxury and extravagance with which they now squander hundreds of dollars on needless food and dress, if not in a still more questionable manner. The Indians now place such high prices on any meat or fuel, or other things which they supply to the whites . . . and . . . it is hard for your missionaries to live with economy among them.[37]

With the Klondike gold stampede, the situation changed drastically. Following the initial discovery in the summer of 1896, word spread first to Fortymile, then to Circle City, and finally to the outside world. Almost immediately, hundreds of prospectors abandoned the claims they had been working and flocked to the Klondike River eager to stake new claims or purchase land on speculation. By the spring of 1897 prospectors had overrun the area displacing the band of Han in the fishing village of Tr'ochëk at the mouth of the Klondike River. Soon after, Dawson City took shape, and by the winter of 1897–1898 it had a population of between 20,000 and 30,000. In 1898, the height of the stampede, an estimated 50,000 people arrived in the North.

While most stampeders headed for Dawson and the Klondike, a group of American miners left Dawson to start a settlement on the American side of the border. They fixed on a site at the mouth of Mission Creek and started the town of Eagle, Alaska. In 1899, the United States Army acquired land adjacent to the town as the site for Fort Egbert, which was established to monitor the border and keep order. In the process they displaced another band of Han.

In less than two years, from 1896 to 1898, the Han had become a minority in their homeland. Where the Han had faced little or no competition, they were now forced to compete for vital resources as their hunting and fishing grounds were overrun. They also found themselves at the economic and social margins of society and displaced from their traditional villages to make way for development. Yet the entire Klondike stampede lasted only about three years, from 1897 to 1900. Fortune-seekers found no streets of gold or places to stake mining claims, and many rushed off to new discoveries at Nome and Fairbanks.

Competition Over Resources

With such a huge influx of people into Han territory, the demand for natural resources increased to the point that the Han had to compete for the basic staples of their existence as well as for jobs. Stampeders' demand for meat, fish, fur, and firewood led to shortages that forced the Han to travel miles in search of food and to ask for relief. The situation was exacerbated by non-Natives who shot animals without taking the meat and by their careless use of wildfire to clear the land.

In Dawson, journalist Tappan Adney wrote that during the summer of 1898 the demand for fresh meat was so great that "numbers of white men proceeded to the upper Klondike in canoes and hunted moose with considerable success." He also noted that some of the hunters wasted the meat. They "were not lacking men even here, who forfeited every right to carry a gun by shooting down in pure wantonness numbers of moose which they made no attempt to save."[38]

In January of 1899 Inspector Harper of the North West Mounted Police also commented on the situation. Writing from Dawson to his superiors, Harper reported a widespread decline in game and furbearing animals:

> A great many moose were brought to town during the past summer and sold from butcher shops in town, also lately, ptarmigan, grouse, and rabbits [Arctic hares] had been abundantly exhibited in front of the various restaurants and butcher shops. The Game Ordinance was not enforced here last summer. This I think was a mistake as if the quantity of moose that was brought in last summer is brought in every year very few will shortly exist in the country.[39]

Harper also reported that miners had set fires, either deliberately or through carelessness, which devastated the country. He added that the Indians complained that the fires had driven off game so they had to travel up to twenty miles to "catch" their meat. Since the mounted police were responsible for administering welfare to Native people, Harper's concern was aimed, in part, at whether and how the police would manage to provide food subsidies to destitute Native people.

The Han also found themselves excluded from most non-mining jobs as non-Natives preferred to hire other non-Natives. The Han competed with failed gold seekers who took up commercial hunting, fishing, and trapping. In one instance, Silas, a Han man from Moosehide who had developed a business selling salmon to restaurants in Dawson, was told by local authorities to stop because a non-Native fisherman complained of the unlicensed activity.

The intensity of the non-Native trapping and hunting led Chief Isaac of Moosehide to complain about white men killing too many animals. Chief Isaac reported in 1915 that white hunters had killed three thousand caribou while his hunters had killed only seventy. The chief said it was all right for the "white man" to dig the gold "on my creeks" because the Indians could not eat gold. But the Indians wanted the caribou and they wanted their hunting grounds. Isaac finished by saying that caribou was his meat and that he did not go around shooting horses or the white man's cattle.[40]

On the American side of the international boundary the situation was similar as the non-Native population in the vicinity of Eagle City increased. While commercial companies were able to supply staples to the town and surrounding area, game and fish for human consumption and dog food were in high demand. In addition, some non-Natives took up trapping and wood cutting for steamboats as profitable alternatives to mining.

The garrison at Fort Egbert relied on wild meat, fish, and birds to supplement imported staples. Samuel Woodfill, a soldier stationed at Fort Egbert, said that although he hunted bear, "it was caribou and moose that we counted on for our chief food supply. We used to go after caribou as soon as they started running along in October. There were three months of open shootin' on caribou, with no bag limit for a soldier huntin' for a company mess."[41]

Woodfill also recollected that soldiers hunted ducks at Ford Lake, a favorite Han hunting spot. He said, "whenever we wanted duck we would go down there for a day or two. It was nothing to kill three or four hundred on a trip."[42]

The reports of one post commander repeatedly mention hunting in the vicinity of Fort Egbert and in one instance indicate that soldiers killed fifty-two caribou in one day. While much of the meat apparently went to the fort, some was shared with the nearby Han community of Eagle Village.

However, the Army was not the only problem. Indeed, detachments of soldiers at Fort Egbert were called out three times in October and November 1904, and again in January 1905, "to prevent the killing of caribou for commercial purposes."[43] The sites recorded for these attempted killings were on Comet Creek, a tributary of the Fortymile River, and on Seventymile Creek. It is not clear whether the soldiers caught and arrested anyone in the act of wholesale slaughter, but there must have been a very serious problem.

In addition to hunting game for the needs of the fort, the military also maintained a summer fish camp on the river below Fort Egbert. The fish caught there were used to feed the numerous sled dogs at the fort.[44] Between the caribou and the salmon, the short-term damage to wild fish and game populations in the area must have been enormous.

Social Change

Before the Klondike stampede of 1898, the success, not to mention the survival, of traders and missionaries depended on their intimate familiarity with how Native people lived. The gold rush fragmented this world into the discrete domains of "town" and "bush." The towns were typical frontier settlements with saloon keepers, prostitutes, confidence men, professional gamblers, and government bureaucrats, most of whom had little or nothing to do with Native people and generally regarded them as the bottom of the social scale. Furthermore, when Natives and non-Natives did meet, it was often in situations, such as a town, where Native people were at a distinct disadvantage. As a result, both groups often developed skewed stereotypes.

Drawn by the excitement and opportunity of town, the Han were introduced to a typical frontier lifestyle characterized by a "taste for luxury, love of gambling [not to mention alcohol], coarse, vile language, and . . . the miserable and ruthless degradation of women."[45] The missionaries feared for the Han's moral and physical decay viewing them as passive actors who had to be protected from their own worst instincts. Some Han leaders such as Chief Charley and Chief Isaac also expressed this fear. Anglican Bishop William Bompas believed that it was often the "younger Indians [and what Bompas elsewhere calls the more cosmopolitan element of Indians who] are only too apt to imitate the careless whites in irreligion and debauchery."[46] In turn, Chief Charley "did not fail to point out the baneful effect of immoral intercourse with the whites" and attempted, in some way, to protect his people.[47]

To combat the destructive influences of the towns, missionaries from both the Anglican and Episcopal churches thought of the Natives as children who needed to be isolated in their own communities where they could be properly cared for and educated. Peter Trimble Rowe, the Episcopal Bishop of Alaska at the time of the gold rush, believed the Natives were victims of a system in which no law protected them.

Figure 2. Arrival of Peel River Indians in Dawson, March 21, 1901. Although the missionaries feared for the Natives, some, such as the "Dawson Boys" were not degraded by contact. Gwich'in from the Peel River, the Dawson Boys made numerous trips to Dawson, worked at a number of seasonal occupations, learned to enjoy drinking, gambling and smoking good cigars but always returned home to the Peel River. In later life many of the Dawson Boys became stalwarts of Gwich'in tradition in their community (Slobodin 1963).

It was, in his view, difficult to alleviate the situation because of the way Native people lived scattered across the country in small groups. Rowe wrote that "something entirely different is demanded, and these original possessors of the country thrust to one side, their food-giving preserves encroached upon by the not-to-be-prevented advance of the superior race, are justly entitled to some protection and aid from our Government." After outlining the problem, Rowe then fixed on the answer, which was to gather the scattered bands of Indians and bring them all together in one place where they could be protected and educated:

> What is needed is some law by which all those who live in scattering families shall be brought together in places not already appropriated by the white people, where under wise leadership they can easily support themselves, learn the art of self government, where they can receive such medical help as will save their lives and where education will be to some purpose and cost less then the present unsatisfactory methods.[48]

Displacement and Resettlement

The Klondike stampede provided the missionaries with the opportunity to put Rowe's ideas into practice. In 1897 prospectors displaced a group of Han living in the village of Tr'ochëk at the mouth of the Klondike River. Eventually a majority of the Han moved to Moosehide and Eagle Village. Moosehide remained a viable community until the 1960s when the last resident moved to Dawson City.

Living in Moosehide and Eagle Village represented a complete change in lifestyle for the Han and an opportunity for the government and church to begin the process of assimilation. Families no longer moved with each change in the season. Communities became central locations from which men went out to hunt and trap and then returned to their families. Instead of living in tents or traditional dwellings, the residents of Moosehide and Eagle Village were expected to live in log cabins, and they were expected to maintain their homes and keep them clean.

In both communities, the government and the missionaries expected children to attend school and to learn the English language. As a result, some parents left their children in the care of the missionaries and schools while they went out and trapped. This had a disruptive effect on Han family structure. As Allen Wright has noticed, "the schools, therefore, also played a welfare role."[49]

The Han were expected to participate in electoral politics by electing village councils. The councils established rules regulating behavior, ranging from the consumption of alcohol to personal hygiene. Through the councils the missionaries also attempted to regulate interaction between Natives and non-Natives, and especially between Native women and non-Native men.[50]

Moosehide

In November, 1896, the Anglican missionary Frederick Flewelling arrived in the Han village of Tr'ochëk. That winter he built a cabin and taught school. Before the ice went out on the Yukon the next spring, Flewelling took a trip to Fortymile, and on returning in May, he found the village transformed: "We reached here last night [May 29, 1897] but could hardly recognize the old place because of so many tents. Five or six hundred men have already come in this spring, and their tents are pitched everywhere." According to Flewelling, the Han, "through a piece of bad management and influenced by Whites" sold their land to the miners while speculators had purchased all the land within a two-mile radius of the mouth of the river leaving the Han without a place to live. Flewelling therefore purchased a forty-acre tract two miles down the Yukon where he proposed to resettle the Han and build a mission.[51]

Figure 3. Church and cabins at Moosehide, circa 1910–1920. As identified by Angie Joseph-Rear. Cabins left to right, top row: Ellen Silas, Esau Harper, Jonathon Wood, Kenneth Joseph, Chief Isaac (without roof). To left of St. Barnabas Church is the pool hall and morgue.

Years later an unidentified Han woman from Moosehide presented a different view of the situation. Her account completely ignored the role of the church and instead highlighted the role of the chief in choosing a village site and the role of the government in providing the land. Both accounts viewed the majority of Han as innocents, unable to resist the temptations of town, and in this respect the chief viewed resettlement as something positive for his people. But unlike Flewelling, who viewed the miners as interlopers who somehow swindled the Natives, the narrator recognized them as human beings who, despite their odd interest in gold, were welcomed as friends. In this way the Han, instead of assuming the position of dispossessed refugees, as Flewelling saw them, became active agents determining their own destiny. The woman said:

> My father was chief at the time of the gold rush. He was the first chief there is. He came along from Alaska, drift up with a few of his people, must have been Eagle, Alaska was their main place.
> He never see any white people in his life before then. But, he knew that they were human beings, and he was friendly with them

and welcome them. And he told his people to be good to them too. So they are, and they good friends.

But my dad didn't want my people to get mixed up with them. Because he thought it would ruin their lives and spoil them, and they'd get drinking and things like that. And so he figured he'll move them down to Moosehide about three miles away from Dawson. He was afraid of alcohol because he saw that they were drinking and things like that, so he thought it wasn't good enough for his people. They live quite simple lives.

Moosehide was a little reserve, I would call it. They moved down there and then started to build cabins to live in. The government give them land there so they figured it would be far enough away from Dawson. Where it was civilized. The government wanted them to live across the [Yukon] river, but my father thought it was too handy to come across back and forth.

My people knew all about the Klondike, but they never knew nothing about gold. Lots of big nuggets along the creeks. But what do they know about gold? Nothing. So the White people come to the country and they found nuggets all around the place. Very strange, very strange to my father that all those people come for gold. Too much money. The way my dad use to say, they throw the money around; they threw the gold around. There's too much of it.[52]

While the Han moved to Moosehide toward the end of 1897, it was not until 1908 that St. Barnabas Church was built in memory of Bishop Bompas. Jonathon Wood served as the Native catechist assisting Benjamin Totty, an Anglican missionary who had been recruited by Bompas and who served the community until 1926. By the 1930s Moosehide had a school, a parish hall, and houses for the priest and Native teacher.

The establishment of Moosehide did not solve the problems of the Han, especially in regard to resources. From the outset, the boundaries of the reserve were in dispute over woodcutting rights. Benjamin Totty requested a survey in 1898 to clarify the issue, and in 1907 Chief Isaac requested, through Totty, an additional timber reserve located up Moosehide Creek. Almost all of the timber in the area had been cut for the steamboats, leaving little for the Han. In the late 1920s the borders of the reserve were altered, probably by the territorial government, to enable local non-Native woodcutters to utilize the good timber that was considered to be of little use to the Han.[53]

Whether or not the creation of Moosehide served the needs of the Han, it did serve the agenda of the Anglican Church by separating and isolating the Han from non-Natives. The rationale for involving the Anglican Church was articulated by Bishop Bompas: "To abandon them [the Han] now that the place is overrun by miners would involve their destruction by more than a relapse to heathenism, namely their being swallowed up in the miners' temptation to drink, gambling, and immorality."[54]

In keeping with their attempts to mold Native character, the missionaries established a number of social organizations including the Moosehide Men's Club and the Senior Women's Auxiliary. In 1932 they opened a branch of the Anglican Young People's Association in Moosehide, which is believed to have been the only all-Native A.Y.P.A. in the Dominion of Canada. The missionaries also hoped to shape the character of the Han by persuading them to regulate behavior in their own community.

In March 1921, the Moosehide people established a village council. Esau Harper was elected chairman, while Chief Isaac was vice chair, James Woods was secretary, Sam Smith the "inside guard," David Robert "children's guard," Tom Young and David Taylor were house inspectors, Jonas Thompson "village inspector north-end," and Peter Thompson "village inspector south-end." Council members served one-year terms and gave themselves the authority to keep the village clean, care for the sick and aged, enforce school attendance, regulate relations between husbands and wives, and punish people who broke the community standards, particularly those regarding drinking.

During its first meeting the council passed seven laws governing the village.[55] The first law prohibited all girls from interacting with non-Natives and stopped non-Natives from coming to the community except for business. The fourth law, reflecting trouble with alcohol, said that a man could not stay in town (Dawson) for more than one day and that he had to have a comrade; if either one saw the other doing wrong he was required to tell the council. In the course of the year the council addressed domestic disputes between husbands and wives, fined people for drinking, and interceded in a case between a Native girl and her non-Native employer. Though remarkably intrusive, the laws were intended to keep families together, limit the Moosehide people's access to Dawson, and enforce standards of behavior.

However, there were disagreements within the community as to the effectiveness of the council. According to one council member,

"The people don't like the council because they want to do what they like—they don't like the council telling them to keep their homes clean and clean the village."[56] Eventually the council relaxed its strict regime.

Eagle Village

In May 1898 a group of twenty-eight American prospectors staked out a town site at the mouth of Mission Creek. Just a few months later, the new community of Eagle City already had more than 500 cabins and a population of 1,700.[57] In Elva Scott's history of Eagle City there is no mention of the Han being displaced by the establishment of the town.[58] U.S. War Department records also make no mention of the Han when the Army obtained a military reservation for Fort Egbert in 1899 (see Figure 4).[59]

However, according to oral testimony from Willie Juneby, Eagle City and Fort Egbert displaced the Han from areas they traditionally used at the mouth of Mission Creek. Willie claimed that before the gold rush the Han had a village there and the "Army got in and moved the Natives upriver."[60]

Louise Paul was told by her aunt Sarah Malcolm that before the coming of white people the Han inhabited the area around the mouth of Mission Creek and that they had a graveyard there. She also said that one of the important landmarks, which marked the presence of the village, was Eagle Bluff located at the mouth of Mission Creek: "First time when there was no white people, this Eagle town was just full of Indians, that was their village. Years ago you could even see their graves where they buried their dead, down there by old nation, in birch bark. You could see the bones, beads and things like that. They called that Eagle Bluff, in Hän Language *Heet'awdlenn* [*Tthee Täwdlenn*], Eagle Bluff." Then the white people started coming, she said, even before her time. Louise went on to say that

> since the white people started coming they kind of shoved the Indians
> up a little at a time. You know where Patty Austin cabin is built, right
> down that bank, there used to be a lot of wigwams. . . . So that's where
> the Indians were shoved up, three miles up there. And then they used
> to have an old chief by the name of Chief Philip, and he got a cache
> three miles up, full of Hudson Bay [blankets] and some beads and
> things like that. He talked my people to go up where his cache was. So
> that white people just took this place over from the Indians. The Army
> came and they really took it over.[61]

Figure 4. Indian village at Fort Egbert. Missionary, soldiers, and Han Indian with dip net, circa 1900.

As in Moosehide, the church came to play a prominent role in Eagle Village. In the summer of 1898, Bishop Rowe staked a site for a mission in Eagle City, but on returning a year later found the site occupied by the U.S. Army. He also found the Catholic and Presbyterian churches active, so he decided to confine his church's activities to Eagle Village. A succession of Episcopal missionaries served Eagle Village in a variety of capacities.[62] In 1905–1906 the Church built St. Paul's Mission in Eagle Village. Around 1925 Bishop Rowe appointed a Han man named Walter Benjamin to assist the missionaries and serve as lay reader. Walter Ben, as he was known locally, served the church in Eagle Village until 1946.

A major concern of the missionaries was protecting the Han from abuses by unscrupulous military personnel and other whites. To do this the missionaries tried to regulate Han behavior by stopping them from associating with most whites and involving the Han men in a temperance society. George Burgess, an Episcopal missionary who served in Eagle Village from 1909 through 1920, blamed white men "of the lower class" (soldiers) for trying to "procure the downfall of the natives."[63]

To stop the fraternization, Burgess ended the dances that had been attended by Natives and non-Natives, a move that angered both groups. Burgess also organized a temperance society to which every male member of the village twelve years and older belonged. There was a one-dollar initiation fee and dues were twenty-five cents per month. To become a member, each man had to agree that for a period of one year he would not touch a drop of alcohol. Members elected their own leaders, and these leaders were supposed to pass sentence on those who violated the laws and regulations. The Han men, according to Burgess, were "learning to get up and talk, expressing themselves as to the best means of livelihood and health to protect their race from sickness and a certain class of whites who seek their downfall. When a person visiting the village is found to be undesirable, he is asked at once to leave by the police, and the older members watch him until he does."[64]

Sarah Malcolm, who lived in and around Eagle Village all of her life, remembered that there was an invisible boundary between Eagle City and Eagle Village. According to Sarah, this was because "there's lots of soldiers someplace [sic] come to the village with liquor, so council don't like it, and if they get caught they say they going to put them in jail because we got lots of young girl in the village go school."[65]

For years the Han were not legally able to purchase liquor in Eagle City, even though it was readily available in Dawson. Matthew Malcolm remembered when they could finally purchase alcohol:

> I remember [when] it first came, oh shucks, it been off and on, and the people downtown, they voted for people here. They're [the Han] not allowed to buy it. So people around here got money, so they just go downtown. Like for instance, you Steve [Steve Ulvi] live downtown, and I got some money, I want booze. I go downtown and give money to you, and you go to the store and get me booze. That's how they worked it. And a couple years after that why they knew what's going on, so hell, people downtown council members, they voted to let the people in the village buy their own booze as long as they got the money. So they let them buy booze, I remember.[66]

Along with the mission, the school came to play a central role in village life (see Figure 5). In 1902 Mrs. Ensign, the wife of the Presbyterian minister, began a day school in Eagle City for the Han children. Then in 1905, the Episcopal Church opened a day school in Eagle Village that remained in operation until the 1940s. While often staffed by missionaries, the school was supported by the U.S. Department of the Interior, Bureau of Education. A major focus of the school was to teach the children English. In 1926 Borghilde Henriksen Hansen came to teach school in the village. Matthew Malcolm remembered Mrs. Hansen forcing the children to speak English:

Oh, them days when I went to school here, you know Mrs. Hansen? She was our teacher. Quite a lot more kids that time than right now. We always go to school, all morning till school's out. We always talk our language. Our teacher [imitating the teacher] "Speak English! Speak English!" And sometime we forget, then we start jabbering away in our Native language. Our teacher got a little stick so long that it was "Speak English! Speak English!" [inaudible sentence] Kids they started speaking English, you know. Now we're all here right now. Some of them young kids they hardly speak their own language.[67]

Figure 5. Indian school at Eagle. Students with Mrs. Ensign, Presbyterian missionary's wife and teacher, circa 1902–1905.

Dr. Schmitter, the Army doctor at Fort Egbert, recorded his detailed impressions of Eagle Village. Like most non-Natives at the time, Schmitter thought the church fostered unnecessary dependency by doling out charity to the Han. In his view there were plenty of opportunities for the Han if they were properly educated and taught to "despise instead of to seek assistance."

Schmitter also noted a variety of health problems, which he attributed to the Han's recently adopted sedentary lifestyle. He noted that many of the men were unable to hunt on account of old age or consumption: "A great change has taken place and conditions could scarcely be worse than they are now. . . . Tuberculosis far outweighs all other ailments. . . . Tonsillitis, respiratory disease, digestive troubles and myalgia are ever present.[68]

Illness and death were also part of Willie Juneby's earliest memories. Willie remembered that when he was a child "quite a few kids died. Biggest part of kids gone with TB. . . . Right after first [World] war we had whooping cough. Everyone. You had to wear it out because they had no medicine." In 1925, "during July, the whole village was down." He and Harry David weren't as sick as the others and "we helped the school teacher that first started to teach us, Miss Stabler. She went around with aspirin. She made a big pot of soup and they packed that around. Everyone was sick."[69] Sarah Malcom recalled that tuberculosis was blamed on unclean houses, and one time "they painted every cabin in the village with whitewash. The door, bed, table legs, walls, everything."[70]

With the nearest hospitals located in Dawson and Fort Yukon, we can only speculate how many lives were lost to such epidemics.

Conclusion

This chapter has outlined major social changes that occurred in the upper Yukon valley between 1840 and 1940. For the Han, the pre-gold rush fur trade created a predicament. On the one hand, as soon as they joined the fur trade, the Han became enmeshed in a world economy over which they had no control. From the outset, they developed a desire for goods they did not make and which they could obtain only through trapping or manual wage labor. To accommodate these desires, they would eventually have to make choices that led to profound changes in future years.

On the other hand, the early trade created an economic interdependency between traders and Natives as fur prices remained high and the trade profitable. In fact, the years between 1840 and 1886 could be considered a golden age in Han cultural history. Despite infectious diseases that ravaged the Native population of the upper Yukon, the Han remained a distinctive people and persisted in their political and economical autonomy. Han culture did not disappear.

The early fur trade was a period of the middle ground when there was as yet little pressure on the Han to conform to white expectations.[71] They were free to choose those aspects of the non-Native belief system and technology that fit comfortably into their life style. They readily accepted innovations in technology to enhance aspects of their culture, including the potlatch.[72] They also created new forms of personal adornment and innovations in styles of clothing (see Chapter 6) which demonstrate a lively creativity rather than a demoralized people.

In sharp contrast, the gold rush placed the Han squarely in the path of unfettered capitalist development. The Klondike gold rush was the defining moment in Han history. More than any other event, it transformed the economy, society, and culture of the upper Yukon valley and subordinated the interests of the Han to those of the mining industry and majority non-Native society. Pressure to change became intense. By the turn of the twentieth century the Han had been marginalized and resettled into permanent villages adjacent to the once-thriving mining towns. Most of the non-Natives soon left for new diggings in Nome and Fairbanks. Wild resources, however, were severely depleted by the miners and soldiers, leaving the Han with a residue of disease, dependency, and alcoholism.[73]

Nevertheless, the Han were not simply victims of the gold rush. They were active participants who made conscious choices and engaged in the economy and society of the time. They adapted and survived. During the gold rush and the several decades that followed, the Han were presented with an alternative way of life not oriented toward life on the land. A living based on hunting, fishing, and trapping became only one of several choices, and subsistence became a component of a mixed economy, not the entire economy.

Notes

1. Ferdinand Schmitter, *Upper Yukon Native Customs and Folk-Lore* (Washington, D.C.: The Smithsonian Institution, 1910). Reprinted by the Eagle Historical Society, Eagle, Alaska, 10.

2. See Cornelius Osgood, *The Han Indians: A Compilation of Ethnographic and Historical Data on the Alaska-Yukon Boundary Area* (New Haven: Yale University Publications in Anthropology No. 74, 1971), 78–79.

3. Shepard Krech III, "The Eastern Kutchin and the Fur Trade, 1800–1869." *Ethnohistory* 23, No. 3 (1976): 213–253.

4. Kenneth S. Coates, "Furs Along the Yukon: Hudson's Bay Company-Native Trade in the Yukon Basin, 1830–1893." *B.C. Studies* No. 55, 1982:56. Robert Campbell complained that he could not match the prices or the acumen of the Tlingit who came to trade with Athabaskans in the Yukon. The Tlingit not only offered better prices but also understood the language and the customs of the Athabaskans. See Julie Cruikshank's *Dan Dha Ts'edenintth'e Reading Voices: Oral and Written Interpretations of the Yukon's Past* (Vancouver & Toronto: Douglas and McIntyre, 1991), 83–86.

5. "*Gens du fou*" was a popular nineteenth-century French ethnonym for the Han, meaning "crazy people." This pejorative name may have been bestowed on them by Murray's young Métis translator, Antoine Hoole. It is no longer in use today. See also Chapter 7, note 2.

6. Alexander Hunter Murray, Unpublished letter to Murdoch McPherson, Peels River, May 16, 1847. Alexander Hunter Murray Fonds. Glenbow Museum Archives, Calgary, Alberta.

7. Krech, "The Eastern Kutchin and the Fur Trade," 214.

8. Murray, *Journal of the Yukon*, 27, 51–52.

9. Ibid., 58–59.

10. Ibid., 60–61.

11. Ibid., 62.

12. François Mercier, *Recollections of the Youkon, Memoires for the Years 1868–1885*. Translated, edited, and annotated by Linda Finn-Yarborough. Alaska Historical Commission Studies in History No. 188 (Anchorage: The Alaska Historical Society, 1986). For more about Catseah see Chapter 4.

13. R. J. Bowen, *Incidents in the Life of the Reverend Richard John Bowen among the Natives, Trappers Prospectors and Gold Miners in the Yukon Territory Before and After the Gold Rush of the Year 1898* (MS in the National Archives of Canada, Ottawa. n.d.), 110.

14. Ibid.

15. Ibid., 116.

16. Ibid., 131.

17. Ibid., 124.

18. Coates, "Furs Along the Yukon." For a more detailed look at the early Han fur trade it is helpful to consult Donald Clark, *Fort Reliance, Yukon: An Archaeological Assessment*. Mercury Series, Archaeological Survey of Canada Paper No. 150 (Ottawa: Canadian Museum of Civilization, 1995).

19. Kenneth Coates, *Best Left Indians: Native-White Relations in the Yukon Territory, 1840–1973* (Montreal & Kingston: McGill-Queen's University Press, 1991), 117.

20. John Webster Grant, *Moon of Wintertime: Missionaries and the Indians of Canada in Encounter since 1534* (Toronto: University of Toronto Press, 1984), 229.

21. Vincent Sim quoted in Mary E. Wesbrook, "A Venture into Ethnohistory: The Journals of Rev. V.C. Sim, Pioneer Missionary on the Yukon." *Polar Notes*, No. 9 (1969): 42. For general information on the Church Missionary Society which supported Sim's work and that of other Anglican missionaries, see John Grant's *Moon of Wintertime: Missionaries and the Indians of Canada in Encounter since 1534* (Toronto: University of Toronto Press, 1984). Chapter 6 of Kerry Abel's *Drum Songs* (Montreal & Kingston: McGill-Queens University Press, 1993) offers a critical assessment of nineteenth-century Christian missionary work among the Dene.

22. Wesbrook, Ibid.

23. Bowen, *Incidents in the Life*, 86.

24. Ibid., 122.

25. William Ogilvie, *Exploratory Survey of Part of the Lewes, Tat-on-duc, Porcupine, Bell, Trout, Peel, and Mackenzie Rivers, 1887–88*. Annual Report for the Dept. of Interior 1889, Part VIII, Section 3 (Ottawa: B. Chamberlin, 1890), 47–48.

26. Vertical File: First Nations: Dawson Teachers' notes and letters file on the Wood Family, letter dated 1928. Dawson City Museum, Dawson City.

27. Kenneth Coates, *Best Left Indians: Native-White Relations in the Yukon Territory, 1840–1973* (Montreal & Kingston: McGill-Queen's University Press, 1991), 154.

28. Quote taken from Sarah Jane Essau to Bishop, 31 August 1919. Anglican Church, Moosehide File, Yukon Territorial Archives, Whitehorse.

29. Canham's remarks are quoted from Kenneth S. Coates, *Best Left Indians*, 11.

30. Robert McDonald is quoted in Coates, *Best Left Indians*.

31. Frederick Schwatka, *Report of A Military Reconnaissance in Alaska Made in 1883* (Washington, D.C.: Government Printing Office, 1885), 99. For a full accounting of the early epidemics impacting Alaska Natives see Robert Fortuine's *Chills and Fever: Health and Disease in the Early History of Alaska* (Fairbanks: University of Alaska Press, 1989).

32. Vincent Sim in Wesbrook, "A Venture into Ethnohistory," 41.

33. Schmitter, *Upper Yukon Native Customs and Folk-Lore*, 18.

34. Osgood, *The Han Indians*, 136.

35. Melody Webb, *The Last Frontier: A History of the Yukon Basin of Canada and Alaska* (Albuquerque: University of New Mexico Press, 1985), 144.

36. Harold Goodrich, "History and Conditions of Yukon Gold District in 1897." In *Geology of the Yukon Gold Districts, Alaska, Part III Economic Geology*. Eighteenth Annual Report of the United States Secretary of the Interior, 1896–1897 (Washington: U.S. Government Printing Office, 1898), 161–162.

37. William Bompas quoted in Hiram Alfred Cody, *An Apostle of the North: Memories of the Right Reverend William Carpenter Bompas* (New York: E. P. Dutton, 1908), 139.

38. Edwin Tappan Adney, "The Indian Hunter of the Far Northwest on the Trail to the Klondike." *Outing* (1902): 633.

39. Inspector F. Harper, as quoted in Robert G. McCandless, *Yukon Wildlife: A Social History* (Edmonton: University of Alberta Press, 1985), 32.

40. *Dawson Daily News*, 4 November 1915.

41. Lowell Thomas, *Woodfill of the Regulars: A True Story of Adventure from the Arctic to the Argonne* (New York: Doubleday, Doran & Company, 1929), 152.

42. Ibid., 99–100.

43. See United States Army, Adjutant General's Office, Post Returns. Fort Egbert (Alaska); 1899–1911. Microfilm. University of Alaska Anchorage, Consortium Library Archives.

44. Anne D. Shinkwin, Elizabeth F. Andrews, Russell H. Sackett, and Mary V. Kroul, *Fort Egbert and the Eagle Historic District: Summer 1977*. Technical Report No. 2, Fortymile Resource Area (Tok, Alaska: U.S. Department of Interior, Bureau of Land Management, 1978), 17.

45. F. A. Archer, *A Heroine of the North: Memoirs of Charlotte Selina Bompas (1830–1917) Wife of the First Bishop of Selkirk (Yukon) with Extracts of Her Journal and Letters* (London, 1929), as quoted in Osgood, *The Han Indians*, 130.

46. William Bompas quoted in Cody, *An Apostle of the North*, 139.

47. Ogilvie, *Exploratory Survey*, 48.

48. Peter Trimble Rowe, "Report of the Bishop of Alaska." In *Annual Report of the Board of Missions of the Protestant Episcopal Church in the United States of America 1910–11*, 68. Copy on file at Episcopal Church Archives, Austin, Texas.

49. Allen A. Wright, *Prelude to Bonanza: the Discovery and Exploration of the Yukon* (Sydney, B.C.: Gray's Publishing, 1976), 254.

50. Coates, *Best Left Indians*, 177. See also Doyle McDonald, "First Nations: Council Notes, 1921–1934." Vertical file, Dawson City Museum, Dawson.

51. Acc. 82/176 Flewelling Diary Box 51, File 6, Yukon Territorial Archives, Whitehorse.

52. Unnamed woman, apparently the daughter of Chief Isaac, interviewed by Julie Cruikshank in *Athapaskan Women: Lives and Legends*. Mercury Series, Canadian

Ethnology Service Paper No. 57 (Ottawa: National Museums of Canada, 1979), 47.

53. Anonymous, "Moosehide, a Brief History." Dawson Band Land Claims Office, Dawson City, n.d.

54. William Bompas to Church Missionary Society, 4 May 1898. National Archives of Canada, MG17, B25. As quoted in Kenneth Coates's *Best Left Indians*, 84.

55. Vertical File: First Nations: Council Notes 1921–1934, by Doyle MacDonald. Dawson City Museum, Dawson City.

56. Ibid.

57. Melody Webb, *The Last Frontier: A History of the Yukon Basin of Canada and Alaska* (Albuquerque: University of New Mexico Press, 1985), 137.

58. Elva Scott, *Jewel on the Yukon: Eagle City* (Eagle City: Eagle Historical Society and Museums, 1997).

59. Shinkwin et al., *Fort Egbert and the Eagle Historic District*, 37–38. See also United States Army, Adjutant General's Office. Post Returns, Fort Egbert (Alaska); 1899–1911. Microfilm. University of Alaska, Anchorage Archives.

60. Willie Juneby interviewed by Regina Goebel on 9–10 December 1980. Typescript. Eagle Historical Society Archives.

61. Louise Paul in *Proceedings, Historical Symposium*. Edited by Elva Scott, 2–4 July 1986 (Eagle City: Eagle Historical Society 1986), 39–40.

62. Personal communication, Elva Scott to William Simeone, 1997.

63. George Burgess, "St. Paul's Mission," *Alaska Churchman* 5 (August 1911):24.

64. Ibid.

65. Sarah Malcolm, interviewed by Yvonne Howard, 21 June 1990. Private Collection of Yvonne Howard, Eagle City.

66. Matthew Malcolm, interviewed by Steve Ulvi and William Schneider, tape recording H91-22-18, 8 August 1991, National Park Service Collection-Yukon Charley. Rasmuson Library, University of Alaska Fairbanks.

67. Matthew Malcolm, interviewed by Craig Mishler, 20 July 1997, Alaska Department of Fish and Game, Anchorage, Alaska.

68. Schmitter, *Upper Yukon Native Customs and Folk-Lore*, 22. The missionary George Boulton, who was in Eagle at the same time as Schmitter, also complained that "Nearly all the Indians have consumption [tuberculosis] in one form or another." See Boulton, "Letter to John Wood," 25 March 1907. Episcopal Church Archives, Austin, Texas.

69. Willie Juneby, interviewed by Mary Matthews, tape recording H91-12-317, 8 March 1973, National Park Service Collection–Yukon Charley. Rasmuson Library, University of Alaska Fairbanks.

70. Sarah Malcolm, interviewed by Jerry Dixon and Reggie Goebel, 6 September 1980. Transcript, p. 6. Eagle Historical Society Archives, Eagle.

71. See Richard White, *The Middle Ground: Indians, Empires, and Republics in the Great Lakes Region, 1650–1815* (Cambridge: Cambridge University Press, 1991).

72. Richard F. Salisbury, "Affluence and Cultural Survival." In *Affluence and Cultural Survival: 1981*, 1–11. Proceedings of the American Ethnological Society, edited by Richard Salisbury and Elisabeth Tooker. (Washington, D.C.: American Ethnological Society, 1984).

73. See for example, Albert Hurtado's *Indian Survival on the California Frontier* (New Haven: Yale University Press, 1988). An important difference in this comparison is that the Han, unlike the California Indians, were apparently not subject to violent attacks and killings by the miners.

Han Bands and Historic Settlement Patterns

TRADITIONAL HAN camps extended from the southeastern limit of the Yukon Flats just above Circle City, upriver to the Sixtymile River, some fifty miles above Dawson in the Yukon Territory (see Map 2). The Yukon River dominates the landscape and cuts through rounded hills that rise abruptly from the riverbank. Several large tributaries flow into the Yukon in this area including the Seventymile, Klondike, Fortymile, Nation, Kandik, and Charley rivers. These, along with a number of smaller streams, provide access to the hills adjacent to the river and the mountains farther back. There are a few lakes near the main river and at the heads of some of the major tributaries.

For the Han the landscape is not simply an inanimate backdrop, but something alive with spirit and memory. Many features of the landscape are named for a particular activity, physical characteristic, or other attribute. For example, Old Man and Old Woman rocks on the Yukon River are named for the two culture heroes whose deeds are described in the stories told by Louise Paul and Sarah Malcolm in Chapter 6. And according to Angie Joseph-Rear, the big rock slide on the mountain above Dawson City is locally known as *Ch'ëdhàä Dädëtaan* ("Moosehide"). "That is our people's marker," she says, "our sign by which other Dineh know where we come from."[1]

Another geographic feature that figures prominently in Han culture is Eagle Bluff (Plate 1), known in Hän as *Tthee Täwdlenn* or "water moving around the bluff," or "the water is hitting right into it." Sarah Malcolm said the chief "always said lots of things about the bluff," that it was always referred to in speeches, and that the chief would even say he was chief of Eagle Bluff. Her comments suggest that the Han thought of certain prominent geographic features in a patriotic way, as did other Athabaskan groups such as the Upper Tanana and Ahtna.

Population

Little is known about pre-contact or historic Han populations. There is scant evidence in the archaeological record for the pre-contact population; historic populations are also difficult to assess. The Han were almost certainly exposed to infectious diseases before they came into direct contact with Europeans, and until the beginning of the twentieth century they were extremely mobile. Therefore, population counts could be made only sporadically.

Table 1 represents population estimates for the Han from 1871 to 2000. Not represented on the table is Alexander Murray's estimate of the number of Han men trading at Fort Yukon in the late 1840s. Murray thought the Han were the largest group trading at Fort Yukon, with 230 men.[2] If this number is adjusted for sex and age, and if we assume a stable population, the total number of Han would be approximately 812. The accuracy of Murray's assertion is difficult to determine and it appears that this estimate is higher than later records show.

The population numbers for 1871 represented on the table are those made by Anglican priest Robert McDonald on his way up the Yukon River from Fort Yukon. The fish camps that he visited probably existed for only one or two years before they were moved to another location and were subsequently never counted again. The population of the Nuklako band was counted only during the years that Fort Reliance was active. The line labeled David's Band/Eagle Village has so many entries for two reasons: first, in the years 1880, 1888, and 1890 non-Natives passed by David's summer fish camp and counted the members of the band that had congregated there, and second, at the end of the nineteenth century a site at or very near the fish camp became Eagle Village and the population was counted on a fairly regular basis. This was also the case for Moosehide village. Note that numbers represented in Table 1 do not include all the settlements for any single year and are probably low.

Historic Bands

Anthropologists have identified three kinds of socio-territorial groups among Northern Athabaskans: the regional band, the local band, and the task group.[3] The regional band occupied a territory identified by tradition and use. Members of the regional band shared a common language and were related through ties of blood and marriage. They spent most of the year in smaller groups or bands dispersed over a wide area. These small bands came together only in times of the year when they could exploit a resource that was plentiful enough to allow a larger group to congregate. For example, a large number of Han would have gathered to fish, to hunt caribou, or to hold a potlatch.

The local band occupied and used a specific territory within the limits of the larger Han territory. Throughout their territory the local band had an assortment of hunting and fishing camps that they occupied at different seasons of the year. In addition to these camps, each of the Han bands seems to have had a principal winter village that it occupied during the darkest, coldest months of the year.

In size, the local band was much smaller than the regional band; whereas the latter may have had as many as five hundred people, the former may have averaged twenty or thirty. All members of the local band were closely related by blood and marriage. A typical band consisted of a core of siblings, male and female, and their spouses and dependents. Membership in a local band was fluid with members shifting from one local band to another. A family might shift its residence because of social discord within a band or move in with in-laws if food became scarce in one area.

A task group came together to harvest a specific resource and did not survive beyond the required period to perform that task. The composition of a task group varied and might include two related families or simply a group of men. Kinship and/or friendship often played a significant factor in the formation of a task group. The difference between the regional band, the local band, and the task group was one of degree rather than kind since a regional band and local band could also act as a task group. But as noted above, most of the year was spent in small, autonomous bands.

Nineteenth-century literature attests to the presence of at least three Han bands. These include Charley's Band, David's Band, and

Table 1
Han Population Estimates

Band/Settlements	1871	1880	1888	1890	1897	1899	1900	1904	1910	1911	1920	1930	1931	1938	1940	1950	1951	1954	1966	1980	1990	1997	2000
Charley's Band/Charley Village				66					24														
David's Band/Eagle Village		106	70	66			63	90	69		60	89		63	62	45		57	64	54	28	24	30
Fort Reliance/Nuklako Band			70	82																			
Isaac's Band/Moosehide					60	55				125			76				60						
Charley River Band							17																
Han Summer Camp #1	52																						
Han Summer Camp #2	19																						
Han Summer Camp #3	20																						
Han Summer Camp #4	44																						
Totals by Year	135	106	140	148	60	55	80	90	69	125	60	89	76	63	62	45	60	57	64	54	28	24	30

(Note: populations for each census have been adjusted to exclude non-Native residents)

Sources:

1871: Rev. Robert McDonald; 1880/1890: Ivan Petroff; 1888: William Ogilvie; 1897: Tappan Adney; 1899: Yukon Archives;
1900/10/20/50/80/90/2000: U.S. Bureau of the Census; 1904/1930: Episcopal Church Records; 1911/1951: Statistics Canada;
1931: Anglican Church Records; 1938/40/54/66: Bureau of Indian Affairs; 1997: Alaska Dept. of Fish & Game Div. of Subsistence

Data compiled by the Alaska Department of Fish & Game, Division of Subsistence, Anchorage the Klondike Band, more appropriately referred to now as *Tr'ondëk Hwëch'in*. It is uncertain whether there was a fourth band composed of people living at *Nuklako*, a settlement located downstream from the mouth of the Klondike River near Fort Reliance, or whether it was a site used seasonally by the Klondike Band.

The earliest information about these bands comes from the observations of traders, missionaries, and explorers who did not describe the composition of the groups or their activities and movements but instead wrote about their fish camps or winter villages. In the twentieth century, anthropologists have collected more specific information about band territories.

Charley's Band

The northern-most band of Han was known as Charley's Band, after its leader, Chief Charley. The band's major winter settlement was called Charley's Village at the mouth of the Kandik River, also known as "Charley Creek." Probably the earliest description of "Charley's Village" is by Frederick Schwatka, a military explorer who conducted a reconnaissance of the Yukon River in the 1880s.[4]

It is confusing to many people that Charley River and "Charley Creek" (the Kandik) both empty into the Yukon River within a few miles of each other, the former coming in from the west and the latter from the east. When the 1900 U.S. Census was taken, the only enumerated village in the area was identified as "Charley River" and not "Charley Creek." While it is tempting to lump this community in with the "Charley Creek Indian village" visited by the next census taker in 1910, there is good reason to think that at least two and perhaps three distinct Han settlements were located in the area. One of these was just above the mouth of "Charley Creek" (the Kandik) on the right bank of the Yukon, and another was just across from the mouth of the Kandik on the left bank, near Biederman Camp.[5] A third settlement may have been established ten miles farther down the Yukon near the mouth of the Charley River. The small and temporary town of Independence, a gold rush community, was established at this location, with eight to ten cabins, and there may have been some Han among them.[6]

Such an interpretation helps resolve the conflict between Schwatka's account of "Charley Village" being located on the western side of the Yukon River and its modern-day archaeological discovery on the right bank or eastern side of the river. Charley Village is identified on the

Alaska Heritage Resource Survey (AHRS) as CHR 001.[7] National Park Service archaeologist Richard Bland thinks the Han actually lived on both sides of the Yukon River at different times.[8] A site with four house depressions (CHR 037) located on the western side of the Yukon River just below the mouth of "Charley Creek" (the Kandik), for example, has been interpreted as a possible satellite settlement of Charley Village.

Yet another reason for thinking there were two or more distinct Han settlements in this area is that the list of names recorded for the "Charley River" Indian village in the 1900 U.S. Census, which included the Johnson, Ginnis, and Philip families, does not match the list of names recorded for Charley Creek Indian village in the 1910 U.S. Census. In 1910 there was no census at all for the Charley River village, and the inference is that the Charley River people moved downriver to Fort Yukon between 1900 and 1910, before Charley Village itself was abandoned. One of their direct descendants, Elliot Johnson, Sr., lived most of his life in Fort Yukon and considered himself to be Han but does not appear to be connected to any of the other Han family trees we have compiled (see Appendix D: Johnson family tree). While Ginnis is an active surname in Fort Yukon, it is unknown whether the present-day Ginnises were from Charley River or elsewhere. To our knowledge there are no Phillip families living anywhere in the region.

Figure 6. Chief Charley, center, with two of his men, 1883. Photo by Edward Schieffelin.

It is also noteworthy that Willie Juneby once talked about a few Indian people living on Sam Creek and on Washington Creek, tributary streams farther down the Yukon River from the mouth of Charley River. Hudson Stuck mentioned baptizing two children at a camp near Woodchopper Creek, but there are no other written records of these families, and apparently the families themselves have not survived. Certainly there is a need for additional archaeological surveys to verify the presence of these camps. A flood reportedly destroyed Charley Village in 1914 and, according to Eagle residents, Chief Charley moved some of his people to Eagle. They are said to have camped at *Nibaw Zhoh* before deciding to move farther upriver to the vicinity of the present Native cemetery.

David's Band

Oral history gathered by Schmitter and information provided by Sarah Malcolm indicate that in the nineteenth century David's Band may have wintered up Mission Creek and on the Seventymile River.[9] Evidence also suggests this band had caribou hunting camps at the head of Comet and Eureka creeks and a moose fence on American Creek. Schmitter relates a story that sometime in the 1880s David's Band was wintering on Mission Creek when it was overtaken by smallpox, and most of the people died.[10] At that point many of the survivors reportedly moved to Fortymile.

Figure 7. A band of David's Indians who camped about 3.5 miles above Camp Davidson during the winter of 1890–1891.

According to Han oral accounts, David's Band also occupied the land around the mouth of Mission Creek at various times. Sarah Malcolm, for example, recalled that many people lived "by the BLM station" (the present Yukon-Charley Rivers National Preserve headquarters) by the [Mission] creek. "Some of the high bank is a burial ground," she said. "Some people are buried way back where there is a good place, but nobody knows where."[11]

David's Band had, as one of its principal places, a fish camp located near the site of present-day Eagle City. Probably the earliest and most complete reference to this community comes from Schwatka, who mistakenly called the place "Johnny's Village." Schwatka described the village as follows:

> The first Indian village we had encountered on the river deserving the name of permanent, and even here the logs of which the cabins, six in number, were built, seemed mere poles and by no means substantially built. . . . It was perched high up on a flat bank on the western side of the river, the gable ends of the house fronting the stream, and all of them very close together, there being only one or two places wide enough for a path to allow intimates to pass.
>
> The fronts of the houses were nearly on the same line, and this row is so close to the scrap of bank that the street in front is a very narrow path, where two persons can hardly pass. . . . This street may have been wider in times of yore—for it seemed to be quite an old village. . . . The roofs are of skins battened down by spruce poles, which projecting beyond the comb in irregular lengths, often six or eight feet, gave the whole village a most bristling appearance. A fire is built in the dirt-floor.[12]

He also noted that below the village was the trading station of Belle Isle, which was deserted. Beside the houses were scaffolds for drying fish and caches upon which were "Hudson Bay toboggan sledges."

In July 1891 Anglican missionary Robert McDonald visited David's Village and wrote, "Reached David's, the chief's fishing place, at sunset. A good many families with him. They are making a good salmon fishing."[13] McDonald gave the location of David's as three days' travel above Willow River. Willow River probably refers to "Charley Creek" (i.e., the Kandik River), better known in Hän as *K'ay Juu* or *K'ay Ndek*, which means Willow Creek. This would place David's fish camp just about where Eagle Village is today.

Located near David's summer fish camp, on the same left bank of the Yukon River, 2.5 miles downriver from the present-day Eagle Village, was a semi-permanent Han winter camp known as *Nibaw Zhoh* or skin house in the Hän language. The site consisted of eight house pits and was probably occupied intermittently during the decade of 1880 to 1890.[14] Oral accounts and genealogical research connect this site with David's Band. Adults residing at this site were "Old Henry" and his wife Isabel; "Old Alec" and his wife Mary; David and his wife; Joe and Maggie, who were brother and sister to Isabel; Simon and Susan, who were the parents of Big Stephen, Sarah Malcolm's father, and "Old Peter," Willie Juneby's grandfather.

The Klondike Band (*Tr'ondëk Hwëch'in*)

The Klondike Band was the uppermost of the Han bands. This band had a summer fish camp at the mouth of the Klondike River called *Tr'oojuu Ech'in*, better known today as *Tr'ondëk* Village or *Tr'ochëk*.[15] Figure 8 shows dwellings at the mouth of the river before the Klondike stampede. It is uncertain whether this, or another band, inhabited the village of *Nuklako* located across the Yukon River from Fort Reliance (see Map 2).

In 1898 the leader of the band was Chief Isaac. According to him, the ancestors of the Han then living at the mouth of Moosehide Creek had a tradition that somewhere up the Klondike River, in the vicinity of the Ogilvie Mountains, lived a large and savage group of Indians they called

Figure 8. The place called Tr'ochëk, near the mouth of the Klondike River, circa 1895.

the "Mahoneys." The Mahoneys were supposed to be relentless in war. So afraid were the Han of the Mahoneys, that until the arrival of the Europeans they would not extend their hunting expeditions any farther away than what is known as All Gold Creek, a tributary of Flat Creek. All Gold Creek is approximately thirty-five miles up the Klondike River from Dawson.

In the 1960s Han elders living in Dawson City outlined the historical hunting area of the Klondike Band for the Canadian ethnologist Richard Slobodin.[16] They said that at the end of the fishing season, before the rivers froze, the people traveled by canoe or steamboat down to either Coal Creek, the Tatonduk River, or the Nation River. After freeze-up the band trekked up one of these valleys into the Ogilvie Mountains where they spent the winter. They moved in such a way that near the end of winter they arrived at the head of the Klondike River. When the ice went out they built moose-skin boats and traveled down to the mouth of the river where they prepared for salmon fishing.

In 1896, at the beginning of the Klondike stampede, the *Tr'ondëk Hwëch'in* were displaced from their traditional site at the mouth of the Klondike River. They later moved to a new village located about two miles down the Yukon River from Dawson, at the mouth of Moosehide Creek. Archaeological evidence indicates that the Moosehide village site had been previously occupied during three separate time periods, the earliest about 6,500 years ago and the latest about 1730 AD.

Twelve-Mile

Twelve-Mile, located on the Canadian side of the border at the mouth of the Chandindu River, is a relatively recent Han community, created at the time of the Klondike gold rush when the Han were displaced from their ancestral home at the mouth of the Klondike River. Most of the Han moved to Moosehide, but some people moved to Twelve-Mile. Some of these residents were either from Alaska or had close ties to Alaska.

Twelve-Mile village was about twenty miles below Dawson and twelve miles downriver from Fort Reliance. The Han call this village *Tthedëk*. Charlie Adams and his wife Ann were the major figures in this move. Oral tradition indicates that at least ten families lived in the village. The settlement was located close to a caribou migration route, which gave people access to plenty of meat and skins. For a time Twelve-Mile thrived, but most people eventually moved to Dawson, and in 1957 a flood destroyed all of the remaining houses.[17]

Figure 9. The Adams and Taylor families at Twelve-Mile Village, identified by Michael Mason. Front row (left to right): Clara, Lydia and Ida Adams (twins), three unidentified toddlers, Emilia Taylor, Bessie Taylor, Ben Taylor; second row: Jimmy Wood, Rowena Stringer, Wilfred Stringer, Charlie Adams, Ann Adams, Bishop Isaac Stringer, Annie Taylor (with unidentified infant), Ellen Taylor, Charlie Mason, Dave Taylor, Martha Taylor (with unidentified infant), circa 1909–1934.

Settlement Patterns and House Types

Han settlements were strategically located for the harvest of game and fish. In 1932, Walter Benjamin of Eagle Village told Cornelius Osgood that in the past the Han constructed three types of shelter according to activity and season of the year.[18] The most substantial houses were built out of blocks of moss and used during the winter when frequent travel was unnecessary. A second type of shelter, used when traveling in the winter, was a domed tent made of caribou skin with the hair left on. The third type of shelter, used in mild weather, was a tent made of skin with the hair removed. According to Osgood, a teepee-like secondary structure was also built.

The moss house served as a permanent winter structure and was built and occupied by two families. In constructing the house, the Han first excavated a twenty-five-foot square to a depth of about one-and-a-half feet, or down to frozen ground. They then raised a poles between four and six feet high at each corner of the square, and one pole about ten feet high between the corner posts at two ends of the house. A ridgepole was then placed between the two center posts, and horizontal beams, parallel to the ridgepole, were set up to connect the corner posts. Rafters were then set in place connecting the ridgepole with the horizontal beams between the corner posts. Once the framework was finished, split poles were set vertically, side by side, all around the house and lashed to the horizontal beam. An opening for a door was left at one end of the house. Squares of moss, cut as large as possible, were then placed against the sides and ends. Moss was laid, with roots facing upward, on the roof. A hearth was placed in the center of the house on a raised bed of gravel. The house was considered complete when a bull caribou hide or bear skin was set for a door.

When moving about during the winter, the Han lived in domed tents constructed of caribou skins, with the hair on, stretched over a frame of wooden poles. These were two family dwellings with a common hearth.

Several very good descriptions of these skin tents are found in the literature. Perhaps the earliest comes from the geologist William Ogilvie who describes Han tents he observed during the winter of 1887–1888.[19] These are identical to those described by the journalist Tappan Adney.

Adney accompanied Chief Isaac's band on a hunting trip up the Klondike River in the winter of 1898. The group camped several times and each time the women set the domed tents. Seven were in this camp. In Chief Isaac's tent, where Adney stayed, there were two households

Figure 10. Indian toboggans stopping at Camp Davidson, 1890–1891. Adney (n.d.) observed that "the Tro-chu-tin with whom we hunted in the upper Klondike in the winter of 1897–1898 packed their numerous long curved ten[t] poles on the toboggan in such a way that they formed a sort of "canoe" with the caribou skin tent covers arranged as a long receptacle in which were carried the smaller children, babies, and pups, as well as various articles of the household economy."

Figure 11. An Indian family and brush house, 1890–1891.

with a total of eight people and eleven dogs. Each household had one side of the fire to itself. People knelt or reclined before the fire, which was built to throw heat in two directions.

Adney described how, when the band arrived at a campsite, the women first removed the snow from an area before they set the tent:

The women took long-handled wooden shovels and removed the snow off the ground an elliptical space eighteen feet long by twelve feet wide, banking it all around two feet high. While some covered the exposed river gravel with green spruce boughs and kindled a fire in the center, other cut sticks three to five feet long and set them upright a foot apart in the bank of snow, the long way of the intended house, leaving an opening at one side two feet wide for the door.

The house poles, an inch thick and ten or twelve feet long, whittled out of spruce and previously bent and seasoned into the form of a curve, were then set up in the snow at the ends of the camp to the number of sixteen or twenty, their upper ends pointing toward the middle in the form of a dome ten feet high. These were strengthened by two arched cross-poles underneath, the ends of which were lashed to the side-stakes with withes of willow twigs thawed out and made pliant over the fire.

Over this comparatively stiff frame-work next was drawn a covering of caribou-skin, tanned with the hair on, made in two sections, and shaped and sewed together to fit the dome. The two sections, comprising forty skins, completely covered the house, except in the middle, where a large hole was left for the smoke to escape, and at the doorway, over which was hung a piece of blanket. The toboggans with the balance of the loads were hoisted upon pole scaffolds on each side of the house, out of reach of the dogs.[20]

During the late spring and summer, when a fire could be built outside, the Han made tents with moose-hide coverings. Figures 11, 12, and 13 are photographs taken in 1890–1891 of such shelters. Brush was used to construct the walls while the roof was made from a piece of canvas (as shown) or skin. They were built with two parallel compartments, one for each family, and space in between for a common hearth. Such tents were probably used at places like Ford Lake where people had temporary camps in springtime.

One other type of traditional structure, which may be the teepee-like structure, was a smokehouse or smoke cache used in the summer (Figure 14). This kind of structure is still used today in Eagle Village. It is built of poles with a canvas or plastic tarp cover. People may have lived in these during the summer, when a smoky fire was desirable for keeping mosquitoes away.

On occasion, the Han slept in the open with minimal shelter, especially if there were only men in the traveling party. Anglican missionary

Figure 12. An Indian brush house and meat cache, located about 3.5 miles above Camp Davidson on the Yukon River, 1890–1891.

Figure 13. Indian canvas-covered house and woodpile, circa 1910.

R. J. Bowen described a trip he took from Fortymile to Fort Reliance with some Han in winter 1895.[21] He and his party traveled by dog team on the ice of the Yukon River, and every afternoon they made camp. When camping on the river, the Han men first dug a hole in the snow with their snowshoes, almost down to the river ice. The removed snow was used as a windbreak. They did not dig nearly so much if they camped in the brush. While some dug out the hole, other men gathered spruce boughs, spreading them on the bottom of the hole, and fur robes were then spread over the boughs. The men used river ice for their tea water. When preparing for bed they banked the fire with green logs.

Figure 14. Fish drying racks, girls, dogs, and dip net, Moosehide, 1897–1898.

By the end of the nineteenth century most Han had settled into permanent communities and built small, one-room log houses heated by wood stoves that had a hole cut for a cast iron door and chimney pipe. While out on the trail, people slept in white canvas wall tents heated by a small sheet-iron stove. In the early 1970s elder Bob Stacey was still living year-round in such a tent, and in 1997 several men were sleeping in one during the summer.

Up until the 1960s most Han living in Eagle Village had no electricity and relied on the outhouse and the "honey bucket" instead of flush toilets. Now at the turn of the twenty-first century most of the Han live in homes of log or frame construction, many of which are still heated by wood stoves. Some homes have small efficient oil heaters and most have propane cook stoves and electricity, but in 1997 almost no one in Eagle Village had running water or flush toilets. That situation is changing rapidly, however, as new government-funded housing is being built upriver along the Dog Island road.

Notes

1. Angie Joseph-Rear, quoted in Norm Easton, "Students Enjoy Moosehide Hospitality." *Yukon News* (30 July 1999), 15.

2. Alexander Hunter Murray, *Journal of the Yukon 1847–48*. Edited by J. J. Burpee (Ottawa: Publications of the Public Archives of Canada, No. 4, 1910), 82.

3. See James W. VanStone, *Athapaskan Adaptations: Hunters and Fishermen of the Subarctic Forests* (Chicago: Aldine Publishing Co., 1974), 45. For more on bands see Chapter 4.

4. Frederick Schwatka, *A Summer in Alaska* (St. Louis: J. W. Henry, 1893), 262.

5. A preliminary inventory of historic and archaeological sites in this area is included in Melody Webb Grauman's *Yukon Frontiers: Historic Resource Study of the Proposed Yukon-Charley National River* (Fairbanks: Cooperative Park Studies Unit, University of Alaska, 1977).

6. The town of Independence was observed by Lieutenant Wilds Richardson in 1899. See Melody Webb, *The Last Frontier: A History of the Yukon Basin of Canada and Alaska* (Albuquerque: University of New Mexico Press, 1985), 138.

7. Schwatka, *A Summer in Alaska*, 262. The Alaska Heritage Resource Survey is a database maintained by the State of Alaska's Office of History and Archaeology in Anchorage.

8. Richard Bland, "Charley Village: Has it Finally Been Located?" Unpublished manuscript. Anchorage: National Park Service, 1994.

9. Ferdinand Schmitter, *Upper Yukon Native Customs and Folk-Lore* (Washington, D.C.: The Smithsonian Institution, 1910). Reprinted by the Eagle Historical Society, Eagle, Alaska, 18. See also Sarah Malcolm, interviewed by Jerry Dixon on 6 September 1980. Transcript, Eagle Historical Society Archives.

10. Schmitter, *Upper Yukon Native Customs and Folk-Lore*, 18.

11. Sarah Malcolm, interviewed by Jerry Dixon on 6 September 1980. Transcript, Eagle Historical Society Archives.

12. Schwatka, *A Summer in Alaska*, 251–252.

13. Robert McDonald, Journals, 1891. In *Letters and Papers of the Church Missionary Society, London* (microfilm copy at Rupert's Land Provincial Archives, Winnipeg).

14. Elizabeth Andrews, "Archaeological Evidence of European Contact: The Han Athabaskans near Eagle, Alaska." *High Plains Applied Anthropologist* 7, No. 2 (1987): 51–63.

15. Helene Dobrowolsky and T. J. Hammer. *Tr'ochëk: the Archaeology and History of a Hän Fish Camp* (Dawson City: Tr'ondëk Hwëch'in First Nation, 2001), passim.

16. Richard Slobodin, "Notes on the Han." Appendix II to Preliminary Report on Ethnographic Work, 1962. Unpublished Manuscript. (Ottawa: National

Museum of Man, Ethnology Division, 1963), 5.

17. Most of the information we received about Twelve-Mile comes from Charles Mason, whom we met in Dawson in 1997. At the time Charles had compiled a history of the village and was organizing a family reunion for later in the summer. His effort to document the history of his ancestors' community is one example of how the Han today are recapturing and learning to understand their past.

18. Cornelius Osgood, *The Han Indians: A Compilation of Ethnographic and Historical Data on the Alaska-Yukon Boundary Area* (New Haven: Yale University Publications in Anthropology No. 74, 1971), 84–85.

19. William Ogilvie, *Exploratory Survey of Part of the Lewes, Tat-on-duc, Porcupine, Bell, Trout, Peel, and Mackenzie Rivers, 1887–88*. Annual Report for the Dept. of Interior 1889, Part VIII, Section 3 (Ottawa: B. Chamberlin, 1890).

20. Edwin Tappan Adney, "Moose Hunting with the Tro-chu-tin." *Harper's New Monthly Magazine* 100, No. 598 (1900), 499.

21. R. J. Bowen, *Incidents in the Life of the Reverend Richard John Bowen Among the Natives, Trappers Prospectors and Gold Miners in the Yukon Territory Before and After the Gold Rush of the Year 1898*. Typescript in the National Archives of Canada, Ottawa, 112.

Chapter Three

Making a Living:
The Han Subsistence Economy

O VER THE LAST 150 years the Han economy has slowly changed from a purely subsistence economy based on hunting, fishing, and gathering wild resources to a mixed economy in which traditional subsistence activities are supported more and more by commercial fur trapping and/or wage labor. This chapter begins with a brief description of the subsistence economy, the seasonal round, and specific subsistence activities described in the literature and in interviews with Han elders. This period pertains to the late nineteenth century and the first three decades of the twentieth century.

The economy of the entire Upper Yukon basin changed during this period from one based on the trade in furs to one based on mining and transportation. The second part of this chapter describes, in the words of Han elders, fur trapping and involvement in wage labor.

One key feature of a subsistence economy is flexibility, and the Han were expert at using most of the animal and plant resources available to them. The most important animal resources were caribou and salmon. Relatively abundant at different seasons of the year, both provided essential calories and fat. In addition, caribou skins were indispensable for the manufacture of warm clothing.

Other animals important to the Han diet were moose, Dall sheep, black bear, arctic hare, porcupine, beaver, and muskrat. Lynx were also eaten, as were marmots. Birds harvested by the Han included several species of ducks, Canada geese, swans, grouse, and ptarmigan.

In addition to salmon, the Han caught arctic grayling, northern pike, and burbot. They also used many different kinds of plants including berries, Labrador tea, moss, white spruce, balsam poplar or cottonwood, aspen, birch, and several species of alder.

A second characteristic of a subsistence economy is a pattern of seasonal movement. During the short summer season the Han lived and traveled along the major waterways, catching and putting up fish (Figure 14). In winter they made extensive trips overland, moving long distances in search of big and small game. The transitional periods of "breakup," in late spring and "freeze-up" during the fall were the most difficult. It was during these periods that travel was restricted, making it extremely hard for the Han to find game.

Sharing resources is yet another feature of a subsistence economy, and sharing within the band was imperative. How these resources were shared depended, in many instances, on who killed the game. The hindquarters of a moose, for example, belonged to the man who shot it, and it was his prerogative to designate who would get the shoulders. The rest of the meat belonged to the community.[1]

Among the Han, work was generally organized around gender and age while the sharing of resources was structured along kinship lines. Young men, directed by their elders, did the more strenuous tasks associated with hunting and killing big game. On occasion, however, women, elders, and older children were employed in hunting activities such as caribou drives. Women were responsible for processing the meat and skins once game was killed. They were also responsible for processing fish caught by the men. Women gathered plants and, more often than men, hunted and snared small game such as arctic hares and porcupines.

When European fur traders entered the upper Yukon valley in the 1840s, the Han economy changed. Trapping furbearing animals took on an added significance because it became the primary means by which the Han could obtain European manufactured goods and items such as tea, flour, and sugar. The Han also sold meat and other products, such as tanned caribou and moose skins, to the traders. Later, as the regional economy developed around mining and construction, wage labor became an important component of the Han economy.

As a result, by the early twentieth century the Han had developed a mixed economy in which the traditional pursuits of hunting, fishing, and gathering were combined with commercial trapping and wage labor. Today commercial trapping among the Han has declined, but they continue to practice traditional subsistence activities while working for wages either seasonally or year-round.

The Seasonal Round

Availability of resources required the Han to move at different seasons during the year. In the summer they fixed all of their attention on fishing for salmon in the Yukon River. From June until August Han families lived in fish camps, catching and drying large quantities of salmon that they stored for the winter. At the end of the fishing season, periodic trips were made upland to hunt game and gather berries. Hunting continued into the fall until a supply of meat had been dried and cached in the hills. As freeze-up approached, the Han returned to the river to prepare for winter.

In early winter, when movement by dog team was possible, all of the cached meat was brought down to the river and the people remained there until their supplies of dried meat and fish were gone.[2] To augment the supply of dried foods, men made periodic trips to hunt moose and other game while the women snared hares close to the village. Once food supplies dwindled, the Han moved away from the river in search of caribou, and throughout the winter months they moved from place to place in search of game. As the weather moderated, they moved to lakes where they could hunt returning migratory waterfowl, muskrats, and moose. Once breakup was complete they returned to the river to prepare for the summer salmon fishing season.[3]

In the early 1960s Richard Slobodin interviewed several Han men and women living in Dawson City, Yukon.[4] Their accounts relate seasonal movements that took place in the late nineteenth and early twentieth centuries. They describe a seasonal round that included salmon fishing at the mouth of the Klondike River and long winter treks into the mountains. At the end of the fishing season, before the rivers froze, the entire band traveled by canoe or steamboat down to one of the side streams feeding into the Yukon, such as Coal Creek, the Tatonduk River, or the Nation River.

After freeze-up, using dog teams and snowshoes, they traveled up these valleys into the Ogilvie Mountains where they spent the winter. The people traveled in a way that brought them to the head of the Klondike River near the end of winter. At spring breakup they camped on the larger lakes in the upper drainage and hunted migratory waterfowl, muskrats, and beaver. After breakup, they built moose-skin boats and descended to the mouth of the Klondike River to prepare for salmon fishing.

Those interviewed by Slobodin said that they sometimes varied their route of winter travel by going beyond the Klondike to the headwaters of the Stewart River and then going down that river to the Yukon. Another variation was to ascend a tributary flowing into the west side of the Yukon River, such as the Ch arley River, and travel along the mountains to the head of the White River. They would then descend the White River to the Yukon River and follow it downstream to the mouth of the Klondike.

Routes that led into the Ogilvie Mountains followed Eagle Creek or Last Chance Creek. According to Bob Stacey, people used Eagle Creek more often during the fall and mid-winter because of the danger of overflow there during late winter. From Eagle Creek people went over the divide into the Tatonduk drainage by way of Lieutenant Creek. They used Last Chance Creek to reach the head of the Porcupine and Peel rivers. A good trail went up Last Chance Creek, then down Stacey Creek and over to the Tatonduk River drainage, then down that river to Andrew Creek and over the ridge to Sheep Creek and the headwaters of the Porcupine (see Map 3). The international boundary had little effect on these seasonal movements until the 1930s when a new duty on furs imported into Alaska from Canada made trapping across the border un-profitable. Richard Caulfield writes that Eagle Village people last used Eagle Creek in 1941. After World War II, the Han living on the Alaskan side of the border shifted many of their subsistence activities to areas such as American Summit, south of Eagle Village.[5] During the post-war era Tim, Jacob, and Matthew Malcolm took dogs and a toboggan to trap marten on Champion Creek. Champion Creek flows along the route of the old telegraph line from Eagle to Valdez.[6]

Bob Stacey, an elder resident of Eagle Village, said that in the 1920s he traveled and trapped extensively in the Ogilvie Mountains at the headwaters of the Blackstone and Whitestone rivers, spent Christmas at Eagle Village and then headed back to the mountains until spring. After breakup he floated down either the Kandik or Nation River to the Yukon where he caught a steamboat on its way upriver to Eagle City.

Sarah Malcolm recalled that when she was a child, just after the turn of the century, her whole family walked in the summer from Eagle Village to Ford Lake, located down the Yukon River near the mouth the Seventymile River.[7] There they hunted muskrats, beaver, ducks, geese, and moose. In the fall, several families traveled together with dogs either up the Tatonduk River, up Sheep Creek, or up Eagle Creek, which crosses the international boundary just east of Eagle Village. On these hunts they pursued sheep and caribou. Sarah said they liked to dry the meat, because that way it was lighter and easier to carry.

By the middle of the twentieth century the Han living at Eagle Village continued to hunt, fish, gather, and trap, but they no longer moved with the seasons. When hunting or trapping, the men seldom spent more than one day away from the village. Rather than accompany the men, the women and children remained in the village, although women did undertake extensive trips into the hills around Eagle Village to pick berries in the fall.

These changes have taken place for four reasons. First, children are required by Alaska law to remain in school until they are sixteen years old, so parents cannot leave on extended trips away from the village. Second, state and federal hunting regulations restrict the hunting of big game to specific times of the year. Seasons for moose and sheep, for example, are now limited to short periods in the fall and early winter. Bag limits set by the state are also restrictive. An individual hunter is limited to one animal of a specific sex. Third, wage labor is much more important today than it was at the beginning of the twentieth century. Finally, the availability of processed, commercial foods makes it less imperative that people hunt and fish.

Research conducted in the 1970s at Eagle Village showed that the Han fished primarily for salmon and whitefish during the summer.[8] In 1971 and 1972 they had fish camps at the mouth of the Nation River, but by 1976 they had abandoned these camps and fished only in front of the village. In the fall, hunters from Eagle Village hunted black bear and moose on islands along the Yukon River such as Wood Island, the islands across from Trout Creek and just below the Nation River. They also hunted at the mouth of the Seventymile River, at Ford Lake, Eagle Creek, the flats around Eagle Village, and along the Taylor Highway, when caribou from the Fortymile herd crossed the road. Han men sometimes killed Dall sheep in the Glacier Mountain area southwest of Eagle Village. Hunts for bear, moose, and sheep usually lasted from one to several days and were often conducted by partners or small groups of men. During the winter, some men trapped marten, lynx, wolf, and fox, and in the early spring switched to trapping beaver and muskrat (Figure 15). They also occasionally killed a moose or black bear at this time of year. In the late spring, once the ice melted from the edges of lakes, the men shot muskrat and returning waterfowl.

Figure 15. Mike Potts's early winter fur catch (wolf, marten, and lynx), Eagle City, December 1973. Left to right: Archie Juneby, Oliver Lyman, Mike Potts, and Danny David.

Fishing

Historically fish—and especially salmon—were a vital source of food for the Han who, at different times of the year, caught whitefish, arctic grayling, northern pike, burbot, longnose sucker, and salmon. The most significant of all fish were the king (Chinook) salmon and chum (dog) salmon (Figure 16). King salmon begin running at Eagle Village around July 1 and continue for about a month. Then there is a short break before the chum salmon run begins in mid-August. Chums continue to run into late September.

Osgood wrote that fresh salmon average one thousand calories per pound. He estimated one salmon would average about fifteen thousand calories and that based on these numbers fifty fish were enough to supply one person two thousand calories a day for a full year.[9]

Figure 16. Charlie Stevens, Sophie Stevens, and Hannah Stevens cutting fish (date unknown).

Han salmon fishing techniques and technology have varied over time. In aboriginal times the Han used basket traps and dip nets to catch salmon. In the early twentieth century non-Native prospectors introduced the Han to fishwheels, and later on the Han took up the use of gill nets.

Traditionally, the Han used long-handled dip nets, primarily to catch Chinook salmon that swim in the deep water away from the riverbank. Sarah Malcolm described how a dip net was used from canoes to catch these fish. She noted that once the salmon's head was pulled over the side of the canoe the fisher killed it with a club:

> people got no fish net, no fishwheel, so they use dip net. Dip net they go out with canoe, and they got dip net. They do like this. Pretty soon king salmon. King salmon is strong. They hold handle, then fish go like this [gesturing]. They put fish head right here in canoe. They club it. They kill it. It's good fish. Dip net is good fish. It dry good too.[10]

According to Willie Juneby, Shade Creek was a good place to dip net for king salmon because the water was the right depth for a man in canoe to see the wake of the swimming fish.[11]

In the nineteenth century the Han made funnel-shaped basket traps of spruce wood tied with spruce roots to catch chum salmon, arctic grayling, and burbot. These traps were set in shallow eddies near the banks of the Yukon River, at the mouth of tributary streams, or in lakes. A weir made of brush was set out from the bank and a gap left in the weir near the trap. As the fish swam upstream, they tried to crowd through the gap but many were forced to swim into the trap. When the fish were running, someone had to constantly attend the trap so that it would not break from the weight of the fish. As the salmon was lifted out of the trap, the fisher hit the fish on the head with a club.

Today fish traps are illegal under state and federal regulations. The Han now use dip nets, fishwheels, and gill nets to catch salmon. Dip nets are no longer used with canoes. Instead the fishers stand along the shore waiting for king or chum salmon that swim in the shallow water near the riverbank. The fisher waits for the telltale wake of the swimming fish, and then quietly, so as not to disturb the salmon, sweeps the long-handled dip net downstream with the current and into the path of the fish. This kind of fishing is most effective during the evening when the sun is low so that the wake of the fish creates a shadow visible to the fishermen. In an eddy, where the current temporarily swirls upstream, the current fans out the dip net's webbing, so the fisher may conserve energy by holding the net firmly in one position and waiting for fish to "bump" into the net.

The majority of Han fishers now use fishwheels to catch salmon. There are fishwheels at Eagle Village and Moosehide and at several fish camps situated along the Yukon River between Eagle Village and Dawson City. Only a few people use gill nets today. In 1997, Matthew Malcolm used a gill net for catching salmon because it was easier for him to maintain than a fishwheel. Matthew set his net in the slack water of an eddy downstream from the village and checked it with his partner once or twice a day, depending on the strength of the run (Figure 17; see also Chapter 7).

Up until the mid-1970s, Han families usually moved to their fish camps while the salmon were running. In the early twentieth century, fish camps were located up and down the Yukon, and several were situated close to Eagle Village. One was near the present Eagle Village cemetery. Willie Juneby remembered "seven or eight canoes down there and the kids snuck down in the evening to get their bellies full of fish head or fish eggs."[12] Sarah Malcolm also talked about this place. She remembered how she prepared fish eggs for babies, and how quiet the camp was on a drowsy afternoon:

> They cook fish eggs for baby, and they make gravy in it and pass around to little baby. Even that little baby eat that fresh fish. They mix it with a little gravy. Whitefish eggs, I talk about, not fresh fish.

And so they helped them. They like it. "And don't put too much salt in," mother say, "not too much salt, just a little bit flavor." And they cooked good for baby, and after that baby just go to sleep. Camp is quiet. People have a little food to eat. That was down cemetery, this side, where they fishing for fish.[13]

Figure 17. Matthew Malcolm's fish camp at Eagle Village, July 1997.

In the past, all of the salmon were dried and smoked. The women split them lengthwise and made transverse cuts in the meat about one inch apart so the salmon would dry more thoroughly. Sarah Malcolm said that cottonwood was used to smoke fish: "Cottonwood, that one strong smoke. Fly don't like it. . . . Night time they dry fish good. No fly bother it. Sometimes two boys they sleep in tent and they take care of those cache fire for fresh fish."[14] According to Silas Stevens, the Han at Eagle Village processed king salmon for human consumption while they used chum salmon primarily for dog food.[15]

Fish eggs, especially salmon eggs, were sometimes dried for storage by either laying them on the same racks as the drying fish or placing them in a sack made of fish skin with some hot water added. In time, the eggs turned into a paste that acquired a strong taste like cheese. Today the Han still smoke salmon, but instead of drying whole fish they cut the fish fillets into long thin strips that are then smoked and dried. They also kipper and freeze salmon and use smoked salmon eggs in a chowder made with macaroni and tomatoes.

Tim Malcolm told us that right after the ice goes out northern pike swim upstream in the Yukon River and can be caught with a dip net during the early spring. Suckers can also be caught then, but the old-timers would eat only the front half of them because the back ends are considered too bony.[16]

Arctic grayling were important fish caught in the fall and spring. Silas Stevens recalled that when he was young he would go grayling fishing at the mouth of the Fortymile River in April or the last part of March. The fish were caught using a jig or small pole with line and barbless hook that allowed the fisher to flip the fish off the hook (Figure 18). As soon as it was out of the water the fish froze.

Figure 18. Chief Isaac fishing for grayling through the ice at Dawson, circa 1900.

We used to go up fishing in the springtime, bunch of us guys, you know, with dog team. About five, six, seven, eight, dog team[s] go up to the Fortymile.... They had village there, but at that time I remember, they only had a store there. They stocked things like cigarettes, candy, things like that. Then we get our load of fish and head home.... It's fun too. Once you get your load [of fish], you just let it freeze, if it's cold enough. And put it in these gasoline boxes, these wooden gasoline boxes. Just fill with snow and ice. It keeps.... Fished right through the ice, jig with a hook. Heck you can just pull them out and flip them. Usually you file the barb off [the hook], you know so just flip them out.... Sometimes you can get a load of fish in two days.[17]

Caribou Hunting

The caribou of the Klondike region occurs in small bands over the country on the higher hill tops where it feeds on the gray moss; but it is generally local in its range, migrating at times in bands so vast as to stagger belief. One such range is on the head of Fortymile River, and from there they migrate, it is said, across the Yukon in winter to the eastern or Klondike side, and are found on the bald foot-hills of the Rocky range.

Once in their migration they passed by the mouth of the Fortymile and 400 were shot by the miners...yet so variable and uncertain are these eccentric animals that the Indians sometimes fail to strike them, and in two cases while I was in the Yukon, a village, one at Porcupine and one at Tanana, was obliged to flee for very life [because they were starving].

—*Tappan Adney (1902: 633)*

Two major caribou herds, the Porcupine and the Fortymile, range within the traditional territory of the Han on both sides of the international border. Today the Porcupine herd, which winters in small groups in the Ogilvie Mountains, the Eagle Plain, and the Richardson Mountains, is the larger of the two. In the past, however, the Fortymile herd may have been larger and at different times ranged from Alaska into western Canada as far as the drainages of the Lewes and Pelly rivers and into the Ogilvie Mountains.

Historically the fall migrations of caribou were important to the Han because they provided quantities of skin, meat, bone, and antler (Figure 19). Of particular significance in the fall were the soft fawn skins that Han women made into winter undergarments and socks. After the animals were gutted and skinned, the women cut the meat and some of the fat into strips so that it would dry quickly. They then cached the dried meat and fat for use in the winter. The forelegs and hooves were also cached in case of starvation, in which case older women boiled them to make glutinous soup.

Figure 19. Indians at a caribou hunting camp, circa 1900–1934.

Before the Han obtained repeating rifles at the end of the nineteenth century, they killed large numbers of caribou by constructing a system of wooden fences and corrals. At the beginning of the twentieth century the military doctor Ferdinand Schmitter collected information about these fences from Han living in Eagle Village. According to Schmitter's sources the fences were used in the fall to intercept the migrating herds, which sometimes contained several thousand animals:

> During the fall, when a run of caribou is expected, two long rail fences are built converging into a corral. Snares are placed in the fence about fifty yards apart and also thickly interspersed in the corral space where the herd is driven. The Indians line up at the entrance

and shoot with their arrows those that try and escape.[18] Some are caught in the fence snares, but most are captured in the corral.

The snare consists of a loop of strong braided moose-skin rope, the end tied to a loose log, the loop being held in place with small strings of caribou skin that break easily. It is a natural opening through which it is presumed the animal will try to pass. As the caribou jumps through the loop the strings break, the loop tightens, and thus caught, he tries to run, dragging the loose log after him, which soon exhausts him. If tied to something firm the rope breaks too readily; hence a loose log is preferred.[19]

Babiche is made from untanned caribou or moose skin. After the flesh and hair have been removed from a skin, it is completely dried. The skin is then soaked again and a knife is used to cut it into long strips. The width of the strips depends on what they are going to be used for. Besides being used to make snares, babiche is also used to fill snowshoes, and to weave into bags used to store clothing or to carry small items.

Louise Paul said she was too young to remember caribou fences, but her mother, Eliza Malcolm, told her that her father "used to make caribou fence and her mother and her two brothers they would chase the caribou. And then they set snares every place that they go and her mother with a big spear just killed them off while they hunt up other snares."[20]

Charlie Stevens recalled that Eagle Village people used a caribou fence, fifteen or twenty miles long, on the Fortymile River.[21] He remembered as a child sitting on the rails of the fence and watching as caribou bulls ran by. Usually the people caught about sixty caribou. Packing the meat out was hard work and dog packs were often used. Mary McLeod, in an interview with Richard Slobodin, recollected that Indians from Dawson and Fortymile gathered at a long caribou fence built in the mountains near Chicken, Alaska. Robert Stacey, an elder from Eagle Village, said that caribou fences were located at Comet Creek about twenty-five miles west of Eagle Village, at Eureka Creek, at Pittsburgh Creek, Gold Creek, and "Teddy's Fork" of American Creek. According to Stacey, the fence at Eureka Creek was erected in 1845 and used until 1900.[22]

In the winter the caribou herds scattered and the Han opportunistically killed single animals or small groups. When they encountered a large number of caribou tracks the Han first made camp and then sent the young men ahead to search out the group of caribou. Once they found the animals, the men tried to herd them back toward the camp and the waiting people. Charlie Isaac of Dawson described this process at length to Richard Slobodin:

> The people would be moving along, looking for caribou sign. Then they might find some caribou tracks that might be one, two, three days old—maybe weeks old. They would look around for the nearest open space of clear ice, maybe an overflow or a glacier. Most of the people would camp there. Five or six young men would be sent after the caribou. They would take very little food—maybe the people had very little food anyway—and would follow the caribou two, three days, maybe a week. Young men were trained to be good runners and to get along without much grub. All this time they slept in the snow, didn't make a fire, kept running all day.
>
> Finally they caught up with the caribou, and then they got on the other side of them and turned them and began to herd them back toward the camp. The first day, the caribou went fast, the next day slower; the third day they were just walking along. Especially if there was deep snow, it was hard for them. As they got closer to camp, every night one of the boys ran back to camp and give word how far away they were, and then ran back to the caribou.
>
> Finally they got close. All the people made a circle around the clear ice—old men, women and children, besides the regular hunters. Some had bows and arrows, some spears, some knives. The young men drove the caribou into the circle of people, and then the circle was closed and all the people hollered and yelled: Wow-wow-wow! And kept the caribou running around in a tight-packed circle, around and around. The kids yelled and waved sticks and hit the caribou's legs. The men used the weapons. Usually they killed the whole bunch, maybe 35—40—50—60 caribou.[23]

If the Han encountered caribou while the animals were swimming across a river, men in canoes wielding a spear pursued them. Matthew Malcolm recollected that:

> Some places near this village [Eagle Village], lot of caribou always crossing. I remember my grandfather had a canoe. All the old timers got their own canoe...canvas canoe. My grandpa's right out in front close to the other side.... There was a bunch of caribous, and boy he's fast and cut the neck like this [gesturing], in the windpipe. They just die off. And just take them to the shore. He does that because he wants to save shells.[24]

From 1955, when the Taylor Highway was completed, until the 1970s, hunters from Eagle Village hunted caribou from the Fortymile caribou herd as they crossed the highway on their annual migration. In 1970 hunters from Eagle Village harvested at least one hundred caribou, and until that time people had not purchased much meat from stores in Eagle City. By the mid-1970s, however, out-migration, poor calf survival, and over hunting caused a sharp decline in the Fortymile herd. These factors, coupled with increased hunting restrictions, have drastically reduced significant use of caribou by the Han.[25] However, village hunters continue to hunt caribou when they have the opportunity.

Moose Hunting

The best-recorded and most vivid description of a Han moose hunt is by Tappan Adney, who accompanied Chief Isaac on a month-long trip in the winter of 1899. At the time, Dawson City was facing a critical shortage of food, and Captain Hansen, manager of the Alaska Commercial Company in Dawson, commissioned Chief Isaac to supply the town with meat. Over a four-week period the band moved forty miles up the Klondike River and killed about eighty moose and sixty-five caribou.

Adney wrote that the band left camp early in the morning: "a wild, screaming, howling cavalcade of Indians—men, women, boys, girls, and babies—and dogs of all degrees of leanness, the dogs hauling birch toboggans, on which were piled smoke-browned house poles, skins, blankets with babies and pups, the women driving the dogs, and nearly every man hauling a miner's sled."[26] The men were pulling sleds because they had already sold most of their dogs to gold miners.

The group traveled up the Klondike River and camped two nights before reaching the hunting area. Early in the morning of the third day Chief Isaac directed his hunters to hunt on the left side of the river. Before Adney realized it, the men had left camp, and by the time he caught up with them they had already killed several moose. Adney wrote that all he saw were the figures of

> Isaac and several others around a long fire, and two others nearby skinning a large moose which lay in the snow. . . . The two Indians soon had the moose skinned and proceeded to separate part from part, using only their hunting knives. After cutting off a chunk of ten to fifteen pounds of meat for each person present, the rest of the meat was covered with snow, and smaller pieces were wrapped in

spruce boughs and made into a pack, a braided rawhide cord, which each carried, being used as a sling.[27]

The men left camp at daybreak, ahead of the women, and, using snowshoes, broke trail to the next campsite. After locating a suitable site, they looked for moose tracks. The best hunters preferred to hunt alone, following the tracks until the trail grew "warm." Then they moved cautiously, peering into the brush, hoping to catch a moose while it was lying down. When the trail became "hot" the hunter removed his snowshoes and crept slowly ahead until he saw the head of the moose and then "with a well-placed shot" killed it.

The next day the band moved camp to be closer to the kill so the women could easily haul the meat into camp. All of the meat was distributed and every edible part of the moose was eaten. Adney wrote:

> The shin bones were roasted and cracked for the marrow; the ears, although nothing but cartilage, were roasted and chewed up; the rubber-like "muffle" or nose, and every particle of flesh, fat, or gristle that could be scraped from head or hoofs, were disposed of. Even the stomach was emptied of its contents and boiled and eaten; but the very choicest of delicacy was the unborn moose, which was suspended by a string around its neck and toasted over the fire.[28]

Adney described the process after the men brought the moosehides into the tents:

> The women at once set to work dressing them. The hair was shaved off; then the skin turned over and all the sinew and meat adhering was removed by means of a sort of chisel made of a moose's shin bone; and finally scraped, a work requiring a whole day of incessant and tiresome labor. The skin was washed in a pan of hot water, and then wrung dry with the help of a stick tourniquet. After which the edges were incised for subsequent lacing on a frame, and then hung outdoors on a pole. The tanning, with a "soup" of liver and brains, is done next summer. After which the skin is smoked and made into moccasins, gold sacks etc.[29]

Over the next month the band moved forty miles up the Klondike River and killed about eighty moose and sixty-five caribou. Meat not used by the band was sold to the miners for $1.25 to $1.50 a pound. The Han used money, according to Adney, to purchase repeating rifles and blankets, some of which were traded to other Natives.

Today the Han seldom undertake long trips to hunt moose and instead hunt close to home. Charlie Biederman, a Métis elder from Eagle City, explained that when the snow in the mountains became deep the moose were driven down onto islands in the Yukon River. The wind along the river blew the snow from these islands uncovering food, and moose congregated or "yarded up" on the islands where they could easily be killed by hunters.[30] For this reason Han hunters from Eagle Village currently hunt moose on Wood Island, the islands across from Trout Creek, and just below the Nation River. They also hunt moose in the flats around the village and across the river.

Bear Hunting

In the past, hunters killed black and brown bears using spears. As Schmitter reported,

> A hunter attracts the bear by making a raven-like noise, causing the bear, as the Indians say, to think the raven has discovered a dead moose.... As the bear approaches, the Indian holds the spear in position facing the bear as it draws nearer to him, and as the bear springs the Indian sticks the spear into its throat at the top of the breast-bone, at the same time shoving the handle of the pole into the ground, thus causing the bear to spear himself with his own weight. Sometimes three men hunt in this manner, two of them attacking the bear on either side as it rushes forward.[31]

Today hunters have given up the spear for the rifle, and people do not go out of their way to hunt bear. Sarah Malcolm said that most Han do not like the meat "because they see big hungry bear always gets on beach, knock down old stump and eat lots of those spider, ants. The bear tries to lick up all the ants." People also do not like to eat bear, she said, because "bear is not clean animal. He kills men."[32] When people do hunt bears, they hunt in the same area as moose, on Wood Island, Montauk Bluff, and on Yukon River islands below Nation River. Joanne Beck's grandmother told her that bear meat is good for men to eat but is too strong for women.[33]

Dall Sheep Hunting

The Han have always taken Dall sheep in the late summer or fall when the sheep are fat and their meat in good condition. In the past, sheep were most often caught with babiche snares, but hunters sometimes killed them with bows and arrows. Women dried much of the meat and cached it for later use and made the skins into sleeping blankets or into warm winter pants and coats. Sheep horns were steamed and bent to make spoons, which were highly prized. Sarah Malcolm remembered that as a girl, her family hunted sheep during the fall in the Ogilvie Mountains. Today, if people want to hunt sheep they go into the Glacier Mountains located south of Eagle Village or travel up Eagle Creek.

Hunting Birds and Small Game

In the spring and fall, people killed Canada geese and various species of ducks. Sarah Malcolm recalled that when she was young, her family went to Ford Lake every spring to hunt ducks, geese, swans, and muskrats. Silas Stevens said that people killed ducks at Cuban Lake, located near Eagle Village, and that mallards were their favorite:

> Up at Cuban Lake, they call it. That's just above the village. There's a lake there. That's where they got duck houses [blinds] all around the lake. They all go up there too, about eight or ten of them. And the ducks, when they start flying, they usually come in between two and three in the lake. All you hear is: Bang! Bang! Bang! Bang! Ducks all over the lake then. They got old raft that they pick up their ducks with.[34]

Joanne Beck, the chief of Eagle Village, stressed how important ducks taken in the spring are to the community, especially since geese are rarely found near the village. She remembered that ten or fifteen years ago hunters killed fifty to one hundred ducks in the spring, but people stopped that for a while because they were chased off by game wardens. Joanne said that the people have resumed their spring duck hunting, which she considers the village's "grandfather right," insisting that they never take more than they need.[35]

Grouse and ptarmigan are two other species harvested by the Han. Willie Juneby remembered that his grandfather used to make a snare fence out of willows to catch ptarmigan:

> Grandpa set snares and built willow fence. They pile snow on the willow and the ptarmigan flying around think they are seeing other ptarmigan so they land there. Grandpa would break off willow about a foot long and set it all around and then use twine to make a snare.

> Get two or three of them [ptarmigan]. Thompson at the store would
> buy them and sell to steamboat people in summer.[36]

Arctic hares, or rabbits, as they are referred to locally, were snared or
killed with a blunt arrow. Hares were an important food source because
they were relatively abundant at most times of the year and required
little effort to harvest, especially with snares. However, because hares
follow a seven-year population cycle, they could not be depended on
every year. Porcupines, while not numerous in the region, could also
be easily killed with a stick or club. In addition, the Han traditionally
snared or shot muskrats and beaver, particularly in the spring and early
summer.

Gathering Plants

The ethnographer Cornelius Osgood was told that people harvested
and ate blueberries, lowbush cranberries, gooseberries, salmonberries,
raspberries, wild celery and onions, wild rhubarb, and Labrador tea.[37]
Mary McLeod of Dawson City told Richard Slobodin that people picked
berries in the late summer, cleaned them thoroughly, and packed them
in birchbark baskets sewn with spruce roots (see Figure 20). The baskets were then stored in underground caches and covered with willow
branches and moss.[38] Later, after it had snowed, someone was sent to
retrieve the baskets and, according to Willie Juneby, the berries tasted
just as fresh as when they were picked.

Louise Paul remembered picking berries in the summer with dogs:

> Put six cans each side of the dog pack. We used to go out Wolf
> Creek to pick blueberries. Cranberries up on wireless station too.
> And then they bring it back. In them days they use to have wooden
> butter barrel and they put it in that and put it someplace it won't be
> bothered and they freeze it. In the winter time they dig it out. In the
> old days they use birch bark, my mom tell me. Birch bark basket and
> then they put their berries in that and sew another birch bark on top
> and keep it clean and put it under the ground.[39]

People also used a kind of root that botanists call *Hedysarum americana*,
which they boiled with grease. The Tutchone, Upper Tanana, and Ahtna
also used the root, which is similar to a potato. It grows near water and
people dig it up either in the autumn, after a hard frost, or early in the
spring. Louise Paul said:

We used to dig roots, wild roots.... In the old days, my mom said when they had nothing to eat, they dig the wild root and they clean it, just like parsnip. Wild rhubarb they eat that too ... didn't keep the rhubarb in the winter, just the berries.... In those days when people get old, they pick that Labrador tea. They boil it a long time and make it strong. They put some sugar in that and it help them not to cough so much. And then if someone get cut or pain, they used to fix spruce pitch, real white one, and then they put it on the canvas and heat it up and put it on the pain. Whenever they had pain. I remember old people used to do that, put it on their body and their back.[40]

Figure 20. Han women with birchbark baskets at Moosehide, circa 1900. The woman on the left is identified by Percy Henry as Henry Harper's wife.

Women also looked for caches of roots stored underground by mice. After they had taken what they needed, the women always made it a point to leave some roots for the mice.

The Changing Economy

As the fur trade developed in the mid-nineteenth century the Han created a mixed economy by combining hunting, fishing, and gathering with commercial trapping. Between 1840 and 1900 commercial trapping developed into an integral component of the Han economy, providing the Han with the means to obtain an assortment of manufactured goods that enhanced their lives. The discovery of gold shifted the emphasis of the regional economy away from commercial trapping to mining and transportation. While most Han continued to trap, many diversified their economic activity by working at various forms of wage labor. But commercial trapping and wage labor are susceptible to fluctuations in the broader market economy, so to make ends meet the Han continued to pursue traditional subsistence activities.

Trapping

At the end of the nineteenth century the Han spent considerable time on trap lines that radiated hundreds of miles out from the villages. Fox, marten, mink, ermine, wolverine, land otters, and wolves were trapped for their fur, but with fluctuations in price and demand, certain species were targeted more than others in a given year.

Entire families spent the fall and winter trapping in remote areas. It was typical for families to move to their trap lines in the fall and return to either Eagle Village or Moosehide for Christmas. After New Year they returned to the bush to complete the trapping season and then in the spring moved back to the Yukon River to await summer fish runs. Money earned from commercial trapping was used to buy staples such as guns, ammunition, traps, clothing, tea, sugar, and flour, but the mainstay of the diet was meat killed by the trappers.

Sarah Malcolm remembered that just after the turn of the century, when she was a small child, her family walked out to the trap lines in the fall using pack dogs to transport their gear. At Christmas time they returned to Eagle Village for the holidays before going back out to their line. Sarah remembered that while on the trap line people lived in canvas tents, two families pitching their tents close to each other. To feed themselves while trapping, Han men hunted sheep, caribou, and moose. Sarah said that they often went to Sheep Creek (the Tatonduk River):

> They hunt sheep, caribou, all we want. They went up to Eagle Creek and Sheep Creek to trapline, until trapping season closed. Lots of moose killed for us to use in winter. Grandma Liza and I have big cache near tent, have lots of fat meat. Fat two inches around kidneys. This was on the side of Sheep Creek. Up into Ogilvie River to trap.[41]

In the spring the family constructed a boat with a birchwood frame, covered it with untanned moose skin, and floated down to the Yukon River and back to Eagle Village. Along the way they killed beaver, muskrat, ducks, geese, and swans.

Louise Paul said that when she was young (in the late 1920s and early 1930s) her family lived between Dawson and Eagle Village and Fort McPherson. Louise described a typical season in which the family moved between the trap line and the village:

> They go on trapping and then they have to come into town, into Eagle town, to get some grocery again: tea and some things that we use out in the camp, like tea and dried fruit and things like that. And then we live there all winter.
>
> And then around Christmas time we come in for Christmas too. Whole bunch of us, we got two [dog] team. Got quite a bit. I go with my Dad, and my mother, she go with my brother. So we got two team, and we go to holiday. And after holiday we go back again. So I never done much schooling, never. I went up to eighth grade, that's all.
>
> So we stayed out there till spring, and then they go beaver hunting while we're out there. We go way down, way down river. They call [it] Peel River, I think. I don't know. That's a big river over there. They go down there and been going about a month, I guess, down there. And we live out there all by ourselves. We're not scared. If that was now, I'd be scared [laughs].
>
> And they bring back some beaver skin, and well there's my uncle live with us too, my uncle and his family. And then we come into Eagle. May [month], we come in. And then they sell their beaver skin and things like that. And then we go fishing in Eagle in the summer time. That's in June, July, August. And then we lived for a while, go fishing, and then we go over again, over to our trapline. So I never been much to school. And they start trapping again.[42]

While whole families often went out together to their trap lines, at the beginning of the twentieth century pressure mounted from missionaries and government officials to keep the children in school. By the late 1930s women and children frequently stayed home while the men went out on the trap lines.

Of course not all children stayed home. Silas Stevens remembered that when he was about twelve years old, around 1938, he skipped school to go trapping with his family around the mouth of the Tatonduk River (Sheep Creek). He recalled that from the main cabin they went to Twelve-Mile Creek and then into the Nation River drainage:

> We left to go over to check our trap line, over the hill down to Twelve Mile Creek. We got stranded at that first tent. That's about fifteen or twenty miles from the river. It turned sixty below. Couldn't go no place. Just kept us busy trying to keep warm you know. It's too cold for the dogs to travel then. We got stranded for one week. It finally warmed up, forty below, and then we headed home. Sixty below, maybe sixty-five, it got that cold. Gosh, your camp stove don't turn out much heat. You got to keep turning. Your front end would warm, then your back would be freezing.[43]

Wage Labor

> *We usually head down no matter what hour; we always go downtown and wait for the [first steam] boat [of the year]. Three miles down, downtown. Build a campfire and watch for the boat. You could hear it too, when it's puffing away, puffing away. Three or four miles away you could hear it. And pretty soon that big white stack would be coming around the bend up above the village. Everybody shouting for joy: "Fresh fruit! Fresh fruit!" They go crazy for that—apples, oranges, and bananas!*
> —Silas Stevens (1997)

The discovery of gold on the Fortymile River in 1886 provided the Han with a number of opportunities to engage in wage labor, and for the first time they had an alternative to hunting, fishing, and trapping as a way to make a living.

During the gold rush Chief Isaac was one of those who staked placer claims, but there is no evidence that he ever developed these claims, and

Han participation in gold mining appears to have been minimal. During and after the gold rush, many of the Han men living in Moosehide and Eagle Village participated in some form of seasonal wage labor. As the market in furs declined, more and more Han switched from trapping to wage labor. Early on the Han were employed as wood choppers, deck hands, winch operators, and pilots for the Yukon and other steamboats going up and down the Yukon River (Figures 21 and 22).[44]

Matthew Malcolm of Eagle Village talked about how people combined subsistence activities with work by fishing in the summer, hunting in the fall, and cutting cord wood in the winter to sell to the steamboats or to residents of Eagle City (Figure 23). Trees that had been scorched and dried by a forest fire were especially good:

> In the summertime up here [near Eagle Village] "Dog Island." You know "Dog Island?" Behind there in the slough on the upper end they got a place for a fishwheel. Every other year I guess they build their own fishwheel, put it in, get some fish there. Then come September he always hunt. Right across from Dog Island, long time ago it burned quite a bit. The people cutting wood there, and they bring wood down for sale, dry wood. Oh about four or five cord at a time, one raft. Take it downtown and sell it.[45]

Cutting firewood for the river steamers was one of the major forms of wage employment for the Han. According to Willie Juneby, in the early part of the twentieth century several of the Han lived in tents at Sheep Creek (the Tatonduk River) where they cut wood for the steamboats. Frank "Heinie" Miller had a contract to supply wood for two boats, so he hired men to cut 900 cords at $4.00 a cord.[46] Silas Stevens recalled:

> We used to cut a lot of wood too, even for the steamboats . . . they move down to Sheep Creek in the springtime. Thirty miles down below Eagle. They all take their dog team, tents, and they set up tent camp. A regular tent city. Down on Wood Island for $4.00 a cord. Good money them days too. Course they get all their grub, their stake, food and grubstake, from the Northern Commercial Company. Then they all head down with dog team, and then they take all their stuff down, four or five hundred pound of stuff, food, regular staples. Course, you can get your meat anytime down there.[47]

Silas said that Willie Juneby operated an old Caterpillar tractor, hauling the wood down to the beach. Willie also trapped when he was not driving the Cat.

Figure 21. Indian Paul and son, 1890–1891. Indian Paul was one of the riverboat pilots of the upper Yukon River.

Figure 22. Steamboats wooding up at Dawson City, 1897–1898. Left to right are the A. Jedoboard, *the* Portus B. Weare, *and the* Col. W. Hamilton.

Figure 23. The steamboat Florence S. *at Eagle, July 1904.*

> He usually did all of the hauling from up the creek, about three or
> four miles up the creek, at Sheep Creek they call it, and then they
> haul it down and beach it. They used two sleds. And then same way
> down there at Wood Island . . . about six miles below Miller Camp,
> this side of Nation River, downriver from "Sheep Creek." That's
> where they did lot of their wood cutting too.[48]

Caterpillar tractors were new to the country in 1937, and the idea
that a local Native could drive a Cat seemed to amaze the Han people at
Dawson. News correspondent Ernie Pyle made a visit to Miller Camp
in 1937 and penned this account:

> Heinie and the Indians who worked for him [at the mouth of Sheep
> Creek] would cut about seven hundred cords of wood each winter.
> They stacked it on the riverbank to feed the fireboxes of the Yukon
> steamers during the summer. . . . An Indian named Willie [Juneby]
> drove Heinie's Caterpillar tractor, dragging the logs down from the
> hills. "Hell, them Indians come all the way from Dawson, a hundred
> miles, just to watch Willie drive the cat," Heinie said, "and I have to
> feed 'em."[49]

At some point Han families made the decision to move into town
permanently and to work more or less regularly at wage labor. Louise

Paul remembered when her family made the transition from living on the trap line through the winter to living in Eagle Village:

> We were out in the woods, and finally we move into town...we lived in Eagle [Village] ever since. That's where I met my husband and marry him. And then after I had three kids, I guess. Mary, Matthew, Ethel, and Bert: four kids. After we had four kids, he worked on the boat, and we chopped wood in the winter time.[50]

Louise said that her husband, Susie Paul, cut firewood for people in Eagle City and worked summers on the steamboats:

> He work on that steamboat a long time, all summer. And then he got a job at Patty's mining camp up here at Coal Creek. . . . That's where we lived. There's our family, and Juneby's family, David's family. Three big families of us lived there all summer. No school them days in Eagle. Not too many children so they don't have school.[51]

From working as seasonal laborers cutting wood, some Han men moved on to more permanent work in mining operations. With skills learned on the job the men went even farther afield working in far-off places such as Fairbanks. The careers of Willie Juneby and Matthew Malcolm were fairly typical. Late in 1938, Willie found employment at Coal Creek mining camp and remained there every year except two years during World War II. He worked on the hydraulic dredge, worked with points, swamping, and helping. In 1940 he learned how to drive a truck. During the war the federal government shut down gold mining activities as a low priority requirement for strategic materials, so Willie went to Fairbanks and worked on the Richardson Highway, driving a Caterpillar tractor during the summers.

When Matthew got older, he worked on gold dredges: "They pay pretty low, so I just worked there a couple of months, and then I went to Fairbanks and join the union and worked there. And afterward when I got married I got a job on the Taylor Highway. Worked on Taylor Highway for about twelve years when I had to give up my work." He went on to say that a couple of them worked on the dredge:

> And what I did I drove truck. And they had a little Cat they drove that and hauled wood and stuff. And Willie Juneby he had a bigger Cat, and I followed him all the time. And some of the other boys worked there. They go out in the field in front of the dredge and

drive points [to thaw the ground]. And a few of them working the dredge. Oiler and deck boy, or whatever they call them.

And the people that stay there [in the] summertime, husband work there, and during the winter they stay there too, and then they get a chance to make a few bucks and they cut wood. Cut a lot of wood there for the dredge, for the same outfit. They need wood for the camp. They tried to save the oil for the dredge. They started April down to the last part of October. When it starts freezing up then they shut down the dredge, and everybody leave except them family guys. They stay there for the winter, husband do a little trapping and cut wood. Sometimes they go to town, and sometimes they visit up here [Eagle Village]. Then go back down.[52]

In the 1950s, 1960s, and 1970s fighting summer forest fires for the U.S. Bureau of Land Management became an important source of income for men and women living in Eagle Village. After firefighting season, the men hunted and then trapped through the winter.

In the 1960s, public assistance in the form of food stamps and Aid to Families with Dependent Children became widely available. In the mid-1970s villagers found a few high-paying jobs through Doyon Corporation oil exploration in the Kandik River basin and through construction work on the Trans-Alaska oil pipeline, but at the end of the decade those jobs ended. There are still very few jobs in Eagle Village, and trapping for furs is much less profitable than it once was. In fact, no one we talked to in Eagle Village reported trapping in 1997. In 2000 the village opened its own grocery store for the first time, providing steady year-round employment for a few households.

Chapter Three

Notes

1. Tappan Adney, "The Indian Hunter of the Far Northwest." *Outing* 39, No. 6 (March 1902), 628.

2. Ferdinand Schmitter, *Upper Yukon Native Customs and Folk-Lore*. Washington, D.C. (The Smithsonian Institution, 1910). Reprinted by the Eagle Historical Society, Eagle, and the Alaska Historical Commission, Anchorage, 3.

3. Information on the historic seasonal round comes from Cornelius Osgood, *The Han Indians: A Compilation of Ethnographic and Historical Data on the Alaska–Yukon Boundary Area*. New Haven: Yale University Publications in Anthropology No. 74, 1971; and Richard A. Caulfield, *Subsistence Use In and Around the Proposed Yukon-Charley National Rivers*. Cooperative Park Studies Unit Occasional Paper No. 20 (Fairbanks: University of Alaska, 1979). Caulfield's is the only published account of the contemporary Han subsistence economy. Caulfield's report is noteworthy because he conducted extensive interviews with a number of elders, including the late Sarah Malcolm and Bob Stacey.

4. Richard Slobodin, "Notes on the Han." Appendix II to Preliminary Report on Ethnographic Work, 1962. Unpublished Manuscript. Ottawa: National Museum of Man, Ethnology Division, 1963.

5. Caulfield, *Subsistence Use In and Around the Proposed Yukon-Charley National Rivers*, 13.

6. Tim Malcolm, taped interview by Craig Mishler, 11 July 1997.

7. Sarah Malcolm interviewed by Jerry Dixon and Reggie Goebel on 6 September 1980. Transcript, Eagle Historical Society Archives.

8. Caulfield, *Subsistence Use In and Around the Proposed Yukon-Charley National Rivers*.

9. Osgood, *The Han Indians*, 115.

10. Sarah Malcolm, interviewed by Yvonne Howard on 20–21 June 1990, private collection, Eagle City.

11. Willie Juneby interviewed by Reggie Goebel on 9–10 December 1980. Eagle Historical Society Archives.

12. Ibid.

13. Sarah Malcolm, interviewed by Yvonne Howard on 20–21 June 1990, private collection, Eagle City.

14. Ibid.

15. Silas Stevens, Tape 1, interviewed by Craig Mishler on 7 April 1997. Alaska Department of Fish and Game, Division of Subsistence, Anchorage, Alaska.

16. Tim Malcolm personal communication to Craig Mishler, 20 July 1997.

17. Silas Stevens Tape 1.

18. Hunters made their bows and arrow shafts out of birch wood. The bows were about five feet long, and the arrows approximately two feet long, with points

made from caribou horn, stone, and later iron. The heads were hafted to the shafts with fine sinew. Sarah Malcolm recollected that men packed lots of arrows. The quivers were worn on the back or at the side. Sarah's father made quivers decorated with white lined beads and blue beads, which were used for identification. Eagle feathers were used to fletch the arrows.

David Salmon, a highly respected Gwich'in elder born in 1912 and residing in Chalkyitsik, says that during the early days the best arrows and projectile points in the region came from the Han. The reason is that the Han found a special kind of quartz from their area which allowed them to cut and incise flat bone points. After being polished, these bone points proved to be excellent and effective for killing moose. The Han accordingly traded these points with the Gwich'in living on the Yukon Flats (David Salmon, personal communication to Craig Mishler, 24 March 2001).

19. Schmitter, *Upper Yukon Native Customs and Folk-Lore*, 8.

20. Louise Paul interviewed by William Schneider, 25 March 1993. Tape recording H91-22-63, National Park Service Collection.

21. Charlie Stevens interviewed by Mertie Baggen. Mertie Baggen Papers 1964–67. Field notes, Box 1, Rasmuson Library, Alaska and Polar Regions, Fairbanks, Alaska.

22. Slobodin, "Notes on the Han"; Caulfield, *Subsistence Use In and Around the Proposed Yukon-Charley National Rivers*, 18.

23. Slobodin, "Notes on the Han," 7–8.

24. Matthew Malcolm interviewed by Steve Ulvi and William Schneider, 27 August 1991. Tape recording H91-22-18, National Park Service Collection.

25. Caulfield, *Subsistence Use In and Around the Proposed Yukon-Charley National Rivers*, 31.

26. Edwin Tappan Adney, "Moose Hunting with the Tro-chu-tin." *Harper's New Monthly Magazine* 100, No. 598 (1900), 498.

27. Ibid, 502.

28. Ibid.

29. Ibid.

30. Charlie Biederman interviewed by Larurel Tyrell, 29 November 1994. Tape recording H95-14. Oral History Collection, University of Alaska Fairbanks.

31. Schmitter, *Upper Yukon Native Customs and Folk-Lore*, 22, 8.

32. Sarah Malcolm interviewed by Jerry Dixon and Reggie Goebel on 6 September 1980. Typescript. Eagle Historical Society Archives.

33. Joanne Beck interviewed by William Simeone at Eagle Village, 23 July 1997.

34. Silas Stevens, Tape 1 interviewed by Craig Mishler on 7 April 1997. Alaska Department of Fish and Game, Division of Subsistence, Anchorage, Alaska.

35. Joanne Beck interviewed by William Simeone at Eagle Village, 23 July 1997.

36. Willie Juneby interviewed by Reggie Goebel on 9–10 December 1980. Typescript. Eagle Historical Society Archives.

37. Osgood, *The Han Indians*, 19.

38. Slobodin, "Notes on the Han," 7.

39. Louise Paul interviewed by William Schneider, 25 March 1993. Tape recording H91-22-63, National Park Service Collection.

40. Ibid.

41. Sarah Malcolm interviewed by Jerry Dixon and Reggie Goebel on 6 September 1980. Typescript. Eagle Historical Society Archives.

42. Louise Paul interviewed by William Schneider, 25 March 1993. Tape recording H91-22-63, National Park Service Collection.

43. Silas Stevens, Tape 1 interviewed by Craig Mishler on 7 April 1997. Alaska Department of Fish and Game, Division of Subsistence, Anchorage, Alaska.

44. See photographs of Susie Paul, Porcupine Paul, Arthur Stevens, and Willie Juneby during the late 1930s and early 1940s in Arthur Knutson's *Sternwheels on the Yukon* (Kirkland, WA: Knutson Enterprises, 1979), 139, 182, 190, 203, 221.

45. Matthew Malcolm, tape recording H95-69-06, 26 August 1991. National Park Service Collection.

46. Willie Juneby interviewed by Reggie Goebel, 9–10 December 1980. Typescript. Eagle Historical Society, Eagle, Alaska.

47. Silas Stevens, Tape 1 interviewed by Craig Mishler, 7 April 1997. Alaska Department of Fish and Game, Division of Subsistence, Anchorage, Alaska.

48. Ibid.

49. Ernie Pyle, *Home Country* (New York: William Sloane Associates, 1947), 583e, 583f.

50. Louise Paul interviewed by William Schneider, 25 March 1993. Tape recording H91-22-63, National Park Service Collection.

51. Ibid.

52. Matthew and Martha Malcolm interviewed by Steve Ulvi, 26 July 1989. Tape recording H95-69-06. National Park Service Collection.

Chapter Four

Social and Political Organization

K INSHIP IS what holds a small society together even when it is politically divided by an international border, as the U.S.-Canada border
divides the Han. Through kinship rights and obligations, people who live
in the same place are entitled to share in a common ethnicity, language,
history, and destiny. Kinship also provides people with access to subsistence hunting and fishing sites. The result is that they have a collective
vision of their place in the world. They become deeply attached to the
land and its resources, and they look out for one another.

In historic times, the Han exhibited several levels of social organization and integration, from the nuclear family, to the household, the
band, the village, and the descent group. However, due to the impact
of the gold rush, missionaries, and other external forces, much of the
historic Han social and political organization has been transformed.
Two-family households have given way to single-family households.
Descent groups have become less and less important. Band leadership
provided by older male chiefs has been replaced by tribal councils, with
young women increasingly at the forefront.

Household Organization

In one of the earliest missionary visits to a Han camp, two-family house-hold units were identified as a basic part of Han social organization, even though nuclear families (conjugal pairs and their offspring) were clearly the most basic units.[1] It seems likely that many of these two-family households were connected by kinship ties, but it also seems clear that they were not always related and did not always travel everywhere together.

Anglican missionary Kenneth McDonald, for instance, visited a Han camp on February 22, 1874, and found thirteen lodges with two nuclear families in each lodge. Every nuclear family (except one) must have had its own transportation, however, because twenty-five sleds (i.e., toboggans) were loaded when they broke camp.[2]

When the geologist William Ogilvie caught up with a band of Han on the North Fork of the Tatonduk River in March, 1888, he observed that "generally two or more families dwell in one tent."[3] And when Tappan Adney accompanied Chief Isaac on a moose hunting trip up the Klondike River he described the chief's house as containing two families. One family consisted of Isaac, his wife Eliza, and a nursing boy. On the other side of the house were a man named Billy, his wife, two girls, and a boy. In addition to these two families, seven dogs and four puppies also commanded their share of the living space.[4]

A mid-twentieth-century example of a well-functioning, two-family Han household group is the hunting and trapping family of Edward Malcolm, his wife Sarah, and their children, and that of Edward's brother Joe Malcolm, his wife Eliza, and their children, which included Louise Paul. Accompanying them, according to Louise, was her grandmother Carolyn, Joe, and Edward's mother. Each fall these brothers and their families traveled and trapped together on Eagle Creek, and in mid-winter they moved to "Sheep Creek" (the South Fork of the Tatonduk River). Louise was quick to say, however, that each of these two families traveling together had its own tent, a change from what was observed by McDonald, Ogilvie, and Adney.

This bond between brothers continued until recent times when Joe Malcolm's sons Matthew, Jacob, and Tim all trapped fur together (in pairs) on Champion Creek. Although they did not take their wives and children with them, these brothers found themselves to be an efficient and compatible work group.

Another two-family pattern which held strong until recent times was governed by matrilocality, at least during the early years of marriage. For the Han, this second kind of two-family unit consisted of a married couple along with one of their adult daughters and her husband and children.

Matrilocality is the custom of a man moving in with his wife's family, or at least relocating to be near his wife's parents, immediately after marriage. When a Han man married, he was expected to live with his wife's parents. While in the beginning he would learn how to make a living from his father-in-law, it also became his lifelong obligation to look after his wife's parents. Matthew and Martha Malcolm, for example, went out hunting and trapping with Martha's parents, Arthur and Sophie Stevens. The advantage of matrilocality, from the man's perspective, is that by serving his in-laws he is able to expand his own territory and gain access to new subsistence hunting and fishing sites.

Band Organization

The band is a community, localized in the sense that it is associated with a territory; it is experienced by its members both as a kin-group and as horizontally cross-cut— although not class-stratified. The band chief is the senior kinsman.

—*Richard Slobodin (1962)*

At the time of historic contact in the mid-nineteenth century the second level of social organization for the Han was the band (see Chapter 2). Athabaskan bands generally consisted of extended families divided into households which traveled and hunted together on the same seasonal round. Each band was led by a middle-aged or elder male chief, who was a role model to others. The only Han band we have a photograph of, however, is David's band (Chapter 2, Figure 7).

Band size certainly varied from season to season and from year to year and was undoubtedly shaped by several ecological factors: (1) the carrying capacity of the land and rivers in providing meat and fish, (2) the size of task groups such as those needed to build and maintain caribou fences and corrals, and (3) the number of people needed to defend against raids by neighboring groups. While there is obvious strength in numbers, the abundance or scarcity of various wild resources combined to limit the size and number of Han bands.

In the summer months, when salmon were running up the Yukon River, it was much easier for many people to live together in one place than it was in the winter months when they had to disperse and move almost daily to forage for caribou, moose, and small mammals. Undoubtedly, the Han adaptation to commercial fur trapping in the mid-nineteenth century and to the gold rush at the beginning of the twentieth century affected the size, composition, and even the number of Han bands.

Village Organization

Not until the gold rush, which put increased stress on game and fish populations, did Han bands gradually condense into relatively permanent year-round settlements called villages. Charley's band and David's band, for example, merged to form Eagle Village, while the Klondike and Nuklako bands (if they were indeed ever separate) merged to form Mooseshide Village. This localization and consolidation may be attributed at least in part to the building of missions and mission schools, and the required attendance of young children in both mission and public schools. Nevertheless, Indian children were not allowed to attend public schools in the Yukon until the 1960s or later. Other factors that contributed to the change from a nomadic to a sedentary life were displacement from traditional sites during the gold rush and increased opportunities for wage labor.

Figure 24. Eagle Village with woman on bench (date unknown).

Kinship ties between parents and children and between siblings nevertheless continue to be important in Han communities today. In Eagle Village it is noteworthy that in 1997 adult siblings had formed housing clusters within the village. Of the three major families living in the village, the Malcolms occupied one end of the community, the Pauls the other, with the Davids in the middle. In Dawson, Han families have clustered together to form a kind of "neighborhood" on the north end of town.

Figure 25. Harold Paul's log cabin, Eagle Village, July 1997.

When the noted author and journalist John McPhee first saw Eagle Village in 1975, he pronounced it to be "a linear community" with all the log cabins lined up in a long row facing the river (Figure 24).[5] By 1997 that linearity had been transformed into more of an oval. While most of today's frame houses and log cabins still face the river (Figure 25), several are now located on the two-lane gravel road which extends behind the village, and some are being built on the new road going upriver to Dog Island. The two-lane back road allows cars and trucks to make a complete loop around the village or bypass it and proceed upriver. In Moosehide too, the original early twentieth century-log cabins were built in long rows facing the river (see Chapter 1, Figure 3).

Fish are very important to maintaining kinship ties, particularly with respect to their processing and distribution. Most of the fish taken in

Eagle Village the summer of 1997 were caught in the gill net of Matthew Malcolm (Plate 7), whose wife and daughters took turns cutting, smoking, and distributing the fish at their camp on the riverbank (Figure 17).

Matthew's oldest daughter Adeline, who now lives in the Upper Tanana community of Northway, drives up to Eagle every summer to get king salmon for her family because there are no salmon runs in the upper Tanana River. In 1997 a new community fishwheel was built and put in the river, but since it was not very productive in catching fish, distribution according to kinship ties seldom occurred. Most of the few fish caught in the fishwheel were consumed by single men.

Descent Groups

Still another level of Han social organization consists of descent groups. Descent groups are genetic blood lines or lineages which were once woven into every other level of Han social organization: the nuclear family, the household, the band, and the village. Although respected anthropologists such as Cornelius Osgood and Richard Slobodin concluded that the Han formerly traced their descent through exogamous matrilineal moieties or clans, Osgood admitted that by the time of his visit to Dawson in 1932, "the clan system was no longer functioning and it was with difficulty that information on the subject could be obtained."[6]

Moiety is a term used to describe a social organization consisting of two major descent groups. Within each moiety there may also be several distinct subgroups called clans or sibs, but if there are no subdivisions, moieties are virtually the same as clans. Persons from opposite moieties and different clans generally share the same household. A clan is a group of people descended from a common ancestor. Exogamous means there is a rule that individuals must marry someone outside of their own clan. Matrilineal characterizes a formal system of tracing one's heritage through the mother's side of the family. In a matrilineal society, the reckoning of descent is exclusively through the mother's side, so that all of the children are of the same clan as their mother. A bilateral kinship system sits in contrast to matrilineal or patrilineal systems. In a bilateral society, descent is reckoned equally on both the mother's and father's side of the family.

Although today little is known or remembered about Han moieties or clans, it would seem that the Han system of reckoning descent once resembled those of neighboring groups such as the Upper Tanana or the Gwich'in, even though the Gwich'in and Upper Tanana provide contrasting models.

In contemporary Han society we found considerable variation among communities in the use of clan names. In Dawson people said they were either Crow (*TätrÅ'*) or Wolf (*Zhur*). In Eagle Village, however, they said they were either Crow (*Nahtsiin*) or Seagull (*Cheechil* or *Chitsyoo*). The linguistic identification of the Eagle Village Han clans with Crow and Seagull correlates closely with the moieties used by the Upper Tanana. A major difference, however, is that the Upper Tanana system is more complex than the Han; each Upper Tanana moiety has several clans as subunits.

The Han clans of Crow and Wolf found in Dawson, on the other hand, correspond more closely with those of the inland Tlingit and northern Tutchone. Among the Gwich'in, the Han's other neighbors, there are three clans—*Chitsyaa*, *NantsÅ^^*, and *Tejiniratsaa*—but none of these clans is directly associated with birds or animals. We found no evidence to support Catharine McClellan's claim that "most of the Han" were affiliated with these Gwich'in clan names, although a significant number of Gwich'in living among the Han in Dawson may occasionally still use them.[7] Like the Han, the Gwich'in have also largely lost their clan identities.

In former times exogamous moieties or clans were important to the Han for preventing incest, providing funerals, and sharing food. But at the time of our visits to Eagle Village and Moosehide in 1997 the Han clans of Crow and Seagull or Crow and Wolf and their significance for these three functions were all but gone. One Han woman from Eagle in her late forties, for example, confessed that she did not really know her clan affiliation and said that clans no longer mean much "because everybody is marrying white people." The kinship terms this woman used for mother's brother and father's brother were identical (*she'e*), as were the terms for mother's sister and father's sister (*shäk'i*), suggesting more of a bilateral kinship system than a matrilineal one.

Percy Henry affirms that when a funeral potlatch is held today in Dawson or Moosehide, "everybody chips in" for the food. But if the deceased person is Crow, the Wolf people still take responsibility for the casket and burial, and vice-versa if the deceased is Wolf. This is the "only part we try to keep it traditional," he says. And while the funeral pot-latch helps to remind people of their moieties, there is no subsequent memorial potlatch among the Han as there is among the Tanacross and Upper Tanana people.[8]

A Han woman from Dawson whom we interviewed noted that she and her husband were both of the Wolf clan and by tradition were not supposed to marry each other. One elder did say something to them, but they did not fully understand what he was saying. However, they discovered that as compensation and atonement for breaking this rule, they were expected to share more of their fish and game with other people.

In addition to the Crow and Seagull or Crow and Wolf clans, Cornelius Osgood wrote about a third clan, *ta ndu a tsal*, which was not mentioned by any of our respondents. Richard Slobodin, who interviewed Charlie Isaac in Dawson, came up with three entirely different clan names.[9]

Frederica de Laguna, who has compared all of the northern Athabaskan kinship systems but has depended on Osgood and Slobodin for her information, concluded that the Han essentially had a dual system, with a third lesser clan or sib that absorbed people who did not fit into the other two, usually from endogamy, marrying into one's own descent group.[10] De Laguna helps us see at least a nominal similarity between Han, inland Tlingit, and Tutchone clans and between the Han and other Athabaskan groups.

The significance of Han clans is largely lost to memory, but Willie Juneby compared them to political parties, finding them to be like "Republicans" and "Democrats" and saying "the Crow party" built a caribou fence on the Middle Fork of the Fortymile River.[11] Presumably this fence was owned and used only by members of the Crow clan. Louise Paul, who was Seagull, also liked the political party analogy, something we have heard among the Gwich'in as well.[12] This analogy between clans and political parties suggests very strongly that an understanding of kinship leads to an understanding of tribal politics and leadership roles.

This confusion and contemporary indifference toward clans and the nominal lack of consistency between key respondents may suggest that (1) matrilineal clans and clan names are something the Han acquired at a relatively late date from neighboring groups to the south and west (a view which Richard Slobodin advances for the Peel River Gwich'in clans); or (2) if Han clans were indeed once powerful and important, they are no longer so because of female out-marriage and emigration.

One view is that the collapse of Han clans has some rather profound effects, one of which has been the disappearance of the memorial potlatch, an institution based on reciprocity and obligations to kinsmen and kinswomen. As de Laguna has written, "Moieties function in primarily dividing individuals into 'opposites' who intermarry, help each other at life crises, particularly death, and who entertain each other at potlatch-es."[13] If people do not know who their relatives are, or if half of their relatives are non-Indians or non-residents, they are no longer able to give or receive the proper gifts, make formal speeches, and fulfill their funeral obligations to those relatives. Their rights and obligations become diffuse and uncertain.

A second view is that the Han potlatch tradition did not actually disappear but has simply been scaled down and transformed into community dinners, holiday celebrations, funeral feasts, and first-kill ceremonies for young hunters (see Chapter 5). That is, Han people still share, reciprocate, and shoulder social obligations, but more on the basis of community ties than by virtue of descent.

Through all of this, it is also instructive to look at the decline of Han nuclear families. In 1973 only two Han men in Eagle Village were married to Han women. They were the elderly couple Louise and Willie Juneby and the middle-aged couple, Matthew and Martha Malcolm. Since then many young Han women growing up in the village have married white men and moved away. Some have since separated and come back, but by 1997 there was not one married family of Han left in Eagle Village.[14] All of the adult men and women were unmarried.

Political Organization

Shortly after the turn of the last century, the Han in Eagle Village, Charley Village, and Moosehide were all led by elder male chiefs. According to Ferdinand Schmitter, the chiefs had complete authority and were responsible for detailing hunting parties and for apportioning the game meat brought back by hunters. The chiefs were also responsible for looking after elders, widows, and orphans. In the absence of the chief, Schmitter wrote, "all important measures are decided by the old men."[15] Like their Gwich'in neighbors downriver and across the mountain divide to the north, the Han elected a council and second chiefs who were of the opposite clan or moiety from the first chief. Council members nominated and elected the chiefs, although this may be a post-contact phenomenon. In Dawson the elected First Nation leadership consists of a chief and four council members. There is no second chief, as found on the Alaska side, but rather a "deputy chief" who can convene members when the chief is absent. The Dawson Han have just recently made the office of chief a salaried position due to monies received from their land claims settlement.

The importance of leadership to the Han and other Athabaskan tribes cannot be overestimated.[16] The Han believe the leaders of the caribou herd, *jaykaw*, should never be killed, for without them the caribou would wander aimlessly and not know where to migrate to find food from season to season. In this way the political organization of the Han mirrors that of the caribou. The spiritual bond between the Han and the caribou is very strong, and for this reason elder chiefs have always been highly respected.

While information on Han chiefs is limited, brief biographies of the most famous of them advance our understanding of them as individuals. The two chiefs we know the most about are Chief Charley and Chief Isaac, although Chief David is often mentioned in written accounts as well.

Chief Charley

Even though Charley is scarcely remembered today in Han oral history, his prominence is attested to by the location of his home community, Charley Village, in traditional Han territory at the mouth of Charley Creek (the Kandik River). Most of the people he led were Han, and he was also the upper Yukon River chief most white people dealt with in Alaska during the late nineteenth century.[17] Because the Charley River, Charley Creek, Charley Village, and the Yukon-Charley Rivers National Preserve are all directly or indirectly named after him, it is important to recognize and commemorate his leadership role in the region.

This much said, there is some reason to believe there were two different Chief Charleys living among the Han in the late nineteenth and early twentieth centuries. The written records are virtually seamless. They show no inconsistency in identification except for his date of death and for slight changes in the spelling of his Indian name, which appears as *Nootle, Nootł'ee, Nootlah, or Nootł'ët*, all variants of the Han word for "White Man."[18]

The photographic record, however, presents us with a striking paradox. There are six historic photos in which Chief Charley is clearly identified. Three of them show a stocky, dark-skinned, relatively clean-shaven man (Figures 6, 26, and 28), while the other three (including Figures 27, 39, and one other not reproduced here) show a thinner, light-skinned, white-bearded man. Martha Kates, a Han elder who traces her descent from Chief Charley through family oral tradition, claims that her great-grandfather had some Russian blood in him. This would certainly help explain why he was called *Nootł'ët*.[19]

Figure 26. Chief Charley and John Martin, c. 1910s.

In addition to his two U.S. Census-identified children, Grace and Dolphus (see Appendix D), Charley may have had another son. The 1900 U.S. Census enumeration sheets for Eagle Village include a "Robert *Nootlah*," age twenty-three, whose name appears directly beneath that of "Charlie *Nootlah*." Robert *Nootlah*, who also went by the name of Robert Charles, is shown in the census to have a wife, Sarah Jane, two daughters named Mary and Sarah, and a son named David. Grace and Dolphus, rather than moving to Circle as Hudson Stuck suggested, actually ended up in Eagle Village, while Robert and his family moved to Fortymile and then Moosehide. However, because we cannot verify whether Robert was a sibling of Grace and Dolphus, we are including him and his descendants under a separate family tree.

To add to the puzzle, Charley *Nootl'ee* was a Han chief who apparently was not a Han by birth. This is actually not too surprising since

Dawson elder Percy Henry is another modern-day example. According to the 1910 U.S. Census, Charley and his wife Sarah were both Vunta or Vantee Gwich'in ("People Living among the Lakes"), a tribal group whose homeland lies in the upper Porcupine River area around Old Crow, Yukon Territory. It seems quite likely then, that Charley was born in Canada.

With all these caveats in mind, the following narrative is written as though there were only one Chief Charley. This is because there is no one alive who remembers seeing Chief Charley and no one from the historical era in which he lived who ever acknowledged the existence of a second Charley. If indeed there were two Chief Charleys, it is now quite impossible to know which man they actually met and wrote about.

Figure 27. Chief Charley.

Missionary Accounts

Charley makes his first historical appearance in the journal of Robert
McDonald, an Anglican missionary who met him on the Yukon River on
July 27, 1871. During his trip upriver from Fort Yukon (apparently in a
paddled canoe), McDonald stopped at four different Han camps, with
Charley's being the first. Charley is not singled out by name on the way
up but only on the return trip. Even in this first account, Charley appears
to have been a friendly and likeable leader. McDonald simply wrote that
he was "kindly welcomed by Nootle the chief, and the others."[20]

Charley's next appearance is in a letter written three years later by
Kenneth McDonald, Robert McDonald's brother. Kenneth was also an
Anglican missionary who often substituted for his brother and who
visited the Han in April, 1874. In his letter to the Bishop of Athabasca,
Kenneth wrote:

> I saw Notle's party who were encamped on the Black River beyond
> Goat Mountain. On my way out to them, I passed Red Leggings
> camp, on a branch of Black River and spent two days with him.
> Thence I was three days in reaching the Gens des Fous [i.e., the
> Han]. There have been several deaths since you saw them in the
> summer, but when I was there all seemed to be in good health. I
> gave Notle and the boy what you sent for them, and they appeared
> grateful. Ketse, in fall, started to go up in the Yukon for the purpose
> of trading with the Chilcat in Spring, so it is very likely he will visit
> Rampart House. Notle, however, will be there with all his follow-
> ers. He does not intend going to the Yankees again.[21]

Robert McDonald noted at Rampart House on June 8, 1874, that "the
majority of the Han Gwich'in arrived with their chief Charles Nootle."
Apparently on a trade mission, the Indians stayed a little over two weeks
and left on June 25. In a letter to the Bishop on July 2, McDonald noted:
"I baptised 25 adults of that tribe and of children, in all 14. The Lord's
Supper was administered to 16 communicants. Of these, 2 were Han
Gwich'in. There might have been many more but for the great dread
they have of that holy sacrament."[22]

The next year, on May 3, 1875, six Han arrived in Fort Yukon with
two Christian leaders, Joseph Kooke and William Chichuin. About two
weeks later the American trader Leroy "Jack" McQuesten arrived there
with seven Han, including Charles Nootle, and one *Trohtsik Gwich'in*.

Trohtsik has been translated as "Country of the Forks,"[23] while *Gwich'in*,
like *Hwëch'in*, simply means "people" or "residents" of a given place. The

Trohtsik (also identified as the *Trodh tsik*) *Gwich'in* were a group of Han living farther up the Yukon River on the Canadian side of the border near Fort Reliance.[24] In the nineteenth century the Han Gwich'in were called "Lower Gens de Fou" and the *Trohtsik Gwich'in* were called the "Upper Gens de Fou." Percy Henry of Dawson says he has never heard the term *Trohtsik* but once heard an elder in Eagle Village refer to all the Canadian Han as *Tr'oojik Gwich'in*, with *—jik* meaning 'mouth of the river.'[25]

On December 2, 1875, Kenneth McDonald set out to visit the Han again after traveling with a dog team from Rampart House to the Yukon River, probably by way of the upper Black River. Accompanying him were John Titsiklyatho and two Han young men. McDonald's diary from this trip probably provides the best account of Han life during the early historic period.[26]

On December 10 McDonald and his party arrived at the Yukon River only to find the Han camp abandoned. The next day they found the Han camp, consisting of fifteen lodges, including some *Trohtsik Gwich'in*. Chief Charley was among them, and McDonald stayed in Charley's lodge. The only food in camp was a few hares. McDonald learned that a *Trohtsik* woman died in childbirth several days earlier and that a Han woman's baby had just died shortly after birth. The Han woman was thus nursing the child of the deceased *Trohtsik Gwich'in* woman. A small moose was killed that day, enough for one meal.

On December 16 camp was moved north about six miles. The next day there was still no food, so camp was moved north another five miles. Finally a bear and a porcupine were killed. On December 18 camp was moved four miles farther north, but several dogs were dead and more were dying along the way. The hunters were up and gone before daylight. When they returned they reported wounding one moose.

December 19 was Sunday. McDonald refused to give the hunters permission to go after the wounded moose on account of the Sabbath. The following day, camp was moved another six miles north, and the hunters returned with news of six moose killed. McDonald's dogs became very weak. Only one dried salmon had been given to them in the previous nine days. On December 21 two more moose were killed.

On December 23 McDonald left Chief Charley and the Han to return to Rampart House, borrowing two Han boys to help break trail. On December 31 McDonald and one Indian companion finally arrived at Rampart House late at night after twenty hours of continuous travel on snowshoes in extremely cold weather. According to his brother

Robert, Kenneth traveled more than 1500 miles on snowshoes visiting the Indians in their camps during the winter of 1874–1875.

On June 20, 1876, Robert McDonald arrived at Rampart House to find 120 Indians, all starving. The leaders among them were Charles *Nootle* of the Han, *Ketse* of the *Trohtsik Gwich'in*, Red Leggings of the *Dranjik Gwich'in* (Black River people), and Peter Roe of the *Neets'ee Gwich'in* (Arctic Village people).[27]

The Early American Years

In 1879, the trader Leroy McQuesten re-ascended the Yukon to reopen Fort Reliance, which had been abandoned two years earlier. When McQuesten stopped at Charley Village, however, he learned that two old women and a sixteen-year-old blind girl had died from eating some arsenic left behind at Fort Reliance.[28] Claiming that other Han living near Fort Reliance were angry and might seek revenge for their deaths, Chief Charley urged McQuesten to stay and set up his trading post at Charley Village. An Indian by the name of "Shenerthy" (probably the famous Gwich'in trading chief *Shahnyaa Ti'*) came by and told McQuesten, however, that the incident at Fort Reliance did not call for alarm and that Charley was merely speaking shrewdly in his own self-interest. McQuesten then decided he did not want to build a new store and pushed on upriver to Fort Reliance, where he was warmly greeted by the band of Han living there. He shrewdly settled the claim against the young blind girl's wrongful death by allowing her father to take one of his dogs. This quickly cleared the air, and the next day McQuesten proceeded to buy a large quantity of furs.

Lt. Frederick Schwatka of the U.S. Army, during an exploratory trip down the Yukon River in 1883, stopped at Charley Village, which consisted at that time of five or six houses built out of sticks and brush. Schwatka counted forty to fifty Indians living there, and his map locates Charley Village on an island in the river a short distance below the mouth of the Kandik River. There Schwatka met Joe Ladue, a Canadian voyageur with a twenty-foot scow, who was living in the village and prospecting.[29]

It was also in 1883 that Edward Schieffelin, an Arizona prospector who struck it rich and founded the town of Tombstone, made a prospecting trip to try his luck in Alaska. Traveling up the Yukon River with Leroy McQuesten and a party of gold miners on the steamboat *New Racket*, Schieffelin took the earliest known photograph of Chief Charley, standing with two of his men (Chapter 2, Figure 6). This is also the earliest known photo ever taken of the Han.[30]

In the summer of 1887, Billie Moore and Dan Daugherty floated down the Yukon River in poling boats, looking for gold.

> They stopped at Charlie Creek [the Kandik River] a short while and hunted moose, for fresh meat, and obtained some king salmon from a Native encampment. There were about four families living there, and they had caught between four and five hundred dog and king salmon. They had the fish drying in the sun on a cache.[31]

Presumably Chief Charley was among the four families.

What did Charley Village look like? During the gold rush, which started at Fortymile in 1886, a prospector named Arthur Walden visited the village and left the following description:

> It was a small village of three or four houses, built of tiny poles laid one on top of the other, as the timber was very small in this section. The poles were notched together like those of a log house and made into double walls about eighteen inches apart. The intervening space was crammed hard with moss. The roofs were covered with moss and a small amount of earth, with a smoke-hole in the middle.[32]

In many respects this double-wall house type seems to match the *dlaat zhax* moss house used by the Goodpaster-Big Delta Indians in the Tanana River drainage.[33] An interior description of a Han house which must have been located either at Charley Village or Eagle Village comes from an Irish stampeder, Michael MacGowan, who in the winter of 1898–1899 was hiking his way from Circle to Dawson and took overnight shelter in a large house of Indians.

> They gave us little three-legged stools to sit on, but they were so low that we preferred to stretch our bones out on the floor. It was an earthen floor, and it was covered with little branches from the spruce-trees just like the old houses away at home were strewn with rushes. When we were warmed up and had come-to a bit, I looked the house up and down and saw that there was a fair-sized crowd of people (and a dog or two) under the roof. Some were lying down, others sitting, on rough sack beds or branches . . . a fine long wide cabin they had, I may say. If there was an overwhelming smell of fish and dogs—and a few other stenches as well—there, we weren't discommoded. They had a fire lighting in the middle of the floor and that was the first time

I ever saw a hearth or a fire in such a place. There was a huge fire there, and the place was filled with smoke and smuts that failed to find their way out through the chimney hole in the roof.[34]

MacGowan's Finnish partner, who had frostbitten one of his fingers, was attended to by an old Indian woman who came out of "a small room at the head of the house." This old woman applied a poultice and recited a magical charm to heal the Finn's fingers.

During the early to mid-1880s, before Eagle City was founded, Charley and his family, and perhaps other families in his band, moved to the new mining town of Fortymile, located at the mouth of the Fortymile River where it joins the Yukon on the Canadian side of the border. An Anglican Church station called Buxton Mission, established by Bishop William Bompas, was located on an island where the Indians liked to camp.

Bishop Bompas was joined by another Anglican missionary, Richard Bowen, who in January, 1896, traveled by dog team about three days up the Fortymile River to an unnamed Indian village, where he was met and guided by "Chief Charlie." This camp consisted of about seventy people who were trapping and processing fur and tanning moose and caribou hides. The location of the camp was not specified except that it was "built in a semicircular form on a plateau between surrounding hills."[35]

Like others to follow, Bowen was greatly impressed by Chief Charley's leadership. Many years later, he wrote:

> The memory of this old man is dear to me and many old timers would regale you with stories of his honesty, sagacity, and kindness. In one instance he is given credit for saving a massacre of the white prospectors, who had been thoughtless enough to lure the Indian squaws into their home and into the dance hall.[36]

An anonymous note to a letter written by a Han man named Arthur and collected by Frederick Schwatka, said: "The chief of the Fortymile Indians is known by both Indians and whites as 'Chief Charlie,' and the Fortymile Indians are known as 'Charlie's Band.'"[37]

Economically as well as politically, it seems, Charley and his band were more favorably disposed toward Canada than to the United States. This could well have reflected Charley's birth and upbringing on the Canadian side of the border, but it was more likely a result of his long-standing trade connections with the Hudson's Bay Company at Fort Yukon and Rampart House. At least until McQuesten arrived to start Fort Reliance in the mid-1870s, and perhaps even much later, the Hudson's Bay Company attracted a loyal Indian clientele. This loyalty was due to the high quality of its goods and its generous trade policy, which included extensions of credit, distribution of gratuities to chiefs, and at least partial forgiveness of past debt.

The Hudson's Bay Company trading post known as "Rampart House" where the Han did most of their fur trading during the late 1860s and early 1870s actually consisted of two places. The company established "Old Rampart" on the Porcupine River in 1869, two years after Americans took possession of Fort Yukon. However, in 1889, "Old Rampart" was discovered to be on American soil west of the 141st meridian on American soil, so the company had to move again twelve miles farther upriver to a point just east of the meridian. This border location, known as "New Rampart," was active until the early twentieth century but is now abandoned.

Judge Wickersham and Chief Charley

The famous Canadian geologist and explorer William Ogilvie thought as highly of Charley as Reverend Bowen did, calling him "a fine specimen of a level-headed, thoughtful Indian."[38] But Charley also had a temper, and sometimes it boiled over.

In the year 1900, for example, at the height of the gold rush, Charley quickly came to the attention of Judge James Wickersham, who had just set up a federal court in Eagle City. Charley accused a man named "Eagle Jack" of stealing one of his dogs and was prepared to go to war to retrieve the dog. According to Wickersham, Charley paddled one hundred miles up the Yukon River against the current in a birchbark canoe "with a determination to get justice if he had to get it by force."[39] He was accompanied by a dozen other fighting men.

Charley talked to a number of lesser officials, each of whom passed the buck until at last Charley was introduced to the judge. In Wickersham's words, Charley sat down and looked him in the eye and said:

> "Me Chief Charley from Charley River. You big chief here?" "Yes," I told him, I was; whereupon he added; "Any odder chief big as you?" No, I modestly admitted.

> "All light, you big chief, I tell you. Eagle Jack steal my dog at Nation river. He got my dog at Eagle village, one mile. You big chief you get

my dog; bring him me. If you not get my dog, I get my dog. Maybe some Indian get hurt. Maybe you get my dog?"[40]

According to Wickersham, Charley's "fearlessness, simple speech, and apparent honesty had won my confidence." Wickersham then walked with Charley over to the Alaska Commercial Company store and instructed a deputy to go down to the village and fetch the dog and deliver it to the chief. Within the hour Charley had his dog back.

On February 13, 1901, when it was forty-five degrees below zero Farenheit, Wickersham traveled downriver by dog team and stopped for the night at "Charley River Indian roadhouse." Wickersham said Chief Charley was happy to see him again and the judge made himself very popular by giving each of the fourteen Indian children in the village ten cents.

Figure 28. Left to right: Chief Roderick of Circle, Chief Isaac of Dawson, and Chief Charley of Fortymile, circa 1900.

Sometime during his 1900–1901 tenure as federal judge in Eagle, Wickersham or one of his aides took a photograph of Chief Charley seated with his counterparts, Chief Isaac of Dawson and Chief Roderick of Circle (Figure 28). Apparently, Roderick, like Charley, was Gwich'in rather than Han.

William "Billy" Mitchell, a lieutenant in the U.S. Army, claimed that he met Chief Charley in the Kechumstuk area in 1902. Although

Mitchell probably knew Chief Charley fairly well, he may have mistakenly assumed Kechumstuk was Charley's home village. Kechumstuk was more closely aligned with upper Tanana River communities than it was with upper Yukon River communities, and it seems almost certain that Charley was more of a visitor and guide to this country than a full-time resident. As Mitchell describes his meeting with Charley:

> At the edge of the Kechumstuk country I was met by Chief Charley of these Indians. We had tea and a good talk together. He had a beautiful silver tip fox skin which in those days was very rare. We had a great trade over it, which ended by my giving him an order on the store in Fortymile for certain amounts of powder, lead, caps (as they still used muzzle loading rifles), flour, bacon, beads, bright-colored wool, and large buttons....
>
> I accompanied Chief Charley to his village, which was quite a respectable cabin community. On a hill nearby were the graves of his departed warriors. Each was enclosed in a sort of fence, with the body in a cache supported on long poles. Strung round about it were the pots and pans that had belonged to the dead man, intermingled with streamers of various kinds to keep away the evil spirits (Mitchell 1902: 49).

In the winter of 1909, Isaac Stringer, another Anglican bishop, made a trip by dog team from Fort Yukon to Dawson and stopped overnight at Tom King's Roadhouse, located at Charley Creek. On December 14 his companion, a man named McRae, went up to the Indian village and took a census. He counted twenty-five people, including "Old Charlie," whom Stringer had previously met at Herschel Island on the Arctic coast.[41]

When the U.S. census taker visited Charley Creek Indian Village in 1910 he found twenty-five people residing there. This census taker recorded not only the names and ages of the residents, but also their ethnicity (under a column labeled "Tribe and Clan"). Of these twenty-five, seventeen were Han, six (including Chief Charley and his wife Sarah) were *Vunta/Vantee Gwich'in*, one was *Takudh Gwich'in* (from the upper Porcupine River), and one was *Neets'ee Gwich'in* (from the upper Chandalar River and Arctic Village area).[42] Others living at Charley Village at that time were Dolphus and his wife Victoria; William and Grace Stacey and their children Ben, Robert, and Anna; Joseph and Lucy Enoch and their children Agnes and John; and David *K'ay* (shown in the census records as Kkaih but pronounced *K'ay*) (lit. "David

Willow") and his wife Myra (who was another one of the *Vunta/Vantee Gwich'in*) along with their six children.

According to Louise Paul, David *K'ay* was the father of Harry David Sr., who claimed to be born in Charley Village on February 2, 1913.[43] Willie Juneby claimed his grandparents were from Charley Creek, and Louise Paul believed that Willie's grandfather was Chief Charley's brother. One of Cornelius Osgood's key respondents, named Angus Alexander (also known as Angus Alex or Angus Alec), was interviewed in Eagle but claimed to have been born about 1872 on Charley Creek. Alexander believed his parents were also born there.[44]

The End of Charley Village
Hudson Stuck, the Episcopal missionary and archdeacon, stopped at Charley Village on his way to Eagle on June 7, 1911, and baptized a baby. At that time he counted only ten or twelve persons in the community. On his way back down from Eagle later that month, Stuck stopped and celebrated Holy Communion with the Charley Village people. The next April, he stopped again and found "no more than seven adults there, the rest out hunting or gone to Eagle."[45]

Several years later Stuck tells us that Charley Village was washed completely away by "phenomenally high water" in the spring breakup of 1914 and that the handful of remaining residents moved to Circle. Two other visitors tell us that "when the ice broke up last spring . . . the flood completely destroyed Charlie's village, where forty Indians made their homes, and they have since scattered up and down the river."[46]

An oral account by the late Charlie Biederman confirms the 1914 flood story but also indicates that many of the people living at Charley Creek died from a flu epidemic there the year before.[47]

At this point we lose track of Chief Charley. We are uncertain about how long he lived or what became of him if he indeed survived the epidemic and the flood. The 1900 census taker found him living in Eagle Village that year at the age of seventy-five, placing the year of his birth, if that age estimate is correct, at about 1825. Elisha Lyman and Louise Paul were both convinced that Charley died in Eagle Village and was buried there. Episcopal Church burial records show that Old Charley (presumably the same person as Chief Charley) died of tuberculosis on September 1, 1907, at age seventy-five (making his birth year 1832), but this conflicts with Bishop Stringer's 1909 survey and the 1910 U.S.

Census report showing he was still living that same year at Charley Creek.[48] This is additional evidence for the existence of two Charleys.

Willie Juneby claimed to be descended from Chief Charley's brother, Old Peter *K'ay* (see Peter and Juneby family tree in Appendix D). In one family tree descendancy chart, Chief Charley appears to have only one direct descendant, the late Oliver Lyman of Eagle Village. If our genealogies are correct, Chief Charley was Oliver's great grandfather—his mother's mother's father. However, a second chart we have developed with the assistance of Martha Kates shows that Chief Charley has many living descendants, including all of the Roberts family living in Dawson.

In retrospect, Chief Charley was a widely known leader who, although not Han by birth or by marriage, adopted much of Han culture and almost certainly spoke Hän. Charley lived through incredible hardship and maintained a truly nomadic subsistence lifestyle well into the late-nineteenth century. He was hospitable to white visitors and became a devout Christian, due to the efforts of the early Anglican missionaries, particularly the McDonald brothers.

Because Charley was not afraid to confront white people on matters of principle, he accordingly earned their heartfelt respect and admiration. He was willing to negotiate differences but was also prepared to settle those differences by force if necessary. Charley was a charismatic figure. Bob Stacey, Chief Charley's grandson, once said that when his grandfather shook his hand, he felt the heat rise right up his arm and into his shoulder, projecting some kind of mysterious power and energy.[49] Although Charley was the leader of a fairly small band of Indians, his power and influence were such that he felt free to roam a wide hunting and trading territory, stretching hundreds of square miles from his home at Charley Village to Eagle, Fortymile City, Kechumstuk, and much of the upper Fortymile River country.

Chief David

One of the early Han chiefs living around Eagle and Fortymile during historic times was Chief David.[50] Although the Han village at Eagle was identified as "Johnny's Village" by Frederick Schwatka in 1883, this name has never been used by anyone since. It probably was erroneous because there is no other record, either written or oral, of a man by this name. To every other visitor to the region it was known as "David's Camp." Chief David was probably one of the progenitors of the David family living in Eagle Village today and led a band of sixty-five to seventy people said to be living along the Yukon River near Belle Isle, about fifteen miles below the Canadian boundary.

From 1890 to 1891, John McGrath of the U.S. Coast and Geodetic Survey, led a survey of the U.S.-Canadian boundary. The survey party camped for the winter on the Yukon River very close to the border, and Dr. Kingsberry, McGrath's assistant, took a series of documentary photos of the local Indians, including a group portrait of "David's Indians" (Figure 7). Whether David himself is in the photograph is uncertain, but he may be the oldest man, fourth from the left. Another photo with some of the same people taken at Fortymile was published in *Frank Leslie's Illustrated Newspaper* on July 4, 1891, page 370. In that same year, Archdeacon Robert McDonald met and baptized a boy named David who was the son of Chief David Sandysk and his wife Eliza, and they were living somewhere in the vicinity of Eagle Village.[51]

Except for these few anecdotes and the celebration of his memorial potlatch in 1903, little is known about Chief David.[52] It seems likely, however, that he was the father of Harry David Sr.'s father, David *K'ay* (also known as Old David), who lived from 1859 until 1919 (see David family tree). We do know that Chief David was succeeded by another of his sons, named Peter, who was installed as chief at his father's 1903 memorial potlatch at Fortymile. This Chief Peter could well have been Old Peter *K'ay*, who was born in 1849 and is the oldest known ancestor of the Junebys (see Peter and Juneby family tree).

Chief Isaac

Chief Isaac was probably better known to non-Natives than any of the other Han chiefs. He was rather flamboyant. He often wore very formal dress, made frequent public appearances, and gave many speeches, but he was also frequently photographed in the midst of subsistence activities (Figures 18 and 29). Isaac was a devout Anglican and was instrumental in working with the Anglican Church to establish the Moosehide Reserve during the gold rush. He was loved both by his own people as well as by many of the non-Natives in Dawson.

Chief Isaac's brothers, Jonathon Wood and Walter Benjamin, were both preachers. Jonathon served at the Anglican Church in Moosehide for many years, while "Walter Ben," as he is remembered, maintained the Episcopal Church mission in Eagle Village and raised a number of homeless children. As young men, Isaac and Walter Ben worked for the Northern Commercial Company as dog drivers and guides.

According to Chief Isaac's daughter, he and his brothers originally came from the area around Eagle before the gold rush of 1898, but it is not clear how Isaac was able to move into the Dawson band's territory and rise to the position of chief in such a short time.[53] The best explanation is from Percy Henry who said that Isaac married the daughter of Gah Tsy'aa [Catseah or Catsah], the chief of *Tr'ondëk Hwëch'in* before Isaac.[54]

It may be a coincidence that Chief Isaac of Dawson had the same name as Chief Isaac of Kechumstuk and Mansfield Village. Even though the Eagle Village and Kechumstuk people have a history of friendly relations, there is no evidence to suggest the two Isaacs were in any way related. A third Chief Isaac, living at Chilkoot, was a Tlingit leader who contracted with prospectors for packing supplies over the Chilkoot Pass during the gold rush.

Figure 29. Three Han in two canoes near Dawson, 1898. On the left is Chief Isaac and his son; in the other canoe is Isaac's brother, Walter Benjamin.

Tappan Adney, who camped and hunted with the Han Chief Isaac along the Klondike River during the gold rush, described his personality and behavior. Adney was a splendid artist as well as a fine writer. His many sketches of Isaac and his people give us a good sense not only of Isaac the man but also of the nomadic Han life in the Yukon backcountry. In his

article "Moose Hunting with the Tro-chu-tin," Adney reported that Isaac
was a tall man who carried himself "with conscious self-respect" and had
"a flashing eye that gave the impression both of mastery and shrewdness."
Isaac would get up before daylight, step outside, and announce the day's
activities. As Adney described: "He spoke not in the smooth, melodious
tongue of the Eastern Indian, but slowly and deliberately, in short, crisp,
incisive monosyllables. When he was done, he informed me in broken
English that we were to hunt on the left-hand side of the river."[55]

From this description, it becomes clear that it was the chief's duty to
give directions to the people for hunting and traveling. Undoubtedly,
the chief's announcement also served as a general wake-up call. The fact
that all the others were still in their tents at that hour of the morning
pretty well precluded any questions or complaints. At the same time,
Isaac is not remembered for being a bully, but for always talking politely
to his followers.[56]

Although most of the time he spoke Hän, Isaac attempted to learn
English as well, and his flavored speech of "short, crisp, incisive monosyllables" evolved into a distinctive vernacular: "Mull moose, too much
tupp; cow moose, plenty fat stop, he all right" meant that bull moose
meat was too tough but cow moose meat was fat and tender.[57] In Hän
and other Athabaskan languages there is no distinction between female
and male pronouns, so it is common to hear Hän speakers use "he" in
place of "she" and vice-versa when they speak English.

One of the notable events in the life of Chief Isaac was a trip he
took from Dawson to San Francisco in 1901 as a guest of the Alaska
Commercial Company. This free trip was by steamboat to the mouth
of the Yukon and then by steamship from St. Michael to Seattle and San
Francisco Bay. Accompanying him, according to Louise Paul, were the
lay reader Walter Benjamin and the Han medicine man Little Paul.[58]
Although he got seasick both ways, Isaac returned to Dawson standing
on the Texas deck of the steamer *Whitehorse*, wearing a high hard hat,
speckled knickers, a bright red tie with a sparkling pin, and sporting
a big Havana cigar in his mouth. The newspapers reported that he was
greeted by a crowd of thousands.[59]

Some notion of the respect people showed to Chief Isaac comes from
a newspaper account of Christmas Day in Moosehide in 1902.[60] On that
day nearly everyone in the village made a formal call at Isaac's house to
give the chief a present, and he in turn gave each visitor a present. In the
process the chief received many pairs of moccasins. The village took on
a bright and festive holiday look with many residents displaying British

and American flags on flagpoles in front of their houses. One legend is that Isaac was hired by white people to use his "rain medicine" to end a long dry spell at Dawson and was successful.[61]

When Chief Isaac died in April 1932, following a bout of influenza, he left two daughters, Pat and Angela, and two sons, Fred and Charlie. Another son, Edward, died of tuberculosis in 1912. After his death, Isaac was widely praised for his "common sense and justice," and according to one journalist, "his one great object in life and the theme of his speeches was to maintain a friendly relationship between the Indians and whites and between the various bands of Indians residing in different parts of the Yukon."[62]

Isaac's biggest grievance was not against the miners who tore up the country during the gold rush, but against the large number of white men who, having failed to find gold, took up fur trapping and hunting, thereby reducing the Indians' chances for making a living off the land. In 1915, he told a newspaper reporter:

> Injun all return today from Glacier trail, where shoot caribou. All my Injun shootem seventy caribou and bringem to Moosehide and putem in cache for winter. That enough last all winter. Jess you tellem white man killem 3,000 caribou, but Injun he killem only seventy. Me no likeum white man shootem caribou.
>
> Jess you tellem in newspaper that it all right white man come dig deep, catchem my gold on my creeks—that all right. Letem white man have gold. Injun no eatem gold. But Injun wantem caribou—wantem hunting ground. In Alaska white man no huntem game; in Canada side white man he go shootem caribou which belong Injun. Caribou my meat. I no shootem horse. I no shootem white man cattle.[63]

Whatever he thought of gold mining, Isaac was interested enough in gold to locate and file four placer mine applications of his own between 1904 and 1919.[64] Few if any other Han showed an interest in gold mining, and it seems unlikely that Chief Isaac made any of his claims pay, but he may have filed these claims to protect his cabins and subsistence sites. Isaac's claims were located on Moosehide Creek near Moosehide village, on Cary Creek (a tributary of the Yukon River just below the mouth of the Fortymile River), on the South Fork of the Sixtymile, and on Pine Creek (a tributary of Matson Creek which flows into the Sixtymile).

To commemorate Chief Isaac's many years of leadership, the *Tr'ondëk Hwëch'in* First Nation in Dawson named its main office building on Front Street after him. This building, which caught fire and burned down on

August 30, 1996, housed the band's council chambers, social programs offices, and band manager's office.

Other Han Chiefs

As noted above, the chief of the Klondike band just before Isaac was a man named Catseah or *Gah Tsy'aa* ("rabbit skin hat"), who visited Fort Yukon to entice American traders to establish a post in his area at Nuklako. Chief William Silas, a subchief to Isaac, was portrayed as a smart young interpreter for the traders. Silas died in the early 1920s and may have been the father of Andrew Silas (see Silas family tree). Church and cemetery records also show that Chief Abraham, who died in 1898, was buried at Moosehide.

According to Percy Henry, the succession of Han chiefs at Moosehide and Dawson following Chief Isaac was Charlie Isaac, John Jonas, Jimmy Wood, and Percy Henry (1969–1984), followed by Peggy Kormendy,

Figure 30. Chief Walter Benjamin (left) and Tom Young, 1919, at Eagle Village.

Hilda Carr, Angie Joseph-Rear, Steve Taylor, and Darren Taylor.[65] Martha Roberts Kates claims that her grandfather Robert Charles was also a young chief, perhaps while he was living at Fortymile.

Alaskan Han chiefs (not necessarily in complete or in chronological order) include Chief Phillip or Felix from Charley River, Walter Benjamin (Figure 30), Arthur Stevens (Figure 31), Andrew Silas, Susie Paul, Willie Juneby, and Angus Alex (Figure 49), all from Eagle Village. As Silas Stevens recalls, "it seems like they all took turns" being chief.

Chief Roderick of Circle, who had his photograph taken with Chief Charley and Chief Isaac (Figure 28), may have guided Reverend Richard Bowen up the Fortymile River in 1895, and was identified by Bowen as a medicine man. He appears in the 1900 U.S. Census in Circle and was apparently Gwich'in rather than Han. Roderick is listed in the census

Figure 31. Elisha Lyman (left) with Andy Stevens (center) and Arthur Stevens (right), circa 1922.

as fifty-seven years of age, with his wife Emma, age fifty, and daughter Bella, age seventeen. In 1916 Bella met and married Adolph "Ed" Biederman, a Bohemian immigrant, in Circle. The couple first moved to Charley Creek where they built a cabin and then settled permanently in Eagle City in 1918.

Unfortunately there is no good written record of the succession of Han chiefs on the American side, but it seems clear that sometime between the 1940s and the 1970s, power began to be transferred from elder chiefs to younger men. In contrast to former times, however, the first and second chiefs as well as council members are elected by popular vote.

The Tragedy of Two Young Han Chiefs

Today there are no longer any elder chiefs such as Chief Charley, Chief David, and Chief Isaac, and the office of chief itself is elective rather than hereditary. Before World War II, leadership was most often passed on from father to son. Beginning in the 1950s, however, a new kind of leadership emerged in the form of young elected chiefs. One of the biggest issues facing these elected chiefs was the widespread availability of alcohol.

When Mishler first arrived in Eagle Village to do fieldwork in 1973, Tony Paul, a bright, affable, and energetic young man, was chief. Tony Paul had married Hannah Wallis, a Gwich'in woman from Fort Yukon, and they were raising a family. Only a few years later, however, Tony died from pneumonia complicated by alcohol-induced cirrhosis of the liver. He was just twenty-nine years of age.

The next chief at Eagle, Michael David, received national attention because he took the noted author John McPhee out camping in the early 1970s and supplied McPhee with much of the material for his bestselling book, *Coming into the Country*. McPhee was very taken by Michael and his father, Harry David, Sr., who was village chief in the early 1960s. Michael had mixed feelings about the National Park Service coming in and managing a large part of the Han homeland, which the Han have used traditionally for subsistence at least as long as there has been written history and undoubtedly much longer. He liked the Park Service because it opposed any new development, but at the same time he disliked it for introducing and enforcing regulations that restricted the Han's ability to hunt and use the land freely, forcing them to adhere to seasons and bag limits.[66]

Michael dreamed of getting more jobs for his people. He tried to establish a post office in the village as well as a store, and he tried to have bootlegging (the illegal sale of alcohol) outlawed in Eagle City. But before he could accomplish any of these things, Michael David died in an alcohol-related car accident on the Taylor Highway. He lived to the age of thirty, one year longer than Tony Paul.

The loss of leadership and vision provided by these two young chiefs was nothing less than tragic. Their deaths devastated Eagle Village.

Women to the Fore: A New Era in Han Leadership

As the times have changed and two of the most promising young male leaders died prematurely from alcohol abuse, gender roles have also changed. Han women have stepped in to become leaders.

In 1983 Joanne Beck (Figure 32) was elected the first woman chief in Eagle Village and has held that office intermittently since then. During

Figure 32. Joanne Beck, Chief at Eagle, July 1997.

the 1980s Ruth Ridley was elected chief even though, ironically, she recalls being trained as a young woman to remain silent when attending tribal council meetings. The Dawson band has had three woman chiefs in a row starting with Peggy Kormendy, followed by Hilda Carr and Angie Joseph-Rear. In 1997 the Han at Dawson were led by chief Darren Taylor, with Angie Joseph-Rear serving as principal organizer of the biennial Han gatherings, and Georgette McLeod as Heritage Officer. Chiefs are elected by the band council to serve two-year terms.

Even though Han women have stepped forward to assume these leadership positions, Beck still sees the chief's position as gender-based. "If I could find a good man to do it, I would gladly step down and follow two steps behind," she says, "because I really see it as a man's job.... I get into arguments with people because I push them and try to show them something better. I just want them to get their drive back. There are so many young men who are able bodied; I just want them to get their drive back.[67]

On the Canadian side Debbie Nagano, the mother of two young children, is fully dedicated to passing on Indian culture and values to children and young people. Debbie and her staff decided to stop worrying about getting elders or parents involved; they just concentrated on what they could do with youth. Workshops in the 1997 two-week culture camp held at Moosehide Village included substance abuse awareness (drugs and alcohol), arts and crafts, traditional games, self-esteem, healthy parenting and relationships, traditional drum making, the Hän language, songs and dances, and traditional medicine.

Women have also taken a significant leadership role in preserving the Hän language. In the 1980s Ruth Ridley worked with the Alaska Native Language Center to publish a book of Han stories, and since then both Angie Joseph-Rear, Jane Montgomery, and Percy and Mabel Henry have worked for the Yukon Native Language Centre to develop a series of school curriculum materials in Hän. One well-educated male speaker of the language, Isaac Juneby, has also worked with the Yukon Native Language Centre to produce literacy lesson books. In Dawson there have been a number of language workshops and classes, and an ongoing women's sewing circle where only Hän is spoken. Despite these efforts, Hän now has fewer than a dozen fluent speakers and is in great danger of extinction within a generation.

Notes

1. Good notes on Han household organization may be found in the missionary journal of Kenneth McDonald (Journals. In: Letters and Papers of the Church Missionary Society, London [microfilm at Winnipeg: Rupert's Land Provincial Archives, 1874]); in the report of surveyor William Ogilvie, *Exploratory Survey of Part of the Lewes, Tat-on-duc, Porcupine, Bell, Trout, Peel, and Mackenzie Rivers, 1887–88*. Annual Report for the Dept. of Interior 1889, Part VIII, Section 3. [Ottawa: B. Chamberlin, 1890]); in the writings of the young journalist, Tappan Adney ("Moose Hunting with the Tro-chu-tin." *Harper's New Monthly Magazine* 100, no. 598 (1900): 494–507; and *The Klondike Stampede* (New York: Harper and Brothers, 1900); as well as in the unpublished field notes of linguist Gordon Marsh (Fairbanks: Alaska Native Language Center library, 1956). Those interested in the physical layout of Eagle Village in the early 1970s may wish to consult John McPhee's *Coming into the Country* (New York: Farrar, Strauss, and Giroux, 1977).

    The standard reference work on Han kinship and social organization is Cornelius Osgood's *The Han Indians* (1971), a monograph based largely on fieldwork done in the summer of 1932. Osgood also drew extensively on the unpublished field notes of Richard Slobodin's "Notes on the Han" (Appendix II to Preliminary Report on Ethnographic Work, 1962, manuscript. Ottawa: National Museum of Man, Ethnology Division). Slobodin's discussion of sib or clan organization among the Peel River Gwich'in, a group that married extensively into the Han both during and after the gold rush, is also worth reading for its conclusion that clans were a relatively late and weak acquisition from the west (Slobodin 1962: 44–45).

2. Kenneth McDonald, Journals, 1874.

3. Ogilvie, *Exploratory Survey* (1890).

4. Adney, "Moose Hunting with the Tro-chu-tin," 500.

5. McPhee, *Coming into the Country*, 382–383.

6. Osgood, *The Han Indians*, 39–40.

7. Catharine McClellan, *Part of the Land, Part of the Water: A History of the Yukon Indians* (Vancouver and Toronto: Douglas and McIntyre, 1987).

8. Percy Henry, Audiotape 1, 1999.

9. Slobodin, "Notes on the Han," 1963a.

10. Frederica de Laguna, "Matrilineal Kin Groups in Northwestern North America," *Proceedings: Northern Athapaskan Conference, 1971*, Vol. 1, ed. by A. McFadyen Clark (Ottawa: National Museum of Man Mercury Series, Canadian Ethnology Service Paper No. 27, 1975), 79–82, 84–85, 89–90. Those interested in clan and moiety affiliations, and the way they vary among northern Athabaskan groups, should look at de Laguna's comparative study.

    Catharine McClellan's brief discussion of Han moieties seems to us to be mistakenly based on Gwich'in clans or sibs, perhaps because of widespread intermarriage between the Han and the Gwich'in, especially in Moosehide and Dawson. See McClellan, *Part of the Land*, 189.

Interesting comparisons may also be made between Han clans or moieties and those of the Upper Tanana Athabaskans, who are also divided into Seagull and Crow. See especially Marie-Françoise Guédon, *People of Tetlin, Why Are You Singing?* (Ottawa: National Museums of Canada, Mercury Series, Ethnology Division Paper No. 9, Ottawa, 1974), 64–96, and Robert A. McKennan, *The Upper Tanana Indians* (New Haven: Yale University Publications in Anthropology No. 55, 1959), 116–139. Richard Slobodin in his "Notes on the Han" (1963) writes about the practice of matrilocality and cross-cousin marriage.

A puzzling sidenote is that the clan name for Crow in Eagle Village is *Nahtsin*, even though the everyday name for Crow or Raven is *TätrĀ'*. See Willie Juneby's story of The Indian War in Chapter 6 below.

11. Juneby, 1973, Audiotape H93-12-319. The Han's downriver neighbors, the *Di'hĀ^^ Gwich'in*, also found this to be an apt comparison (see Johnny Frank in Mishler, *Neerihiinjìk: We Traveled From Place to Place: The Gwich'in Stories of Johnny and Sarah Frank*, 2nd ed. [Fairbanks: Alaska Native Language Center, 2001], 135). The Tlingit, Tutchone, and Ahtna frequently draw on this analogy as well.

12. Louise Paul, Audiotape 1, 1973.

13. De Laguna, "Matrilineal Kin Groups in Northwestern North America," 89–90.

14. Insights into the life of a young Han woman who became an alcoholic as a result of her failed marriage to a white man can be found in a Fairbanks newspaper column (see Lynn Watson, "Alcoholic Tells of Her Pain and a Reunion." *The Northland News* (April 1988), pp. 5ff.

15. Schmitter, *Upper Yukon Native Customs and Folk-Lore*, 12.

16. Ferdinand Schmitter's observations from Eagle Village during the first decade of the twentieth century help clarify the traditional leadership roles played by Han chiefs. Information about the election of chiefs and second chiefs comes from Angus Alex, Cornelius Osgood's key respondent in 1932 (see Osgood, *The Han Indians*, 41–42), and from Han elder Silas Stevens (Audiotape 3, 1997).

17. The earliest sources on Chief Charley are the Anglican missionary journals of Robert and Kenneth McDonald, preserved on microfilm at the Public Archives of Canada in Ottawa as part of the records of the Church Missionary Society of London (CMSL). Of special interest are the journals of Robert McDonald for 1871, 1874–1876, and 1891, and the journals of Kenneth McDonald for 1874–1875.

Another missionary who met Charley was the Anglican Richard Bowen, who ventured forth to Han villages and winter camps from his base at Fortymile. Bowen's journal, apparently written many years after his sojourn in the Yukon, remains unpublished (see R. J. Bowen, *Incidents in the Life of the Reverend Richard John Bowen Among the Natives, Trappers Prospectors and Gold Miners in the Yukon Territory Before and After the Gold Rush of the Year 1898* [Ottawa: National Archives of Canada, n.d.]). We found a typescript copy of it at the Tr'ondëk Hwëch'in Land Claims office in Dawson.

18. Good information about Chief Charley and his band is found in the household enumeration sheets of the U.S. Census (Bureau of the Census, 1900; 1910) for Charley Village and Eagle Village. His name is often spelled Charlie Nootle or Notle in historic documents and is pronounced *Nootl'ët* or *Nooglit* by Percy Henry.

19. Descendant Martha Roberts Kates alerted us to a close-up photo of her great grandfather, Chief Charley (Figure 27), from the Bunnell Collection at the Rasmuson Library archives at the University of Alaska Fairbanks, which has no contextual information. The man in this photo very closely resembles the man shown below in Chapter 6 (Figure 39), except that he is wearing spectacles.

    Another photo of Chief Charley which we have not attempted to reproduce here is found in William Ogilvie's *Early Days on the Yukon and the Story of Its Gold Finds* (London, New York, & Toronto: John Lane, 1913), 72. This individual also sports a thick white beard and moustache and appears to be light-skinned. He clearly resembles the man shown here in Figures 27 and 39. Taken about 1890, Figure 39 clearly depicts a different individual from the stocky, dark-skinned, clean-shaven man shown in Figures 6, 26, and 28. Ogilvie is the only one who provides both a photo of Chief Charley and written observations of him, but even so the photo and the observations appear in separate publications.

20. Robert McDonald, Journals, 27 July 1871.

21. Kenneth McDonald, Journals, 24 April 1874.

22. Robert McDonald, Journals, 2 July 1874.

23. Robert Kennicott, "List of Kutchin Tribes." MS 203-b. circa 1869. Washington, D.C.: National Anthropological Archives.

24. Mary E. Wesbrook, "A Venture into Ethnohistory: The Journals of Rev. V. C. Sim, Pioneer Missionary on the Yukon." *Polar Notes*, No. 9 (1969): 34–45.

25. Percy Henry, Audiotape 1, 1999. Percy may also have had in mind Tr'ochëk, the old village site at the mouth of the Klondike River.

26. Kenneth McDonald, Journals, 1875–1876. The narrative summary that follows is taken from these journals.

27. According to Ogilvie's observations in the late 1880s (*Exploratory Survey*, 48), the persistent efforts of the McDonalds to convert Charley and his people to Christianity had paid off.

28. Leroy McQuesten, *Recollections of Leroy N. McQuesten: Life in the Yukon 1871–1885* (Dawson City: Yukon Order of Pioneers, 1952).

29. Frederick Schwatka, *Along Alaska's Great River: A Popular Account of the Travels of the Alaska Exploring Expedition of 1883; Along the Great Yukon River from Its Source to Its Mouth, in British North-west Territory and in the Territory of Alaska* (New York: Cassell, 1885), 88, also map sheet 8.

30. Edward Schieffelin's album of photographs of Alaska Natives living along the Yukon River is in the James Wickersham Collection at the Alaska State Historical Library in Juneau. This album constitutes perhaps the earliest collection of photographs of Alaska's Interior Natives.

31. Will H. Chase, *Reminiscences of Captain Billie Moore* (Kansas City: Burton Publishing Co., 1947).

32. Arthur Walden, *A Dog-Puncher on the Yukon* (New York: Houghton-Mifflin, 1928), 59.

33. See house descriptions and sketches in Craig Mishler's *Born with the River: An Ethnographic History of Alaska's Goodpaster and Big Delta Indians* (Fairbanks: Alaska Division of Geological & Geophysical Surveys, Report of Investigations 86–14, 1986), 29–33.

34. Michael MacGowan, *The Hard Road to the Klondike.* Trans. V. Iremonger. (London & Boston: Routledge and Kegan Paul, 1962), 104–105.

35. Bowen, *Incidents in the Life*, 125.

36. Ibid., 35–36.

37. Anonymous, Note to a letter written by a Han man named Arthur and collected by Frederick Schwatka. Manuscript 3704. Washington, D.C.: The Smithsonian Institution Archives.

38. Ogilvie, *Exploratory Survey*, 48. Ogilvie noted that Charley greatly preferred Canada over the United States for political reasons. General insights into why the Hudson's Bay Company was able to maintain a competitive edge in its trade with Chief Charley and the Han even after it relocated from Fort Yukon to Rampart House can be found in Arthur J. Ray's essay, "Periodic Shortages, Native Welfare, and the Hudson's Bay Company: 1670–1930," in S. Krech III, ed., *The Subarctic Fur Trade: Native Social and Economic Adaptation* (Vancouver: University of British Columbia Press, 1984), 1–20.

Kenneth Coates, in his paper, "Furs Along the Yukon: Hudson's Bay Company–Native Trade in the Yukon River Basin, 1830–1893," *B.C. Studies*, No. 55 (Autumn), 50–78, insists that the Hudson's Bay Company trading advantage was short-lived after the purchase of Alaska because the American traders quickly adopted many of the Hudson's Bay Company's policies and practices. However, by 1887, Alaska's territorial governor, Alfred Swineford, charged in his annual report that the Alaska Commercial Company, untaxed and virtually unregulated, had "driven away all competition and reduced the Native population to a condition of helpless dependence, if not one of absolute and abject slavery." It did this, he wrote, by paying "beggarly prices for their peltry" and exacting "exorbitant prices for the goods given in exchange" (Swineford quoted in Gruening, *The State of Alaska* [New York: Random House, 1954], 512, n. 64).

39. James Wickersham, *Old Yukon: Tales, Trails, Trials* (St. Paul: West Publishing, 1938).

40. Ibid., 43–45.

41. Isaac Stringer, unpublished diary, 14 December 1909 (Toronto: Anglican Church Archives).

42. Bureau of the Census, Department of Commerce, Thirteenth U.S. Census, 1910. Microfilm. (Anchorage: National Archives and Records Service).

43. Bureau of Indian Affairs, Department of Interior, Village Census Rolls, 1966, RG 75, Microfilm. (Anchorage: National Archives and Records Service).

44. Osgood, *The Han Indians*, 17.

45. Hudson Stuck, Diary, 1911–1912. Records of the Protestant Episcopal Church in Alaska. Microfilm 91. (Fairbanks: Alaska and Polar Regions Department, Rasmuson Library, University of Alaska).

46. Matthew Sniffen and Thomas Carrington, *The Indians of the Yukon and Tanana Valleys, Alaska* (Philadelphia: Indian Rights Association, 1914), 6.

47. Charlie Biederman, Audiotape H95-14, 1994. This taped interview with Biederman alludes briefly to the 1913 flu epidemic at Charley Village. Biederman also says that he saw about five cabins still standing there in the spring of 1923 or 1924, but these were all leveled by a large Yukon River ice jam in the spring of 1925.

    By the time of the epidemic and flood, if he lived that long, Charley would have been about eighty-eight or eighty-nine. His age as given in the 1910 U.S. Census at Charley Village is only forty-nine, which is surely an error, since he was already a band leader by 1874, and all the turn-of-the-century photographs show him to be an old man.

48. The reports about Chief Charley's burial place in Eagle Village come from oral interviews with Elisha Lyman (Audiotapes 1 and 2, 1973), from Louise Paul (Audiotape H91-22-43, 1991), and from Episcopal Church burial records housed in the Eagle Historical Society archives.

49. Mishler, Eagle Village field notes, 21 December 1973.

50. Notes on Chief David can be found in William Ogilvie, *Exploratory Survey*, 48. Anecdotes about David *K'ay* and other people who were from Charley Village come from Willie Juneby (interviewed by Regina Goebel on 9–10 December 1980 typed transcript of tape recording at the Eagle Historical Society archives), and Louise Paul (Interviewed by Craig Mishler, Audiotape 1, 1973; also Audiotape 2, 1997). Harry David Sr.'s birthplace at Charley Village is confirmed by a household census done in Eagle Village by the Bureau of Indian Affairs in 1966.

    The Kandik River (aka Charley Creek), first reported by Schwatka as a place name in 1888, was probably corrupted slightly from *K'ay'ndik* ("lower Willow Creek"), and David *K'ay's* surname may also have referred to this creek. Ferdinand Schmitter, the medical doctor at Fort Egbert, made a fundamental error in identifying the people of Eagle as "Vun tte kwichin [Vunta kutchin]" ("people living among the lakes"), even though he somehow got the ethnonym right in translation as "the people of Willow Creek" (Schmitter, *Upper Yukon Native Customs and Folk-Lore*, 1, 16). There certainly were several *Vunta/Vantee Gwich'in* living among the Han, and this may have produced the confusion.

51. Anonymous, "Yukon Yarns." *Alaska-Yukon Magazine* 3 No. 2 (March 1907): 84–87.

52. A lengthy description of Chief David's memorial potlatch can be found in the

Yukon Sun newspaper, 18 April 1903.

53. Joy McDiarmid, "Pat Lindgren, Daughter of Chief Isaac," *Yukon Indian News*, 25 October 1977, 9.

54. Percy Henry, Audiotape 1, 1999.

55. Adney, "Moose Hunting with the Tro-chu-tin," 498. Although Adney was only with Isaac and his band for about a year in 1897–1898, his two magazine articles and his artistic sketches provide more sympathetic insight into Isaac's leadership style, personality, and way of life than any other combination of sources.

56. Walter DeWolfe in McClellan, *Part of the Land*, 226.

57. Adney, *The Klondike Stampede*, 631.

58. Louise Paul, Proceedings, Historical Symposium, 2–4 July 1986 (Eagle: Eagle Historical Society), 39–43.

59. Dawson City Museum Library, Chief Isaac file, unlabeled newspaper article.

60. *Dawson Daily News*, 26 December 1902.

61. Robert McDonald, Journals, 7 July 1887 and 17 July 1891.

62. Newspaper obituaries of Chief Isaac appeared in the *Dawson News*, 12 April 1932, and the *Alaska Weekly*, 15 April 1932.

63. Speech quoted in the *Dawson Daily News*, 4 November 1915.

64. Copies of Chief Isaac's placer mining claims are on file in the Dawson City Museum.

65. Percy Henry, Audiotape 2, 1999.

66. McPhee, *Coming into the Country.*

67. Joanne Beck interview by William E. Simeone in Eagle Village, 23 July 1997.

Chapter Five

Traditional Han Religion

Spiritual Power and Shamanism

TRADITIONAL HAN religious beliefs were based on the conviction that the universe is full of power. This power is immense and lodged in all things from a mountain to an animal, an arrow, a gun, a stone, and menstrual blood. Since all things possess power, people believed the world was alive, and within this animate world they warily negotiated their way by enlisting animal allies and observing a multitude of taboos or rules that guided their behavior in everyday life.

One way humans obtained power was by dreaming of an animal, which then became a person's ally. The dreamer learned songs, incantations, or rituals to summon power that he then employed in hunting or other activities. The dreamer did not view the dreamed animal as a spirit or metaphysical entity but as an actual animal being. Ferdinand Schmitter's comment that "the Native believes in a rather concrete existence of dream life, and he sees spirits as if they were real creatures" suggests such a view.[1] Another indication of this view is that people believed that amulets or fetishes, made from some part of the animal, possessed power that protected the owner.

Humans also obtained luck by securing, or even just seeing, an object that was considered to have power. Such objects might be a bit of animal skin, the feather of a bird, or a flower, which possessed power because they were set off from the ordinary, either by appearance or by timing, such as a robin appearing in the dead of winter. While everyone may have considered such an occurrence unusual, individuals alone, not a religious specialist or priest, interpreted the significance or meaning of the event.

Within Athabaskan society, individuals held varying amounts of power, depending on their ability to dream and whether they could obtain objects that contained luck. Those who held the most power were shamans or medicine men who had a gift for dreaming and obtaining strong spiritual allies. While individuals sometimes possessed enough power to ensure their own hunting luck, shamans were powerful enough to fight off or defend against malevolent spirits. To this end they held semi-private or public ceremonies to cure sickness. Shamans sought cures by entering a trance state, singing and drumming, using Native medicines, and removing objects of affliction by sucking or blowing them out of a patient's body.

A shaman is a person who has special spiritual powers acquired voluntarily, through his or her own initiative; or involuntarily, because of the person's mental and physical disposition. These powers are thought to give the shaman special abilities that enable them to deal with supernatural beings. Schmitter's primary interest was in shamanism: "My first inquiry was for a medicine man, but I was informed that there was none now in the vicinity, all of them having died or left long ago. They were very reserved on this subject and it was two years before I won their confidence."[2] According to Schmitter, there were good and bad shamans. Healing was the only interest of good shamans, but bad shamans liked to kill and therefore were not apt to live as long. Shamans had diverse abilities that ranged from healing people to making a prospective hunting trip successful.

The power of a shaman, according to Schmitter, came from his or her ability to dream: "Only the medicine man has access to this dream life, and he alone can transfer animals from real to dream life and vice-versa."[3] Shamans derived their power not only from animals, but also from the sun, the moon, the stars, trees, birds, or even a piece of brush.

Charlie Isaac told Richard Slobodin that one source of power was a certain flower that the shaman might see in the mountains:

Blue flames coming from this flower. You and I couldn't see the blue flames, but he could. He would pick some and keep it, and use it later for power. He could use it to hurt or kill people, too. He would make something from the flower or whatever it was and shoot it, send it, a long distance, and would hit his enemy, say in the chest, and that man would start to get sore there, and then infection, pus, flesh get rotten. Then he would probably die.[4]

Schmitter saw Han fetishes made from a weasel skin, a beaver tooth, and small animal bones with glass beads of various colors sewn around the eyes and mouth. Mary McLeod said that shamans also carry their umbilical cord in their "medicine bundle."[5] Schmitter also learned that shamans dug a certain type of root, which they carried in their pocket and which had the appearance of being alive because it grew larger or smaller.

According to Schmitter's sources in Eagle Village, evil spirits sent by bad shamans caused sickness and epidemics. These spirits entered the body as animals, and by moving around caused illness. To heal a patient the shaman performed a ceremony that included songs learned through dreaming. During the ceremony the shaman extracted the bad spirit by either blowing or sucking it from the patient's body. The shaman then returned the offending spirit to whomever sent it. Schmitter told of a shaman he treated for tuberculosis, bronchitis, and pleurisy. According to this man, his illness was the result of a bad shaman's magic that had caused the quill of a large eagle feather to enter his body. The shaman told Schmitter he had cured himself by removing the quill in the presence of several witnesses.

Disease was not always the result of a bad shaman sending evil spirits but could simply come by itself. In this case the Han used medicinal remedies. Schmitter noted that to cure a cough a person chewed grass roots or spruce bark and in some cases drank a tea made of boiled bark, roots, or brush. A shaman healed wounds by removing the scales from a piece of king salmon skin, then held the skin between his palms and blew it into the wound, where it formed a membrane and stopped the bleeding.

In the 1960s Charlie Isaac told Slobodin that shamans knew about various plant remedies and would do doctoring. A shaman could set a broken leg or arm by wrapping it with fresh birchbark. The bark dried hard and would be stronger than a cast, Charlie said. Shamans used spruce gum as a salve and for chewing, and they made tea from different plants for curing.[6]

125

If a man wanted to become a shaman, he went to sleep in the same blanket with a shaman, and when they were asleep the shaman taught the novice how to become a shaman. Schmitter thought shamans were hesitant to teach others because their power would diminish and make them vulnerable to a more powerful shaman.

The Human-Animal Relationship

In the Athabaskan spiritual tradition animals and humans have a close relationship. This intimacy stems from the belief that at one time animals and humans were the same category of being, able to talk to one another and exchange shape or form. Humans emerged as distinctive beings only through the efforts of the culture hero *Tsà' Wëzhaa* (see Chapter 6) who took away the animals' power of speech and their ability to take on human form, and in the process made animals the legitimate prey of human hunters. Though transformed and separated from humans, animals never lost their ability to know and understand the deepest of human intentions. As a result, animals must be approached with respectful intentions so that they will consciously sacrifice themselves to the hunters. Such a belief is still evident today among some Han people. Joanne Beck of Eagle, for example, stated that the moose killed for her grandmother's funeral potlatch in 1997 stood on the road and waited for the men to load their rifles before walking off the road where they could easily kill and butcher it.

Hunters must not only have respectful intentions toward their prey but also show proper respect toward its remains. If a hunter does not properly dispose of the animal's carcass, the animal's spirit will take offense and make itself unavailable, with dire consequences for the hunter. These rules apply to both game and fish. To please the salmon spirit, the fisherman who catches the first salmon of the season must share the meat with everyone around him.

Walter Benjamin of Eagle Village told Osgood in 1932 that people boiled the first salmon caught each year and shared the broth with everyone in the community, except for females observing menstrual taboos and women with nursing babies. A similar sharing of the first salmon occurred at Moosehide when the first man to catch a fish gave a little piece to everyone.

Chapter Five

Feasts

Dr. Schmitter's description of various ceremonies held at Eagle Village makes it clear that the Han had ceremonies similar to those practiced by Tutchone, Upper Tanana, and Tanacross Athabaskans. According to Schmitter, the Indians of Eagle Village were "quite strong in tradition, and no household event is passed over without ceremonious observances that usually take the form of 'banquets' given by the person immediately interested."[7]

When a child was born, the father gave a feast for the entire village. He also gave a feast after the oldest boy killed his first game, "thereby attaining his majority and proving himself a hunter." Schmitter said that at this time the boy presented a bird to the head man of the community while his father also made a present to the chief "in token of his esteem and pleasure at his son's accomplishment."

People in Eagle Village still hold feasts honoring a boy's first kill. When Joanne Beck's son Jonathan killed his first moose, he gave parts of it to everyone in the village and to some people in Eagle City. His mother also made a feast for him. After the feast, Joanne's son made a short speech and she gave him a new rifle. According to Joanne, it is proper for every young man to share his first kill with everyone in the community because that brings him good luck.

In addition to celebrating the achievements of the son, Schmitter reported that fathers provided a feast to the community when a girl arrived at the age of puberty. In most northern Athabaskan cultures the onset of menstruation signaled to the entire community that a girl would soon be ready for marriage. At the beginning of her first menses she was secluded for up to one year in a special shelter built away from her family. According to Schmitter, the girl was left in the care of a relative of her fiancée. She wore a special hood that covered her face so she could not look directly into a person's eyes and spent her time learning the various duties of a wife, including how to sew.

A number of restrictions were imposed on the girl during seclusion, many of which were connected to the belief that menstrual blood was repugnant to animal spirits and would bring bad luck in hunting. The girl could not eat fresh meat, was required to drink all liquids through a tube, and had to use a special cup and bowl. When away from her shelter, the girl walked with her head down and was not allowed to look at anyone, especially men. She was also restricted from walking on game trails or trails used by hunters because menstrual blood might pollute the trail and offend the animal spirits. Schmitter remarked that in 1906 young women were still isolated, but for only a few months. However, as late as 1960 Slobodin reported that young girls were still isolated in Eagle Village.

As Gordon Marsh observed, "Another type of social ceremony practiced by the Han was the "tobacco party." In the middle of the nineteenth century the Han had to travel all the way to Hudson's Bay Company trading posts on the Mackenzie River to obtain tobacco. After their long trip the people sat and smoked together, passing the pipe around" (Marsh 1956).

Elva Scott, in her book on the history of Eagle City, wrote that during the late 1920s the Han living in Eagle Village held community feasts, which they sometimes referred to as potlatches.[8] Her description sounds similar to the mid-winter festivals held by the Ahtna, Upper Tanana, Tanacross, and Tutchone in which people gathered to tell stories and riddles, exchange gifts, and play a hand game.[9]

At Eagle Village a small group of men went door to door with a blanket. On answering the door, people tossed berries, frozen meat, or cans of fruit into the blanket, and the men took the food to the community hall where they made a stew. Food was served to both men and women. The men ate at one table, the women at another, and after the meal the women took the excess food home. In the evening people had a dance with jigs and reels.

The Potlatch

You see Alaska potlatch, you know holy god.
                                        —*Martha Taylor*

Various occasions in traditional Han culture required the distribution of food. These included the first successful hunt of a young man or the first menses of young girl. Feasts to commemorate these events were usually small affairs involving only members of one community. Other events, such as a death, required elaborate ceremonies that might begin with a small feast and dance immediately following the funeral and culminate, a year or so later, in a larger memorial ceremony that included days, if not weeks, of lavish feasting, singing, dancing, oratory, and a distribution of gifts. These larger ceremonies were major social and religious events attended by people from a number of bands.

In the early literature these death-related rituals were called "feasts for dead." Anglican missionary Vincent Sim reported one such event held in 1883 at Nuklako across the river from Fort Reliance, but he provided no details.[10] In the late-nineteenth century these events became known as potlatches, a word derived from Chinook trade jargon used up and down the Pacific coast and brought north by prospectors. Today people have given the word a much wider connotation, so that it often refers to community feasts associated with holidays.

Among the Han, death bought not only sorrow, but also fear that the ghost of the deceased would try to take a another person, such as a close relative or favorite friend, before departing for the spirit world. To limit this possibility, the corpse was cleaned and dressed by people who were not relatives of the deceased, usually members of the opposite moiety (see Chapter 4). Because of a fear that handling the corpse would contaminate the living, it was considered an act of respect when people prepared the body. Once the body was disposed of, either through cremation or interment, the deceased's relatives held a ceremony in which they distributed food and a few gifts to those people who had taken an active part in the disposal of the corpse.

Charlie Stevens said that in the past, when someone died, the deceased's relatives "hired" two men to cremate the body. These two men had to be "outside relatives" and they got "paid" for their service.[11] Charlie Isaac told Slobodin that "of course the tribe [moiety] of the dead man was supposed to give the presents, not get them—except for the grub at the feasts."[12] In effect, because of the potlatch system, "people were publicly reminded throughout their lives of who they were and how they should behave to one another."[13]

Martha Taylor of Dawson City said that when a person died, his or her body was wrapped and placed in a tree, and people held a "little lunch." When people came together for a funeral during the winter, they turned their toboggans over and laid them side by side in the snow to make a floor. The feast may have been a way of compensating members of the opposite moiety who helped prepare the corpse and grave.

> They don't dance [like] white man. Just Indian way they dance. Just sorrow dance they do, you know. Oh toboggan, the toboggan dance. And after a while the big people finish, they put all the young teenager there, we have to dance too. We have to dance and after we finish they start to eat something.[14]

After a person died the deceased's relatives worked and saved to hold a memorial potlatch (Figure 33). Simon McLeod of Dawson told Richard Slobodin that people held potlatches for various occasions, but the most important were memorial potlatches. According to McLeod, when a person died his or her relatives and family would save up "grub and goods." If an important man or woman died, the potlatch would be very large.[15]

Schmitter witnessed a memorial potlatch held for the chief of Eagle Village. However, instead of the relatives working and collecting the gifts, the chief himself had accumulated the goods. Schmitter wrote that before his death the chief had

> hoarded up much wealth of skins, blankets, traps, rifles, and other property, and, since it is not customary among the Eagle Indians for relatives to inherit the property of the deceased, his kin folk received nothing of his belongings. By common consent Old Peter took charge of the effects.
>
> It was then announced that there would be a "potlatch" in the spring, when the goods of the deceased man would be given away. Invitations were sent east to the Moosehide Indians up the river, west to the Charlie Creek Indians down the river, and south over the hills to the Ketchumstuk [sic] Indians. The Porcupine Indians to the north were not invited because they were not related to the tribe.[16]

Chief Isaac of Moosehide presided over several days of feasting and dancing. At the dinners, Schmitter wrote: "the men first gorged themselves, allowing the women to come in after they had finished and take what was left. Between the ceremonies they assembled in groups about the village and gossiped or sung to tunes resembling those of Japanese operas."[17]

For the final ceremony the potlatch hosts built an enclosure measuring thirty by sixty feet and surrounded by a fence seven feet high. People sat around the edge of the enclosure facing the gifts gathered at one end while Chief Isaac positioned himself next to the pile of gifts and presided over their distribution. Before he distributed the gifts, Isaac and other men gave speeches. Schmitter said that some of the speakers became highly "wrought up," which may refer to the stylized form of speech-making known as "chief's talk." Once the speakers had finished, Chief Isaac handed out the gifts, but only to the visitors; the Eagle Village people themselves received nothing.[18]

Figure 33. Potlatch at Eagle, Alaska, spring 1907. Yukon Archives, Whitehorse. Front kneeling: Edward Wood; Front left to right: Paul Chancy, Henry Harper, Charley Steve, Billy Silas, Ben Harper, David Taylor, David C. Roberts, Peter Thompson; Back row: Kenneth, Chief Alex, Joseph, Jonathon Johnson, Canadian Joe, Esau Harper, Andrew Silas, and Chief Isaac. Identified by Martha Kates. Note the raised ganhook with attached flags. This last great potlatch may have been held in memory of Chief Charley, who died in 1907.

Figure 34. Moose kill, potlatch at Moosehide, 1907.

Potlatch gifts mentioned by Simon and Mary McLeod included Hudson's Bay blankets, fur pelts, Stetson hats (which, Mary said, "costs lots"), shirts, "hankies," scarves, and other clothing. Women might receive the Stetson hats because they liked to wear them in the gold rush days. There was a dance where the women danced wearing Stetsons with a feather stuck in them. Mary McLeod went on to say that there was no dancing at the memorial potlatch. Instead the women put on a march in honor of the deceased.[19]

A brief description of a potlatch held at Fortymile appeared in the April 18, 1903, edition of the *Yukon Sun* newspaper. This report described the occasion for the ceremony as the "succession" of Peter to the position of chief inherited from his father, Old David, who had just recently died. While succession potlatches were not the norm in other Athabaskan groups, Osgood reported "that a chief was appointed at the time of the potlatch given following the death of a chief." [20]

The guests at the 1903 potlatch included people from Peel River, Tanana River, Mackenzie River, Han from downriver, and the Moosehide people led by "subchief" Silas and Chief Isaac. The report said that the potlatch continued for several days and nights and that welcoming dances were done as each contingent of guests arrived by toboggan. Feasts of moose meat, supplied from the forty moose reportedly killed by the Charley River people, also marked the occasion.

Osgood collected some additional information about the Han potlatch from Walter Benjamin in the 1930s. Benjamin said the potlatch hosts made some of their guests drink grease so they could vomit into the fire, but they only did this if the deceased person being honored was particularly well loved.[21]

The *Tr'ondëk Hwëch'in*, or Klondike band of Han, came under intense pressure to change during the Klondike gold rush. One change desired by the Canadian government was abolition of the potlatch. In 1884, the government amended the Indian Act, making participation in the potlatch a misdemeanor. Although created to eradicate the potlatch along the Northwest Coast, the law also took effect in the Yukon Territory. The government, as Catharine McClellan wrote, "thought it unchristian and they feared that a potlatch host would lose everything and become a public charge."[22]

Responding to this prohibition, Chief Isaac of Moosehide "took" many of the Han songs and dances associated with the potlatch and left them with the descendants of relatives and friends who now live in the villages of Northway, Tetlin, Tanacross, and Dot Lake. According to stories told by residents of Tanacross, Dot Lake, Tetlin, and Dawson, Chief Isaac gave the songs, dances, and a dance stick called a "ganhook" or "ganho" to the people of the upper Tanana region. These songs have been retained in people's memories until today, and some of them are still actively performed.

According to Benjamin McCloud of Dawson, who learned the story from Titus David of Tetlin, Chief Isaac attended a memorial potlatch for Chief David of Tetlin about 1917. At that potlatch Chief Isaac taught the Tetlin people Han songs and gave them drums and a ganhook. The "ganhook" or "ganho" (see Figure 33) is a dance stick used by the lead dancer to direct the movement of the other dancers. Ganhooks today are made from flat boards about six or seven feet long and five or six inches wide that have a handle at one end and hole in the board for the thumb. They are painted various colors and decorated with ribbons, yarn, and beads.

Tanacross elders say that the Han from Dawson were noted dancers who taught their dances to relatives from Mansfield Village. Tanacross tradition also says that in 1912 Chief Isaac of Dawson left the ganhook at the old village of Lake Mansfield. Gaither Paul of Tanacross described this event in some detail:

I heard Mansfield had a big potlatch, I guess it was over Chief Isaac [of Mansfield/Kechumstuk]. And people from Dawson is invited and they came all the way from Dawson. And there too my grandmother told me story about it.

They bunch up across the lake, and they start shooting across the lake, and they knew they were coming, and dog team after dog team just line up across the lake. They stop at the edge of the lake someplace and tie up their dogs and there too they had a fire going but nobody went over to the lake to greet them. Man come from Dawson, but nobody greet them!

They dress and they came into Mansfield like, like what I said Copper River [people] did. And this one I heard, you know that Charlie's house over that trail? They comin' up there, and when they comin' over that hill I remember people say they come over just like spruce hen. You know they dance like that, they comin' over just like that, just like spruce hen comin' over. Their leader is the only one standing up and behind him is just like a bunch of spruce hen. That was part of the dance. They used to dance that way. They don't dance like that any more, like spruce hen.

That is probably 1912, they said. That is the year that ganho come to Mansfield. That Moosehide chief brought it up and he left it, he brought it up, and he come ahead with it. Ganho come from Dawson people, started that.

I don't know the meaning, too. I hear speech that Moosehide chief left that at Mansfield as a gift when he came. And he left it there without it, to be used in dance. That is the start of ganho in dance. Moosehide chief brought it in.

I don't know the original one, what happened to it, but I saw it. It was painted really beautiful, beads or yarn hanging down and when you shake it, it kind of rattle, that is what he carried ahead. He left that with Mansfield people. That is the start of use of ganho in Tanacross area. That is what I heard, my father told me this. Just like the chief at Dawson left that as a gift at Mansfield when he came that year. From there they copy it and always use it in dance.[23]

Government restrictions on the potlatch created a difficult situation for the *Tr'ondëk Hwëch'in*. Martha Taylor remembers the police stopped them from making potlatches, but, she said, "when our parents gone [died] we make lots of supper and sometime we get [give] money who they pack coffin around. That's all we do, but we can't do nothing no more."[24] As

Figure 35. Indians at Dawson. Ceremonial potlatch dance in the A.C. Company yard off Front Street, Victoria Day, May 24, 1901. The washtub drummer at left strongly resembles Chief Isaac.

Figure 36. Tim Malcolm with fiddle, July 12, 1997.

Martha indicates, people abbreviated the ceremony, holding feasts and giving money to the people responsible for handling the corpse, but doing nothing more.

In this repressive atmosphere the word "potlatch" came to connote any kind of celebration or community get-together, such as a Christmas party. Various Dawson newspaper articles described "potlatches" as they occurred at Moosehide. For example, the December 26, 1902, edition of the *Dawson Daily News*, reported one that involved a distribution of clothes donated to the village by a Major Wood. Similarly, in January 1924, the Dawson paper wrote about two "potlatches."[25] One of these was a Christmas party replete with Santa Claus, followed by jigging and square dancing in Jonathon Wood's cabin; the other was billed as "the last dance of the season" where, among other things, the "great war dances of the tribe also will be put on." The reporter went on to say that "many whites in this district who have not seen these historical tribal dances, which are fast becoming a vanishing feature of Indian life, will have the opportunity tonight."

Contemporary Feasts

People hold similar feasts in Eagle Village today, which they also call potlatches. Angela Harper, following the tradition of her mother Sarah Malcolm, gave a "farewell potlatch" in 1997 before she left Eagle to return to Fairbanks for the winter. This outdoor feast included barbecued short ribs and chicken, fried king salmon, salads, moose head soup, beans, and desserts. It was followed by Tim Malcolm playing his fiddle (Figure 36), accompanied by Edward David on guitar. In contrast to older memorial potlatches, however, there was no distribution of gifts or other ritualized activity.

Today Han people continue to hold potlatches when someone dies, although in somewhat abbreviated form. Bertha Ulvi described it as follows:

> Everybody help us at grave. Then while they're digging the grave, all the ladies cook, and when they come back they eat. We have food on the stove all of the time. Then after they bury the body, and then we all go to the community hall, and we have big potlatch. We don't have no dance or anything though. Just big potlatch, and people just sit around.[26]

She added that "if it's one of our family, we give blankets" as gifts. But when asked if the people give memorial potlatches, such as those put on by the Tanacross people, Bertha said no.

In his monograph on the Han, Osgood wrote of the disappearance of the old form of the potlatch, which "disintegrated in the first half of the nineteenth century as a result of various pressures and the general dissolution of the Han social organization. The Indians could no longer afford to amass great quantities of gifts, and about the end of the nineteenth century the Canadian government seems to have forbidden potlatching."[27]

Osgood is correct that the potlatch changed; however, the information presented above describes a mortuary ritual with feasting, singing, dancing, oratory, and a distribution of gifts that survived into the early twentieth century. It is also clear that when Schmitter was in Eagle the Han had no trouble gathering the necessary amount of goods to hold a potlatch. Sometime later, a Peel River Gwich'in told Slobodin that

> One time at Eagle I see $15,000 stuff given away. I was standing in the back of the crowd; just a poor boy. The chief—the talker—he calls me up to the front. I feel shy, don't want to go. Then he says I'm good boy and gives me a new shotgun, a .410 [gauge]. They feast for about a week. All the tribes was there.[28]

Today the elaborate memorial potlatches are gone, but the impulse to give remains.[29] Community dinners and funeral potlatches remain important events in Eagle Village. The *Tr'ondëk Hwëch'in* in Dawson are relearning some of the songs and dances Chief Isaac left with people in the villages along the upper Tanana River. For the last several years young people from Dawson have gone to Tetlin and Tanacross to record the songs, and people from those villages have gone to Dawson to teach.

Notes

1. Ferdinand Schmitter, *Upper Yukon Native Customs and Folk-Lore* (Washington, D.C.: The Smithsonian Institution, 1910). Reprinted by the Eagle Historical Society, Eagle, Alaska.

2. Ibid.

3. Ibid.

4. Richard Slobodin, "Notes on the Han." Appendix II to Preliminary Report on Ethnographic Work, 1962. Unpublished Manuscript (Ottawa: National Museum of Man, Ethnology Division, 1963), 19–20.

5. Ibid.

6. Ibid., 19.

7. Schmitter, *Upper Yukon Native Customs and Folk-Lore*, 14.

8. Elva Scott, *Jewel on the Yukon: Eagle City* (Eagle City: Eagle Historical Society and Museums, 1997), 81.

9. A fairly detailed description of the Upper Tanana winter festival and potlatch tradition may be found in Marie-Françoise Guédon's *People of Tetlin, Why Are You Singing?* Mercury Series, Ethnology Division Paper No. 9 (Ottawa: National Museum of Canada, 1974), 200–232.

10. See Mary E. Wesbrook, "A Venture into Ethnohistory: The Journals of Rev. V. C. Sim, Pioneer Missionary on the Yukon." *Polar Notes*, No. 9 (1969), 42.

11. Charlie Stevens interviewed by Mertie Baggen. Mertie Baggen papers 1964–67 field notes, Box 1, Rasmuson Library, Alaska and Polar Regions, Fairbanks, Alaska.

12. Slobodin, "Notes on the Han," 17.

13. Catharine McClellan, *Part of the Land, Part of the Water: A History of the Yukon Indians* (Vancouver & Toronto: Douglas and McIntyre, 1987), 222.

14. Martha Taylor, in Notes from Han First Nations Land Claim Office, Dawson City.

15. Slobodin, "Notes on the Han," 17.

16. Schmitter, *Upper Yukon Native Customs and Folk-Lore*, 15.

17. Ibid., 16.

18. Ibid.

19. Slobodin,"Notes on the Han," 17.

20. Cornelius Osgood, *The Han Indians: A Compilation of Ethnographic and Historical Data on the Alaska-Yukon Boundary Area* (New Haven: Yale University Publications in Anthropology No. 74, 1971), 42.

21. Ibid., 55.

22. McClellan, *Part of the Land, Part of the Water*, 222.

23. Gaither Paul interviewed by William E. Simeone, October 1986. Private collection.

24. Taylor, Notes.

25. See *Dawson Daily News*, 5 January 1924, 2–4, and 7 January 1924, 2. Microfilm copy at the Dawson City Museum.

26. Louise Paul and Bertha Ulvi interviewed by Craig Mishler, 20–21 April 1997. Alaska Department of Fish and Game Collection, Anchorage, Alaska.

27. Osgood, *The Han Indians*, 144.

28. Richard Slobodin, "The Dawson Boys: Peel River Indians and the Klondike Gold Rush." *Polar Notes*, No. 5 (1963), 33.

29. In an effort to revive the tradition, Isaac Juneby and his wife Sandy organized a small honorary potlatch for Han elder Louise Paul in June 1993, while Louise was still living. However, Laura Sanford of Tok was brought in as a singer and consultant because no one in Eagle Village knew exactly what to do. See Mike Pitka, "First potlatch in over 85 years held by Eagle Village," *The Council* 18, No. 6 (July/August 1993), 3.

Chapter Six

Han Expressive Culture: Part One

In Eagle Village, life continues, but the traditions can stay, if we listen and learn.
  —*William Silas,* The Northland News, *May 1988*

E XPRESSIVE CULTURE or folklore is that aspect of life which is largely devoted to play and beauty. It includes stories, songs, instrumental music, dances, games, traditional dress, and folk art. Expressive culture is simultaneously an outpouring of creativity and traditionality, and it is used by a people to announce who they are, what they value, and how they have fun. Some expressive culture is highly verbal (narrative and song), some is rooted in gesture (dancing and games), and some is manifested in material culture (basketry, beadwork, wood carving, jewelry, and dress).

For the Han, all of these forms contribute significantly to their spiritual and artistic identity, and today a revival is underway to document and bring back these traditional arts. A revival is necessary because many of these art forms were discontinued altogether following the gold rush, or survived only through a few individuals. Accordingly, this chapter and the next are devoted to an appreciation of Han artistic expression.

Hän Hòdök / Han Stories

Storytelling is an ancient Han art form, passed down for many generations and is very much alive today. Elder Percy Henry learned stories when he was a little boy: He learned the right to listen by doing chores for the elders. "I used to work like slave to get story," he said. "Pack water or cut wood or empty slop buckets. That's the way I trade the story."[1]

The first Han stories to be recorded are in Dr. Ferdinand Schmitter's collection, a small but impressive volume originally published by the Smithsonian Institution in 1910 and reprinted by the Eagle Historical Society.[2] Schmitter took a strong interest in Han oral traditions and fortunately had the services of a good interpreter named Arthur. Unfortunately, the stories in the Schmitter collection are not attributed to the individuals who told them, and we must come to know the stories without knowing the storytellers. This loss of context greatly limits our understanding and appreciation of the texts.

The folktales collected by Schmitter at Eagle Village are titled "Creation of the World," "The Origin of the Wind," "The Miraculous Little Man," "The Boy in the Moon," "The Camp Robber," "The Raven Restores the Sun to the Sky" (a variant of Raven Steals the Sun), "The Raven and the Coot," "The Woodpecker," "The Robin," "The Wolverine and the Traveler," "The Wolverine and the Hunter," "The Adventures of the Old Man," and "The Old Man and the Old Woman."

Schmitter noted that "The Old Man" and "The Old Woman" are the names of two rocky outcroppings facing one another in the upper Yukon River on the Canadian side of the border between Eagle and Fortymile. As geologic formations, they were observed and drawn by Frederick Schwatka when he first floated down the river in 1883.[3] Schmitter identified the rock on the north side of the river as the Old Man and the one on the south side is the Old Woman, who was supposed to be the Old Man's wife.[4] For some reason there are many stories about the Old Man but only one or two about the Old Woman. But, as we shall see, different storytellers have different repertoires.

William Haskell, for example, relates a legend that he learned from local traders.[5] A poor old man who is tired of being scolded by his wife kicks her across the river, whereupon she turns to stone and becomes Old Woman Rock. This action is made possible by the assistance of a shaman.

Another version of the story appears on the web page of the *Trondëk Hwëch'in* at trondek.com but without any attribution to the storyteller. This electronically published version of Old Woman Rock corresponds loosely to Sarah Malcolm's version, in which a young Han girl stretches out her legs and changes the landscape and the course of the Yukon River. In the online version, the powerful young Indian girl very surprisingly becomes Queen Victoria.

In Han oral tradition, as represented below through Mishler's field recordings in the early 1970s and in 1997, Louise Paul tells only about *Tsà' Wëzhaa*, the Old Man, while Sarah Malcolm tells only about *Ts'àchin*, the Old Woman.[6]

The importance of the Old Man or *Tsà' Wëzhaa* story is that it is multi-episodic and tells about a time when the world was quite different from what it is today. *Tsà' Wëzhaa* lived at a time when all of the animals could talk like people and many species were very hostile to humans and preyed upon them. *Tsà' Wëzhaa* is heroic because as he goes downriver he kills off all of the hostile animals except bear and saves at least one of each kind to perpetuate the species. He makes the world safe for human beings. *Ts'àchin*, the Old Woman, on the other hand, is remembered for removing the rapids from the Yukon River and making it safe for people to travel upriver. *Ts'àchin Ts'ee* (Old Woman Rock) is thus an important place name in the very heart of the Han homeland.

A second collection of Han stories from Eagle was collected by Swedish folklorist Anna Birgitta Rooth in 1966 and published under the title *The Alaska Expedition 1966*.[7] Rooth traveled throughout interior Alaska that year and recorded a large body of tales, all in English. In Eagle she recorded traditional narratives by Bella Biederman, Elisha Lyman, and Charlie Stevens. Biederman, however, was not Han but a Gwich'in woman from downriver near Circle who married a local white man.

The Rooth collection was published without titles. However, it is fair to say that Charlie Stevens told the tales we know today as the *Tsà' Wëzhaa* cycle (related to the adventures of a man called Beaver), as well as variants of "The Boy in the Moon," "Raven and the Geese," "The Wolverine's Trap," "Crow Steals the Sun," and "Crow Loses His Beak." Elisha Lyman told the story of "Crow Spoils the Girl," "The Boy in the Moon," and "The Wolverine's Trap."

Roth discussed motifs and geographic distribution of "The Wolverine's Trap" in another book, *The Alaska Seminar*, published in 1980. She viewed this sometimes-independently told tale as part of the longer cycle about the adventures of "Beaver/Noah/Kayakman" also known as "The Man Traveling About the World," or simply "The Traveler."[8] In Hän this is the *Tsà' Wëzhaa* or Old Man cycle. "The Wolverine's Trap" does not appear in Schmitter but does indeed make up the final episode of Louise Paul's telling of *Tsà' Wëzhaa*.

One isolated but important Traveler text, told in English by Mrs. Taylor of Dawson (presumably the late Martha Taylor), appears in Richard Matthews' book *The Yukon*. Taylor told how Beaver Man (*Tsà' Wëzhaa*), almost like a water witch, went around thrusting his willow stick into the ground to create fresh water streams. All of these springs then came together to form the Yukon River.[9]

A third corpus of oral narratives, collected from Louise Paul and Eliza Malcolm by Diana Greene, is called *Raven Tales and Medicine Men Folktales from Eagle Village*, a small photocopied booklet with very limited distribution.[10] Because Eliza Malcolm did not speak more than a few words of English and was principally a speaker of the now-extinct Takudh language, her stories must have been translated by her daughter Louise Paul. The stories in this collection, which have been "retold" in standard English, include "Raven and the Goose," "How Raven Got His Beak Back," "Raven's Wife," "Raven and the Whale," "The Medicine Man" (parts 1 and 2), and "The Medicine Man and the Caribou."

A fourth collection of Han stories, told in the Hän language, was recorded on reel-to-reel tape from Louise Paul and Willie Juneby during the late 1970s.[11] These tapes are housed in the Alaska Native Language Center at the University of Alaska Fairbanks. Louise Paul's stories, partly transcribed and translated by Louise's daughter Ruth Ridley, remain in unfinished manuscript form. These tapes and transcripts include two autobiographical stories, "The 1939 Trip to Gwazhal Mountain" and "Living at Woodchopper Creek." The tapes also contain a number of Louise's traditional stories: "Raven Spoils Girl," "Raven, Merganser, and Arctic Red River," "Old Woman Murders Daughter," "The Story of Two Brothers" (parts 1 and 2), "Man Marries Bear," and the ever-venerable *Tsà' Wëzhaa*. The Willie Juneby tapes contain a personal memoir called "Potlatch at Kechumstuk (circa 1920)," the *Tsà' Wëzhaa* cycle, and one called "Indian Wars." To date, the Juneby tapes have not been transcribed or translated.

Louise Paul

Louise (Plate 9) told the long story of *Tsà' Wëzhaa* to Craig Mishler on December 27, 1973, while she was peeling turnips and carrots for supper in her old house in Eagle Village, a building that formerly served as the village schoolhouse. The tea kettle was percolating as she talked, and the house was lit with propane gas lamps. On that afternoon she was wearing a green and white checkered cotton dress with short sleeves, had a pink cotton band in her hair, black socks over nylons, and black rubber boots. She told the entire story in English and then upon request repeated it in Hän. Regrettably, the Hän version has not been transcribed.

The Han story cycle of *Tsà' Wëzhaa* is a close correlate of the Upper Tanana cycle of *Tsa-O-Sha* ("Smart Beaver") collected by Robert McKennan during the winter of 1929–1930.[12] In published form, the Upper Tanana cycle appears much more elaborate than the Han cycle recorded by Schmitter, but this probably had more to do with the story-tellers and with the collectors than with what was actually circulating in oral tradition. The version told by Louise Paul to Craig Mishler in both Hän and English, for example, is much fuller and longer than the earlier one recorded by Schmitter.

Tsà' Wëzhaa / The Old Man Story

Louise Paul, December 27, 1973

1. *TSÀ' WËZHAA* AND OTTER WOMAN
   Well, he started down the river,
   And up here, about half way up,
   Up here where they call Cliff Creek, I guess.
   That's where Otter and Mouse were living there.

   Well, like I told you,
   This Otter got a line across the river.
   Anybody pass that,
   [S]he got some kind of bones hanging this end where she live,
   So she could tell somebody pass by there.
   She go out there.
   She see a man.
   She bring them in, bring their canoe up,
   And she try to make them stay.
   That's how she get hold of them.
   She make them stay with her.
   Pretty soon she just kill them and eat them up.

So this man [*Tsà' Wëzhaa*] was coming down,
And he stopped there.
Well, first thing she did, she brought the canoe up,
And that Mouse is up across from her.
You know, they live together, you know, in a wigwam,
Like in the old days, I suppose.
Then she got this hash.
In the old days they make some kind of meat.
They pound it up and they call it hash.
In Indian they call it *jatson*.
So she give this man some,
And then she went down the river,
Get him some drinking water.
And this man said, "I don't drink no river water!
I drink only creek water!"
—Just so she go someplace.

And while she went up little ways,
Every little place she stop,
"Is it here that there's a creek?"
Chaalaa? Chaalaa?
That means, "Is it here? Is it here?"

And he just said, "No!
It's quite a ways up where I passed a creek,"
he told her.

So she went up around the bend.
Then he got his canoe out.
She tie it up real good too.
That's so he won't get away, that canoe?
And here he see that she cut it up with a knife, too!
And that Mouse said, "All that hash she gave you,
That's made out of human flesh."
Meat, you know?
So she gave him something good to eat,
That little Mouse.

So while she's gone this Mouse got her deal out—
You know, them days they called awl,

146

That's the only thing they sew with.
She sew his canoe up quick-like for him,
And he took off.

When she [Otter] come back this man was gone,
So she just took [off] after that man.
And right up here, "Half-Way"[13] they call it, I guess.
And there's twenty-one islands up here.
That's where he just went all around that island,
And he got one beaver while he was doing that.
So he went to sleep, and she found him.
She found him sleeping there.
So while he was sleeping she tanned that beaver skin that night,
they said.
She's real active in work too.
And when he woke up she was sleeping.
So he killed her.
He killed her right there.
He got rid of that one.
He got rid of that one.

CM: Who did he kill?

LP: That Otter.
He killed that Otter that night.
Now he got rid of one that eat human being,
One animal that eat human being.
So he got rid of that one.

2. *TSÀ' WËZHAA* MEETS BEAR, EAGLE, MOOSE, AND MOUSE
And then he start from there down this way.
That's when he got to Ford Lake.
And then he went downriver and stopped at Ford Lake.
That's where Bear is living.
That's down here below Eagle.
And that Bear he kills men too.
He kill human being and eat them.

So he [*Tsà' Wëzhaa*] got there,
And this Bear said—

He got a daughter that he want some good man
to marry—
So he said, "You gonna be my son-in-law!"
So he told that man to stay there,
And first thing he said—
He want to make himself bow and arrow, that man.
So he [Bear] told him [*Tsà' Wëzhaa*] to go out and go up.
"Go out and get something to make bow and arrow with."
So he went out to get that feather, you know,
For bow, for arrow?

That's what I told you about yesterday when he killed them
Eagle[s] too,
And he let one little Eagle female,
That little girl there,
And he give her good meat after he kill the mother
and the father Eagle,
And that little boy Eagle.
And then he give some good meat to that little Eagle,
That little girl Eagle?
He said, "From now on you live on just this kind of meat.
Don't eat human being again!" he told her.
And she said, she will.

So he left that, and then he came back with this feather,
And that Bear said, "Gee, how can you get those feather
and things like that?"
Them animal[s] are bad animal[s].
He [Bear] think he gonna get rid of that man some way,
Through these other bad animal[s]?

And then next he [Bear] said,
"There's a moose out in the lake.
There's a moose out in the lake,
And you could get your sinew from there."
For that string on the bow?
So he [*Tsà' Wëzhaa*] went out there too,
And this moose is just skinny and scrawny-looking moose,
And he kills people too, I think.
So he [*Tsà' Wëzhaa*] just don't know how to get to that moose.

So there's a little Mouse around there.
So he told this Mouse.
He said, "Can you kill that moose for me?"

And that Mouse said, "How can I do it?" (laughs)
So this Mouse said, "If you tell me how to do it, I'll do it."
So the Mouse went up there,
And he went in his, from behind, you know?
[through his anus]
The moose is laying down or something like that, I guess.
And he got inside of him [and killed him].
That's where you could see where the heart that big artery is.
In the moose there's little print-like.
They say that's a Mouse track! (laughs)

And he [*Tsà' Wëzhaa*] got that one too,
And he got his sinew right there.
And then finally he got that one too,
So he got his bow and arrow made.

3. *TSÀ' WËZHAA* AND SNIPE[14]
    That's two deal now he got—a feather and a sinew.
    Then he got to get pitch, you know.
    I don't know what for,
    But he got to get pitch, to pitch something together.
    [Probably to help attach the feather to the arrow.]
    So he went out to get pitch, spruce pitch.
    And when he went out there all the pitch just go
    like this on the tree,
    You know? (gesturing).
    Just something fierce, I guess.
    He got kind of scared, but he got hold [of] a stick,
    And he just knocked them down all over, you know.
    And he stopped that [pitch] from doing that too.
    And he brought some of that back,
    And that Bear said, *"Di do'iy!"*
    That means, "How does he get by with those things?" you know.
    "How do he get them things?" you know.
    He don't expect this man to get them things.

He [Bear] thought sure he [*Tsà' Wëzhaa*] might get killed by one of those deal[s].

And then finally, he [*Tsà' Wëzhaa*] got that [pitch] too,
So he got his bow and arrow made.
And then he said, "O.K. now."
He [Bear] told that man, he said . . .
He's going out with that man, you know,
To where his daughter stayed.
He pretend that, I guess.
He said his daughter is staying someplace,
So they went up together.
So, that's one little place [in the story] I don't understand it too well.
So he went out with him.

And this other Bear tried to get after him,
But he killed that other Bear that he pretend was
his daughter?
He killed that one too.
That's his daughter.
She pretend [to be] this other Bear.
But he killed that,
And then he got mad, this old Bear,
So he got after him,
And then this *Tsà' Wëzhaa* he got real scared,
So he just start running from him, you know?
So he got down there [to] Ford Lake.[15]
He got in that lake.
And then that Bear he told the Frog,
"Drink all that water for me."
So that Frog start drinking that Ford Lake.
That's a big lake!
Pretty soon that Frog keep drinking water,
drinking water.
Pretty soon that lake is going dry,
So he got scared, this man.
And then he [Bear] told a Snipe that went by.
He told that Snipe, he said,
"If you can do it,
Would you hit that Frog in the belly for me?"

150

And he said he'll try, so he went around the Frog,
And Frog look at that Snipe.
He said, "Did somebody tell you something to do to me?"

And that Snipe said, "What you talking about?
I'm looking for something to eat for my little ones.
I'm not trying to cause trouble!"

So, while he [Snipe] got chance he just hit that Frog right in the
belly.
All that water came out.
During that time while that Frog drinking that water, you know?
He [Bear] just tear up all that moss around Ford Lake.
If you go down there [to the lake] you could see it's just
torn up like,
Just like the stories go!
How things goes like that?
I wonder who's the smart guy to tell such a story like that?

And then he don't know what to do,
So he just went, and then that Frog, you know,
That Snipe hit that Frog in the belly,
So all the water splash out again.
So best he can do he went to the outlet [of the lake],
You know, tried to get out to the river.
And then he [Bear] was down there already too,
With his, what they call net.
You know, what they call gill net.[16]
He got that down there already.
So he [*Tsà' Wëzhaa*] put something in his coat,
And throw that in there [in the net], you know.
While he [Bear] dig that out,
He [*Tsà' Wëzhaa*] just went by that net.
That's how he got past that Bear.

But he got the worst Bear that killed people too—
That other one, that other Bear, you know,
That he claimed was his daughter?
That's the one he got rid of.
There he fixed two animals now.

4. *TSÀ' WËZHAA* AND **RABBIT**
   "Fixed Eagle, Moose, even Rabbit in the old days.
   We hear the story of them.
   They kill human being.
   He fixed them too.
   He fixed them too.
   You know them days Rabbit got long tail, they said.

   There's a trail going by,
   And there's two Rabbit sit like this with their tail into the road.
   When a man go by they hit both end on each side and kill him.
   They eat him there.
   So he [*Tsà' Wëzhaa*] put two heavy, two hard [pieces of birchbark
   on his side[s] and pass there.
   When he pass there they tried to kill him,
   But they broke their own tail.
   He fixed, he fixed those Rabbit too (laughs).

   That's as far as I know where he went, down here [to] Ford Lake,
   And from there we don't know where he went,
   But he fixed the Wolverine and the Raven.

5. *TSÀ' WËZHAA* AND **RAVEN**
   "They were stopping someplace on the river overnight,
   And they sleep on the little bluff.
   Well, he [*Tsà' Wëzhaa*] was going along the river with this Raven,
   And this Raven said,
   "Whatever you do to me, don't ever try to do anything to me.
   If you ever try to kill me or do anything to me,
   You won't see no more human being[s]," he said.
   "You won't see no more people."
   So one night he [*Tsà' Wëzhaa*] just try him
   [Raven] out.
   He pretend he was sleeping,
   And they sleep on the bluff on the hillside like this, you know?
   (gesturing)
   He pretend he's stretched out like this,
   And he kick that Raven,
   And he roll over the hill, you know,
   And he just splash all over.

So he start off.
Next he hear sound like a big village, you know.
He hear lot of people.
When he stop there he don't see nobody.
He could see people live there,
But he don't see nobody.
But he could see some fish laying on the beach,
you know?
Some fish laying on the beach.

Next, he'd start up again.
Next he'd hear lot of people again.
When he come to that town, same thing.
He don't see no people,
But he see lot of them fish laying on the beach.
So he went back up.
He went back up to where he killed that Raven.
And he start picking [up] that little piece
[piece by piece].
He put it in.
He got his canoe on the beach,
So he put one little piece [in the canoe],
And pretty soon he's [Raven is] coming back to life.
He say, "How do you feel?"

He [Raven] keep telling him, "Not yet.
You still got to find some more pieces of me!" (laughs)
So he do that and pretty soon he got almost all the pieces back,
And he say he feel better now.
So he put Raven in the canoe,
And they went back down,
And he asked him.
He [Raven] said,

"Like I told you, you won't see no more people,
human being[s].
What did you see every time you come to the village?"

"Oh, all I see is fish laying, lot of fish laying on the beach."

So he start up with him.
"I'll start up with you," he said.
"I'll start up with you."

And he start up with him.
When they come to the village, it's same thing.
So quiet, and here them fish [are] laying.
He said, "Jump out of your canoe and jump on the first fish that's
laying there."
He jump on there.
He keep jumping on there.
Out of them big fish come the people, you know?
They jump out of it?

That's what Raven done for [him] trying to be mean to Raven,
But I don't know if Raven killed people them days.
Raven, they're bad animal in the old days, you know.
They do a lot of things,
And that's all I know about that story.

6. *TSÀ' WËZHAA* AND WOLVERINE
He was coming along this road.
Everybody is out hunting,
So he's out hunting too.
But he knows something [is] ahead of him,
So I don't know.
He's a very smart man, they said.
This *Tsà' Wëzhaa*, he's a smart man.

So it's kind of warm,
So he got his gloves in the road,
And he's kicking his gloves along.
Pretty soon they went over the glacier.
So he looked down.
He could see where that glacier is just deep, like this,
And there's three prongs like it's thick enough.
That Wolverine trap, you know,
Where they kill the human being?
If they don't know, they fall down there.
They get killed.

So this *Tsà' Wëzhaa* he walk down there,
And he make his nose bleed, you know?
He got that all over that,
And he put that prong up inside his skin, his parka?
And he just lay there, pretend he's dead.
Pretty soon this Wolverine come along.
And this Wolverine he's got a lot of little ones too.
And he was coming along, so he said—
He was just happy he got this man, you know?
So he put that man on [his back].
He start packing that man home.
Well, that man is kind of heavy for him too,
And every time he jumped why he grunt-like, you know,
And that man can't help laughing.

So he throw that man down.
He said, "Seems like you're living."
Seems like he's living, he thought to himself.
So he tried to hit that man, but he don't hit that man.
He say, "If I hit him, he gonna be all bloody,
And I don't want to do that."
So he got him home finally, and them little [Wolverine] kids,
When they see their Dad bringing that man,
Packing that man home,
They start bringing in wood, you know?
And then he ask his wife, "Where is my knife?"

Well, this man [*Tsà' Wëzhaa*], in them days they're
medicine people, medicine man.
Some way he [Wolverine] can't find his knife to cut the man up with.
And then he start get mad with his wife because he can't find his knife.
And then them little kids they were out on the tree.
They could climb trees,
And this one little girl Wolverine, the smart one,
She called her Dad.
She said, "That man is looking at me!"

He's looking at them little one,
And he didn't know that little, little Wolverine,

That little girl was looking at him.
And then he [Wolverine] said,
"If you get the prongs into you,
You won't be looking at nobody!"
He told [this to] his daughter, his little daughter.
He should have hit that man then,
But then he said, "If them prongs stick into you,
You won't be living now,"
He told that little girl.

So pretty soon him and his wife they start fighting too.
They can't find the knife.
He blamed his wife,
And just when he start to fight his wife,
That man jump up and hit him [Wolverine] with that hatchet he got?
And then he killed that [Wolverine] woman.

Then he start killing off them little Wolverine.
That little girl he can't do,
He can't, he can't kill her.
He got hold [of the] axe.
He tried chop that [tree] down,
But that little Wolverine keep saying,
"Let the axe get dull!"
And it gets dull.
He can't even cut with it,
And when he start to build fire,
So she'll jump down or something,
Just so he [can] kill her?
She start peeing and everything, you know. (laughs)
So she put the fire out that way.

So finally he said,
"I gonna let you go, but whatever you do,
Don't eat human being again from now on."

And that little girl said,
"Whatever you do from now on,
When you put your things away,
Be sure to put them away good that I don't get into them!"

You know nowadays Raven, Wolverine,
If you cache something away,
I don't care how high or anything,
They'll get into it.
That's why she said that.
"If you put anything away,
Be sure you put it away good."
Now that's the end.

Sarah Malcolm

On the rainy summer afternoon in 1975 when Sarah told Craig Mishler the following story, she was in her house wearing a red scarf held on with bobby pins, a blue flannel shirt with rolled up sleeves, a checkered cotton outer shirt, a purple skirt, thick support hose, red socks, and beaded moosehide slippers. For jewelry she wore a small gold cross on a neck chain and a man's-style silver watch band on her left arm.

Ts'ächin / The Old Woman Story

Sarah Malcolm, August 15, 1975

One woman up this way,
That [old] man went down river, they say.
This woman went up.
They call him [her] Ts'ächin.
This man [who] went downriver they call Tsà' Wëzhaa.
Tsà' Wëzhaa they call him.
Up that way, Ts'ächin, Fortymile.

Downriver this side,
When we go up Fortymile fishing grayling in spring?
There's other side, big open place, no hill?
Open place, big hill like that.
It's shaped like a ship.

How come it look like ship, I say?
I see way up, high as that.
It's shaped like a ship, you know, like this [gesturing].

CM: On the bluff? Rock?

SM: Yeah, rock. I see big tree way up.
Nobody get on top of that thing, they say.
I see some dry wood on,
And this side it [is] just swamp, I think.
Water little bit on the moss swamp and all over,
And nobody will get into it, they say.
When we come down we stop for a while.
We look at it.
It look like ship.

CM: This side of Fortymile?

SM: This side, yeah.
That [is] the one [called] *Ts'ächin*.
They call it *Ts'ächin Ts'ee*.
They call it Old Woman Stone.

And when [s]he sleep,
I don't know why they say that.
When she sleep,
She stretch her leg like this [gesturing],
And she put [pushed] those big rock [a]way,
Push [a]way rock all across the Yukon River,
And big rapid go like this [gesturing].
All awful, they say.
Water go like this,
And then one woman talked to her.

"And *Shizhäts'e'*,
How you think your children gonna float down in this hard rock?
Tuunint'ai, where you think your kids gonna go through right now?
No raft go down; no boat go down; no canoe go down."

"Try again; do something for it,"
[S]he tell that *Ts'ächin*.
And next time she sleep she do something again.
Her leg like this [gesturing],

She stretch it.
And then those stones just like gravel all gone.
Just little bit [of] rapid[s] up there.
Water just go like this little [gesturing].

Then she went up.
There on that side is a rock.
You could see her sled track.
Then I hear she draw moose this side too.
With stone shaped like moose, they say.
But I don't see that.
Maybe some place up above Dawson, I don't know.

And that *Tsà' Wëzhaa* Old Man went down,
Fool around by Ford Lake.
I don't know much about that.
Ts'ächin she do something upriver, lots.
She make some place this side creek too.

CM: Was she like God? Did she make things?

SM: I don't know. That's what they say.
She done something to that rock, big rock.
Pretty near across the Yukon River make too much.
You can't go through.
You can't go down with canoe, raft.
It's hard.
So this woman talked to her,
And "Sometime your kid[s] might go down here,
And it gonna be too hard for them,
And they're gonna have family too.
Do something for it [i.e., for them].

You try to do something about it,
And night time [when] she sleep she stretch her leg,
Lift her leg any way she want.
Lost rock just like gravel.
They make good river again, they say.

CM: Her name again was . . . *Shizhäts'e*?

SM: (Correcting): *Ts'ächin.*

CM: Nice old woman.

SM: That stone just like ship, I call it.
Next time you go up [to] Fortymile [River] you look for it.

CM: O.K. You gave that other word to me, that *Shizhäts'e*.
What's that mean?

SM: [My] daughter.

CM: That's the daughter? Old woman['s] daughter?

SM: This woman talk to that *Ts'ächin*, say *Shizhäts'e*.
She don't want to talk to her nothing,
So she say,
"*Shizhäts'e*, make a good river for your children sometime."
She told *Ts'ächin*.

CM: And Old Man is named *Tsà' Wëzhaa*.

SM: *Tsà' Wëzhaa*, uh huh.
He fool around down Ford Lake.
I don't know much about [him].

Willie Juneby

Willie said he first heard the following story from his grandmother
and that it took place when his grandmother was a young girl, but he
also heard it again years later from Bob Stacey. His grandmother on his
mother's side was named Laura (see Appendix D), and Laura was married to Old Peter *K'ay* (1849–1922). Assuming that he was referring
to Laura and not to his paternal grandmother, and assuming Laura was
somewhat younger than her husband, as most Indian women of that
time were, we would guess that the events described in this story took
place in the late 1850s or early 1860s. From internal references, this
story can also be dated to the period shortly after firearms were first
traded to the Han, which probably followed the establishment of Fort
Yukon in 1847.

In this legend, the two Han moieties, *Nahtsiin* (Crow) and the *Cheechil* (Seagull), join together to gain revenge and fight the raiding *Nä'ya*. Sarah Malcolm identified the *Nä'ya* as the "Stick Indians" living around Fort Selkirk. They were probably northern or southern Tutchone. In a discussion in English after telling the story in Hän, Willie said the *Nä'ya* people lived somewhere near the head of the Yukon River but also mentioned Dawson Creek and Fort Nelson. The *Nä'ya* were considered to be enemies because they kidnapped and killed several Han people. A shorter variant of this story collected from Charlie Isaac in Dawson was published in Osgood (1971:63–64).

The Indian War[17]

Willie Juneby, March 8, 1973
Translated from the Hän by Adeline Juneby Potts

I'm going to tell you a story.
It happened long, long ago, when my grandmother was a little girl.
She told me about a tragedy that happened.
Two parties, Nahtsiin and Cheechil, were from the same Han territory.

During the winters they would travel on foot
together looking for game.
The young men were trained to hunt at an early age.
During the long winter they kept the food supply going.
Besides being expert hunters,
They could track down other men.
As they went about they kept a low profile.

One day one of the hunters went ahead of the others on snowshoes.
He came upon a strange bunch of men,
And found out they could understand each other,
So he stopped to camp with them.
But he never came back.

The men following behind this hunter came to a camp
Where a woman and two children had been left behind.[18]

One man said, "I need to follow him, but who could go with me?"
One of the other guys said,
"Me. I understand both Indian and a little of the white man's
language,
So I'll go."
They left the others along the bank.

While they were there, a stranger appeared.
Suddenly, the stranger said,
"I just witnessed a tragedy.
One man carried a gun, the type that you load up.
And he shot a man, cut him up, and buried him under
the snow."

So they set off on snowshoes again,
And when they came upon the remains of the murdered man,
They turned back towards the woman and two children.
The woman was frantically waving a cane
And came running towards them, crying:
"My family!"
Before they had a chance to explain what happened,
A relative told her,
"Keep quiet!"
Out of shock, she hit one of the men with her cane.
Her relative, without thinking, hit her across the back of the head,
And she died instantly.
Her two children, in their innocent and childish ways,
Didn't even notice what was going on.
Then the men had to make a decision about the welfare of the
children.
As they were in deep thought and discussion,
They fed the children dry fish.
Then they clubbed them to death.

Toward evening the hunters met up with their own kind with
news of the tragedy.
One leader, Tay Thee Chah of the Cheechil,
And his warriors,
Traveled day and night, without sleep.
Going here and there, they came to a house where people

of the Nahtsiin party were living.
As they were visiting, the Nahtsiin tried to make their company
feel welcome.
The recent tragedy was too much for them.
They couldn't even talk or argue.
Finally they suggested that to kill each other over it was
too much to bear,
On top of all their other problems.
So they set off again,
Probably around March, in the springtime.

They walked day and night, still not getting enough sleep.
Then one of the elders spoke up:
"Whoever did this to you, why don't you do the same [to them]?"
While discussing their tragic loss to the *Nä'ya*,
They fell into a deep sleep.

Early the next morning, as the sun was coming up,
The wives brought in spruce wood for the fire.
As the men were eating, the women brought out their pack sacks
And sat them down next to the men.
Out of the clear blue sky, they suddenly sang out in their
language.
Meanwhile the young girls flirted and showed off in front of the
young warriors.
After they ate and finished singing,
It was time for them to leave.
Off they went, picking up the pack sacks the women left on the
floor for them.
They never looked back.
As they walked along the path to a camp underneath
small spruce trees,
They didn't bother to build a fire.
The tough leader Tay Thee Chah also had some tough relatives,
But not very many of them because a lot of them had passed on.

The Nahtsiin only had the same amount of people,
But the Cheechil had doubled in size and there were some things
said that made the others nervous.
So they changed the subject in order to avoid problems.

For some reason, they knew there was going to be a tragic story,
For they were setting off again upriver on a special big day.
They walked and walked all day long.

They came to a house with no one inside.
"It's been figured out.
I'm the one who does all the thinking,"
Said Tay Thee Chah.
With a shortage of food and quick thinking and action,
He killed a bunch of ptarmigan that day as they flew up.

The hungry men nibbled away on the ptarmigan as they trotted
along.
By the time the sun was coming up over the mountains,
They were in northern Canada [i.e., the upper Yukon River].
In this part of the country there were a lot of mountains.

Speaking of the enemy, Tay Thee Chah said,
"I know their ways because I have lived kind of like
the way they live,
And so I know a few things."

The men went back to the area for a lookout on the mountain.
Before they knew it, spring came.
One day as the men were looking out, they spotted some
movement.
Back at camp caribou [meat] was shared by shoving it into each
other's hands.

At this time they had three men on the lookout.
Sometimes they had a little camp fire going towards evening.
There was probably a reason for this.

One evening as they wandered in the middle of the night,
They spotted a light through the trees,
Possibly a camp fire.
With this news the warriors came back.

Tay Thee Chah was happy to hear of this.

He asked for some grease.
And when some grease was handed to him,
He smeared it all over his face.
With long curly hair and bare muscles,
He looked at the others through the smoke.
All were agreed that Tay Thee Chah was a tough man.

In the nearby mountains another caribou was killed.
Some men got the fire going, which had died down to sparks.
Tay Thee Chah knew the country.
Either he or his relatives had probably been there.

In this part of the country you don't expect any visitors.
On they went for many miles, as his friends in later years told
about him.
As they walked along they came across a hut-like structure with a
fire going inside.
Tay Thee Chah stood outside the door and peeked inside
Until his friend pushed him on the side—
A signal to walk back to camp.
All he was doing was trying to see how many men were
inside the hut.

Back at their base camp Tay Thee Chah tied a headband
across his forehead.
Soon he would be going to war.
Night fell with no one falling asleep.
They had to take cat naps while sitting up.

The next morning they put on their snowshoes.
One tribe was going one way,
And the other was going a slightly different route.
There was another important man in the Nahtsiin group.
They called him Hahkhee, meaning boss man or chief.
The men climbed the trees to look out.
All the time they were under the orders of
Tay Thee Chah,
Who was sitting on a tree with his shotgun,
the type that you load up.
It wasn't too long after that the *Nä'ya* were slaughtered.

There were dead bodies everywhere.
Those that survived turned back to get away.
What happened on that day is that the enemy was blasted away.

After the fighting was over,
The warriors and leaders headed back up to their own territory.
Silence came upon them, but one man tried to keep talking
about the war.
When they got closer to home, they livened up a little,
Told stories and laughed.

Back then there were hard feelings, tribes against tribes.
And there were consequences.
Because of Tay Thee Chah all this came about.
They won the war and made a name for themselves.
But Tay Thee Chah never bragged or told about the war himself.
His friends and family, however,
Told it over and over,
And it will be retold once again.

Oliver Lyman

Oliver Lyman, better known in Eagle as "Mr. O" (Figure 15), was a
leading Han storyteller, a respected elder, and a comedian. As far as
we can tell, he was the last surviving descendant of Chief Charley. In
the summer of 1997, Oliver was in charge of building and maintaining
the community fishwheel, which was located just below his bench on
the high bank overlooking the river, and his white Ford truck was one
of three vehicles in the village. Angela Harper elicited the first story
from Oliver outdoors during her annual "farewell potlatch" supper, with
half of the village in attendance. Oliver told the second story the next
evening by a wooden bench on the riverbank, with Bertha Ulvi laughing
hard and repeating the punch line several times.

The Stranger From Across the River

Oliver Lyman, July 12, 1997

This story took place just before my Dad,
Elisha Lyman, was born.

One spring there were some people from Eagle Village right
down here.
They were working in the village cemetery there by the riverbank.
And they were making a fence or something.
When all of a sudden they heard someone shout from the bluff
across the river.
Well, they looked up and saw this man standing up there.
And then the next thing they knew,
This guy made his way across the river,
Climbed up the bank,
Stumbled into the graveyard,
And dropped dead right there in front of them!
They really didn't know what else to do,
So they just dug a grave and buried him right there.
He was an Indian,
But they had never seen him before,
And they didn't even know his name or where the heck he came
from.

The Japanese Tourist

Oliver Lyman, with assistance from
Bertha Ulvi, on July 13, 1997

Albert Carroll of Circle,
When he was here for Louise Paul's funeral,
Told me this story.
He said that Johnny Nathaniel,
Who has a fishwheel about fifteen miles below Circle,
Went out to check his wheel one day this summer.
When he got there he was surprised to find a Japanese tourist.
The man was standing up soaking wet in his fish box.
I guess he was just stuck there.
So Johnny asked him what happened and how he got there.
The Japanese man said he was floating downriver in his canoe,
And he was taking pictures of the fishwheel when he lost
his balance,
Tipped over the canoe,

And fell into the river.
When he fell into the river,
The fishwheel scooped him up and brought him back out of the
water,
And he either climbed into the fishbox or got dumped in there.
So when Johnny came back up to Circle,
And people asked him how many salmon he got,
All he could say was,
"Well," he said,
"I got no salmon, but I caught one Japanese!"

Han stories such as these provide crucial links to Han history, beliefs, humor, subsistence, and world view. As verbal art, they elicit vivid images of the recent and the distant past. In doing so they represent two major kinds of oral traditions: those "handed down" through many generations (such as the Old Man and Old Woman stories) and those quickly popularized and "handed across" within the same generation (such as the Japanese Tourist story).

Although this is not the place for extended folkloristic analysis and interpretation, much of the significance of these stories lies in their multiple contexts. One obvious context is the collective repertoire of other Han stories, and a comparison of their close variants. A second context is embedded in the life histories of the storytellers. In many folklore collections the stories have been sadly separated from the storytellers. As in Dr. Schmitter's early collection, the performers' identities and the performance contexts remain invisible.

Yet another crucial context is the social situation in which the tales are performed. Were the stories elicited or were they offered spontaneously and voluntarily? Who else was there and how were the stories shaped to meet the expectations of the listeners? Was the setting indoors or outdoors? In the daytime or in the evening? In the summer or in the winter? By defining these contexts with our field notes, we can do much to help the texts come to life and lift our understanding and enjoyment of them to another level.

Chapter Six

Notes

1. Percy Henry interviewed by Craig Mishler, audiotape 1, 11 October 1999.

2. Schmitter, *Upper Yukon Native Customs and Folk-Lore*; portions now available online at trondek.com/history/yale-han-mythology.html.

3. Schwatka, *Along Alaska's Great River: A Popular Account of the Travels of the Alaska Exploring Expedition of 1883; Along the Great Yukon River from Its Source to Its Mouth, in British North-west Territory and in the Territory of Alaska* (New York: Cassell, 1885), Map 2.

4. Arthur, Dr. Schmitter's interpreter, was apparently not Arthur Stevens, the father of Silas Stevens, who would have been a very small child at the time. Photos of the rocky outcrops known as "The Old Woman" and "The Old Man" have been published recently in Victoria Joan Moessner and Joanne Gates, eds., *The Alaska-Klondike Diary of Elizabeth Robins, 1900* (Fairbanks: University of Alaska Press, 1999), 262. Percy Henry says in jest that the Old Man and Old Woman rocks are where Uncle Sam got divorced from Queen Victoria.

5. William Haskell, *Two Years in the Klondike and Alaska Gold-Fields* (Hartford: Hartford Publishing Company, 1898), 159–160.

6. The story titles, sections, and subtitles included here are artifacts of the interviewer. Louise, Sarah, and Oliver Lyman did not use them. Editing is indicated in brackets [ ] for clarification.

7. Anna Birgitta Rooth, *The Alaska Expedition 1966: Myths, Customs, and Beliefs among the Athabascan Indians and Eskimos of North Alaska* (Lund: Acta Universitatis Lundensis, Section 1: Theologica, Juridica, Humaniora, 14).

8. Anna Birgitta Rooth, *The Alaska Seminar* (Uppsala and Stockholm: Almquist and Wiskell, 1980), 37. Additional analysis of Han and other northern Dene oral narrative styles may be found in Rooth's *The Importance of Storytelling* (Uppsala and Stockholm: Almquist and Wiskell, 1976).

9. Richard Matthews, *The Yukon* (New York: Holt, Rinehart, and Winston, 1968), 2.

10. Diana Greene, *Raven Tales and Medicine Men: Folktales from Eagle Village*. Privately published, n.d. Copy at the Eagle Public Library, Eagle, Alaska.

11. Further information on the Hän alphabet and language may be found on the Internet at the Hän web page maintained by the Yukon Native Language Centre in Whitehorse: www.yukoncollege.yk.ca/ynlc/YNLCinfo/Han.html

12. Robert A. McKennan, *The Upper Tanana Indians* (New Haven: Yale University Publications in Anthropology No. 55, 1959), 175–190.

13. "Half-Way" is a place on the Yukon River between Dawson and Eagle where the mail carrier Percy DeWolfe lived.

14. An early version of this same episode appears in Schmitter, *Upper Yukon Native Customs and Folk-Lore* under the title, "Adventures of the Old Man."

15. Ford Lake is close to Calico Bluff, only a couple of miles downriver from Eagle Village. There are small frogs living around the lake even today.

16. In Schmitter's version, Bear uses a fish trap instead of a gill net to try and catch *Tsà' Wëzhaa*.

17. The original source of Willie Juneby's "Indian War" story is his audiotape in the Alaska Native Language Center library at the University of Alaska Fairbanks, with circulating cassette copies available at the Oral History Collection at the Rasmuson Library, University of Alaska Fairbanks (tape H91-12-318). This war story is traditional and is a variant of the same one Charlie Isaac (Chief Isaac's son) told at Dawson in English to Richard Slobodin in 1962 (see Slobodin, "Notes on the Han"). For more on Han warfare, see Catharine McClellan's discussion in "Feuding and Warfare among Northwestern Athapaskans." In *Proceedings: Northern Athapaskan Conference, 1971*, 1, edited by A. McFadyen Clark, 214–218. Mercury Series, Canadian Ethnology Service Paper No. 57. Ottawa: National Museum of Man, 1975.

18. Apparently this was the family of the missing man.

Chapter Seven

Han Expressive Culture: Part Two

Traditional Songs and Dances

THE EARLY-TWENTIETH century loss of Han song and dance repertoires (*tr'uts'ä* or *tr'oodz'e*) is indeed tragic, for at the time of white
contact in the mid-nineteenth century, the Han were considered by
Alexander Hunter Murray to be the most exciting and dramatic singers
and dancers of all the Athabaskan tribal groups who frequented Fort
Yukon. Murray said, for example, that the first time he met the Han in
1847, he gave each of them a small piece of tobacco as a token of friendship. Shouting and whooping, they "immediately formed into a half
circle and danced with great vigour for a few minutes, keeping time
with their outlandish songs. They had a very extraordinary and wild
appearance with their greasy [*sic*] dresses covered with beads and brass
trinkets, and long cloated hair fluttering in the breeze."[1]

Sixteen years later, Robert McDonald, Anglican missionary in Fort
Yukon, observed: "The Han Gwich'in arrived this morning. A dance
of welcome was given them by the others, and it was succeeded by
another in return from them. It is from their dancing that they are
called *gens du fous* [Fr. 'crazy people']. Their songs are very exciting and
rather pleasing."[2]

171

Han singing styles have never been described in detail, but one observer described Han potlatch songs as "resembling those of Japanese operas" and the dance motion being a swaying of the body, "alternately bending the right and left knee."[3] In 1932, Walter Benjamin told Cornelius Osgood that the Han had four kinds of songs: love songs, war songs, potlatch songs, and shamanic or medicine songs.

There is no mention in the early nineteenth-century historic literature of the Han ever using a drum, but a potlatch photo taken in 1901 (Figure 35) shows a Dawson man, possibly Chief Isaac, banging away on a big metal washtub to the movements of dancers in what appears to be a skit or play. The washtub here serves as a substitute drum.

There is a good photograph from about the same time of Chief Isaac of Moosehide holding a skin drum (Figure 38), and Schmitter described a potlatch dance where "time was kept by one of the Indians beating on a caribou skin drum."[4] Therefore, the Han were using drums by at least the first decade of the twentieth century, if not long before. Since there are words in the Hän language both for the skin drum, *tsùl tr'oghàl*, and for the drum-beating stick, *tsùl biitr'oghàl*, a case can be made for their antiquity. Today skin drums are considered essential to Han song and dance performance.

Sadly, recordings of traditional Han songs and dances are virtually nonexistent. The only Han song ever published is a memorial song composed by a woman incarcerated in the Dawson jail. Performed by Charlie Stevens for Swedish folklorist Anna Birgitta Rooth in 1966, it was dedicated to the memory of the woman's uncle and was composed when she heard a steamboat go by and blow its whistle.[5]

Han song and dance was once part of everyday life. Rooth talked to Borghilde Hansen, the schoolteacher who served in Eagle from 1925–1938. Hansen observed first-hand that Han medicine men used ceremonial song and dance as part of the healing process, along with the administration of certain plants and roots.[6]

There is a question about whether any of the old dances and songs were lost when the Han discontinued the memorial potlatch in the first two decades of the twentieth century. Elder Mary McLeod had insisted that no dancing be performed at Han memorial potlatches, and so instead the women put on a march accompanied by the beat of a drum. As Slobodin described it: "Every now and then they made hand motions: hands extended, palms down, thumbs touching, moved slowly downward in front of the chest; Mary characterized this motion as a soothing or quieting gesture. The marching women wore two horizontal streaks of red paint across their faces."[7]

Even so, Martha Kates thinks that her 1907 Eagle potlatch photograph shows two young boys (one of them her father David Roberts) holding feathers that may have been used in a "grouse dance" (see Chapter 5, Figure 33). Also, according to Kates, the kneeling man wearing the wolf-head mask and cape in this photo suggests a dance or ceremony associated with the Wolf clan.[8]

For a few years in the early-twentieth century other social events, such as Euro-American and Euro-Canadian holiday celebrations, provided outlets for Han song and dance. In journalistic accounts following the Christmas holidays in 1923, for example, we learn that five young dancers at Moosehide did "historic performances" of the Moosehide dance, the Ross River dance, the Coffee Creek dance, the Selkirk dance, the Tanana dance, the Eagle dance, the duck dance, the caribou dance, the fish dance, and others. An exhibition of Han war dances in Moosehide right after the 1923 holidays, however, was promoted as "a vanishing feature of Indian life."[9]

The photograph taken in Dawson on Victoria Day in 1901 (Figure 35) also helps contextualize Han dance occasions. However, such holidays were not enough to sustain Han musical traditions because none of the dances or the songs with which they were associated seem to have survived to the present day.

The good news is that some of the lost dance songs have been found and returned to the Han from the people at Tanacross, who first received them at the turn of the century and kept them in memory. The gift of songs was accompanied by a Han ganhook, a decorated wooden dance staff (see Figure 33). Kenneth Thomas, Sr. of Tanacross reported that when he attended the Han gathering in Moosehide in 1996, he returned five songs which had been given by the Han to his ancestors at Kechumstuk and Mansfield Village before he was born.[10] Laura Sanford of Tok and Tanacross has also assisted the Han in this song and dance revival. As Dawson elder Doris Adair says, "The heartbeat of the drum is coming back to us."[11]

Fiddle Music and Square Dancing

Not limited to aboriginal-style singing and dancing, the Han were as strongly influenced as the Gwich'in were by the fiddle music brought in by Hudson's Bay Company men and by American prospectors of

Figure 37. Group photo of two couples, n.d. Left to right: Elisha Lyman, unidentified woman (possibly Laura Lyman), Sarah Malcolm, and Edward Malcolm.

the gold rush. During his 1891 expedition to the Yukon and Alaska, Schwatka met two Indians named David and Peter from the Fortymile country (probably David *K'ay* and Peter *K'ay*) who were constantly singing or humming fiddle dance tunes such as *The Arkansas Traveler, Rory O'Moore,* and *The Girl I Left Behind Me.*[12]

Joe Adam, Big Jim Juneby, and Joe Susie Joseph earned a reputation as three of the premiere Han fiddlers of the early twentieth century. Consequently, it is possible that fiddle music and its associated jigs, contra dances, and square dances gradually or suddenly displaced Han aboriginal-style singing and dancing.

It is with some amusement that we read a detailed description by the geologist Josiah Spurr about a so-called "squaw dance" held at Fortymile in the summer of 1896.[13] On this occasion white gold miners gathered in a large log cabin for a dance with Han women without ever speaking a word, since the women did not speak English and the miners did not speak Hän. The only noise all night long was the sawing of the fiddle and the shuffling of feet across the wooden floor. It is unclear whether the fiddler for this event was white or Indian. What is clear is that the Han women loved to dance and the Han men were not invited to participate.

A newspaper account of the Christmas and New Year's celebration held at Johnson [Jonathon] Wood's cabin in Moosehide in 1924 suggests that social dancing was still very popular among the Han at that time. The account describes one dance done in pairs, in which the women keep their feet on the floor while the men leap as high as possible. This would seem to be a local variant of the Red River Jig. Jimmy Wood was one of those demonstrating "the jig dance, a continuous performance." Although most of the white visitors left at 10:30 P.M., "the Indians then took over the dances, and fox trots, square dances, and waltzes were the order until 3 o'clock in the morning."[14]

In the 1970s Willie Juneby and Jacob Malcolm were the premiere Han dance fiddlers in Eagle Village. Some of Willie's tunes included *Neets'ee Tly'aa*, the *Red River Jig*, the *Red Wing Two Step*, *Buffalo Gals*, *Over the Waves*, the *Merry Widow Waltz*, *Silver Bells*, at least two square dances, *Turkey in the Straw* and *Brighton Camp*, and an assortment of polkas and schottisches.[15] Willie played a fiddle made out of birch wood by Frank Hobson, an Eskimo living in Copper Center. He was often accompanied by his son Archie on guitar.

The primary tradition bearer in Eagle Village in the 1980s and 1990s has been Tim Malcolm (Figure 36), who is often accompanied on guitar by his younger brother Micah Malcolm or by Edward David. Tim and Micah's father, Edward Malcolm (Figure 37), who died in 1948, was also an old-time dance fiddler and had a great influence on his sons.

After bowing a chorus or two of a tune, Tim has a unique way of picking out the melody of the tune on the violin using only his thumb, a pizzicato technique we have not witnessed anywhere else in the North. Also, Tim and Micah have a nifty guitar trick that is really fun to watch. Sometimes Tim will play the left hand fingerboard of the guitar while Micah plays the right hand or strumming part, and then right on cue they will switch off with one another without missing a beat.

Musical and Choreographic Revival

Although the performance of aboriginal songs and dances has undergone a small revival in the late 1990s, community square dances accompanied by the fiddle have become rare in recent years. Still, it is important to understand that song and dance and instrumental music lie at the very heart of Han spirituality and power. Restoring and maintaining these musical and artistic forms will contribute greatly to the distinctiveness of the Han as a people.

No one understands this better than the Han themselves. At the Han Gathering held in Moosehide in 1994, Gerald Isaac made this eloquent speech while wearing his grandfather's jacket:

> I want to speak a little bit about this ceremonial jacket I'm wearing today. This ceremonial jacket belongs to my grandfather Chief Isaac of Moosehide. It has been brought back to my family some years ago. It went away. It traveled all around the world. This Nogletstri' took it as a gift from her grandmother that my grandfather gave to her.
>
> And this jacket must be at least a hundred years old, and the last time it was used was probably as long ago as maybe seventy years or more. So it is with great honor and great respect and great pride that today I display it to all of you. And I display it to all the First Nations, and I display it to the public.
>
> We are trying desperately to bring our Han culture back. We are trying desperately, as you heard our elder Percy [Henry] speak, to lay the ground work, to bring our songs back, to learn our songs, to learn to play the drum, to learn to sing and Ay-chÅ, hätr'unohthän, Òaa hozho chodza'. That means "to also learn how to dance." And when we dance, we laugh, and when we laugh we are happy. Tr'öähÒÅy, ay chÅ. We are happy also.[16]

In July 1996, the *Tr'ondëk Hwëch'in* performed a play in Dawson called *Beat of the Drum*. Directed by Kathryn Bruce, the performance featured actors dressed as Bear, Wolf, Beaver, Muskrat, Wolverine, Raven, and a Child. It recounts the loss of the Han cultural heritage and identity. At one point in the drama, someone says, "It's hard to keep time without the beat of the drum or to sing songs when you no longer have the words."

After facing a series of crises ranging from alcohol abuse to the loss of language, the players instruct Raven to fly away with the songs, dances, stories, and drum and to "store them where they can be protected until there comes a time when we can share them with pride and honesty, a time when we have found our power." The things that Raven rescued and stored away are returned to the people at the end of the play, and they regain their lost power. The Child accepts the gift of the drum and leads the other actors in a final dance.[17]

We witnessed the teaching and performance of three local songs at the Han culture camp in Moosehide in July 1997: the Canadian Flag–Yukon Flag Song, the Moosehide Song used to identify themselves at other peoples' potlatches and gatherings, and the Moosehide Welcome Song for welcoming visitors to Moosehide gatherings. Two additional songs were performed by visiting instructors: the Champagne Village Welcome Song, and one that was introduced as Lacey's Song after the woman from whom the singer had learned it.[18] Because the Han have lost so much, their attempt to perpetuate song and dance traditions has by necessity become a process of borrowing and reinvention, and the song repertoire is still very limited.

The youth attending this workshop participated by singing and drumming along with the adult leaders, but on this occasion no dancing accompanied the songs. Debbie Nagano, one of the culture camp coordinators, explained that traditional Han dance choreography consists of an inner circle of drummers plus the holders of the ganhooks positioned in the center of the dance floor:

> The ganhook holder is the person that keeps track of how many times we're going to sing it, or when it's going to end, or it also keeps the movement of the women to go left when they're dancing. Then when they see that ganhook turn over, they rotate over.

This innermost circle is surrounded by a circle of non-drumming male dancers who are surrounded in turn by a circle of female dancers. The closed circle dance formation is a primary characteristic of most northern Athabaskan traditional dances, and the concentric circle set design is very similar to that used by the people of Tanacross, Tetlin, and Northway.

Han Games

Several Han games appear in the historic literature. Leroy McQuesten described a game played on New Year's at Fortymile during the 1880s that is remarkably similar to today's Alaskan Iñupiat Eskimo blanket toss, except that the Han "blanket" was made out of moose skin.[19] He observed that the Han delighted in tossing up both their own men and women as well as white men, and that they kept up this tradition year after year. Ferdinand Schmitter reported at the turn of the century that the Han at Eagle Village once played an outdoor game similar to volleyball. The ball, apparently about the size of a baseball, was made of caribou skin stuffed with hair and had a marten tail attached. Instead of a net, the Han used a line drawn on the ground to separate the two sides.[20] This game was also played by the Gwich'in.

The Han were also fond of a game similar to the Dogrib hand game, which amounted to a form of gambling:

> Two rows of men sit opposite one another, each man holding in his hand a bone marked with a notch. The bones are secretly passed from right to left and vice-versa. Some one on one side would call out which of the opponents' hands contained the bone, and the calling side would get as many sticks, from a pile of about sixty, as the number of opponents' hands guessed correctly. Each side called the other alternately. Sometimes they would hold another unmarked bone in the opposite hand so as to confuse the guesser. The side which lost or got the fewer sticks had to give the other something as a forfeit.[21]

The Han also played a hoop game, similar to the one played by their Gwich'in neighbors, with the hoop made of willows. But while the Gwich'in tried to retrieve the hoop with a hook as it was floating down a stream (a game called *neehilak*), the Han tried to throw spears into the hoop as it was rolling along the ground. This game was used to develop hunting proficiency at a time when spears were still important to subsistence.

Still another game, called *ts'ik'e ootth'an*, was played with caribou toe-bones or hooves. The object was to try to throw the bones up in the air and catch them on a stick. The chief would put up the tobacco, and every man who could catch the bones on a stick was allowed to have a smoke.[22]

Since the 1970s we have not seen any of these traditional games played, although it is possible that some are taught at the Han culture camp at Moosehide. The most popular adult Han games today are card games, which are enjoyed by both men and women. In 1997 we were able to participate in two of them, *Bizhur* and Indian Bingo. These are described in some detail in Appendix C.

Traditional Dress and Adornment[23]

At the time of white contact in the 1840s traditional summer dress for Han men and women consisted of shirts or tunics made of tanned caribou or moose skin; a man's shirt was pointed in front and back while a woman's was pointed only in the back and was a little longer. The lower garment for both sexes was a pair of trousers with attached moccasins. Winter clothing followed the same general pattern except that it was made primarily out of caribou skins tanned without removing the hair. The hair was worn on the inside. Winter clothes and sleeping robes were made of hare skin as well.

Before the Han obtained trade beads they decorated their clothing with red ocher, porcupine quills, seeds, and a few dentalium shells received in trade. By the 1840s the Han were using trade beads as a major form of decoration, and Han men also decorated their shirts with brass ornaments, apparently obtained in trade with the Russians.

> Painting the face, piercing the septum of the nose and lobes and helix of the ears, and arranging the hair were customary among Native peoples of the upper Yukon valley. . . . Each man has hanging from his neck two small bags containing black lead and red earth [ocher] for the painting of themselves (their faces), each one paints according to his own fancy; most commonly the upper parts of the cheeks and around the eyes are black, [with] a black strip along the top of the nose; and forehead is covered with narrow red stripes, and the chin with strips of red and black.[24]

Alexander Hunter Murray observed that at Fort Yukon "every Indian wears them [small dentalium shells] as nose and ear ornaments, for hair bands, etc."[25] Dentalium, a white sea shell, was a form of currency in the nineteenth century, and it is still widely recognized today as symbol of prestige and wealth. Strachan Jones, another trader at Fort Yukon, distinguished the Han from other tribes for wearing a metal ring in the nose. At Eagle, Schmitter also noted that it had been the custom to pierce the nasal septum and that most of the adults still had holes in their noses for wearing pins made from the bones of small birds.

Murray noted that Han mixed into their hair "red earth [ocher], greese [sic], and the down of geese and ducks." The hair was then gathered by a band of dentalium shells and beads into a long queue or tail that hung down the back. Eagle or hawk feathers, according to Murray, were "stuck in the hair behind, and removed only when they go to sleep or to be used in dancing."[26] Schmitter described a similar way of arranging the hair. For winter headwear, the Han wore marten or hare skin caps.

We have never seen any examples of Han porcupine quill work and suspect that it is now largely a lost art. We do, however, have Schmitter's detailed account of porcupine quill decorations:

> Porcupine quills, which are used for decorating their clothing, were dyed red by boiling in cranberry juice, or blue by boiling in huck-leberry juice. When any quills were found which were pure white, they were left so. Various colored flowers were also boiled and their coloring matter used in dyeing the quills. Small geometrical figures were made by sewing the flattened-out quills to a backing of skin, and long stripes were made by rolling the quills into spirals about a sixteenth of an inch in diameter and sewing them side by side. The backs of mittens and insteps of the moccasins were decorated with these quills. Flat strings of caribou skin one-fourth of an inch wide were sometimes wound with porcupine quills. These strings were either sewed to, or tied about the coat wrists and about the breeches below the knees. The coat of a chief was decorated down the front and back and had a special collar, significant of his office, which consisted of a strip of moose skin about two inches wide and nearly a yard long with one margin fringed by cutting it into strips. On this was sewed strands, and strings of quills were suspended from the ends. The collar hung around the neck and down the front like a scarf. A special hunting belt was made of caribou skin decorated from porcupine quills, and from it hung an ornamented moose skin sheath containing a hunting knife.[27]

Although people generally dressed alike, rich Han were distin-guished by their clothes. Murray noted that the wealthy had two suits of clothes, one of which was worn when dancing. Native people also stressed the "close identity between their clothing and their selves."[28] In historic Athabaskan culture, clothes made the person, reflecting social status and correct or ideal behavior. Fine clothing was associated with competent, moral people who took care of themselves and others, and refrained from gossip, boasting, and dishonesty.

Some clothing decorations, such as beadwork, porcupine quills, or dentalium shells, reflected the wealth of the person wearing the clothes and indicated the ability of the woman who did the sewing. Pieces of fur, or animal bones, teeth, or claws were worn as amulets so that a person would take on a particular characteristic of the animal.

Hudson's Bay trader Robert Campbell noted that the Han decorated their clothes with ermine or squirrel skins or tails, duck wings, and long hair. A hawk claw meant swift to the prey, a beaver's shoulder blade indicated strength, a bear claw meant unafraid, and a weasel skin meant the person would be able to walk on snow.[29]

Changing Dress Styles

During the early stages of the fur trade the Han were not interested in altering their personal appearance. They wanted blankets, axes, knives, powder horns, and files, but, as Murray wrote, "it was hard to dispose of clothing, as they consider their own dresses much superior to ours both in beauty and durability, and they are partly right, although I endeavor to pursued [persuade] them the contrary."[30]

However, their disinterest did not last long. Murray reported that at the end of 1847 the Han desired blanket coats or capotes, and leading Han men wanted the chief's coats distributed by the Company. These coats or jackets modeled on military uniforms were given out by the Hudson's Bay Company to encourage chiefs who supported the Company's interests. Those chiefs or leading men who received the coats, and their followers, probably began to identify with the traders.

While the Han or Gwich'in did not immediately accept the woven clothes offered by the Hudson's Bay Company, they did want beads. According to Murray, "there was not an Indian but wears fancy beads, that is blue, and red of various sizes [and] they cost the Indians nearly double what they pay for the common white beads."[31]

By the 1860s western clothing became a trade item, and changes in clothing styles and personal adornment radiated out from the trading posts into the more remote camps. What might be called "transitional clothing" was described by the naturalist William Dall after he encountered a group of Gwich'in just below Fort Yukon. All of them wore clothes obtained in trade at the fort. According to Dall one of the women wore a calico dress. He described the men's clothing as follows: "Hudson's Bay moccasins, leggings, [and] fringed hunting-shirts of buckskin, originally introduced by the English traders, who obtained them from the tribes to the southeast. They had an abundance of fine bead-work in which the French Canadians delight, and which those women who frequent the forts learn to excel in."[32]

One portrait of Chief Isaac (Figure 38) taken in the twentieth century shows him in transitional chiefly dress, wearing a chief's jacket

Figure 38. Chief Isaac in transitional dress with skin drum, 1920s.

and cloth pants. The jacket has an abundance of leather fringe and a flowered beadwork strip down the front seams. His gauntlet-style mittens also appear to be heavily beaded, and his bandolier is the same one he wears while paddling a canoe (Figure 29). One unusual feature is the decorative garters tied with ribbons around his knees. Such garters were traditional among Natives living in the southern part of the Yukon. Perhaps at the photographer's request, his black bowler hat has been removed and placed on a chair beside him.[33]

The earliest photograph of Chief Charley, taken in the summer of 1883, shows him and two of his men standing side by side at an

Figure 39. Chief Charley in winter dress, 1890–1891.

undisclosed location (Figure 6). The photo shows that Han men had by this time largely accepted western-style clothing, including candy-striped cotton dress shirts, heavy flannel shirts, broad-brimmed felt hats, neckerchiefs, suspenders, and cloth pants. Charley's trade bead necklace signifies his social rank. One of his sidemen is wearing a decorated pouch, perhaps made of moosehide, attached to a rope around his waist.

In the winter of 1887–1888 William Ogilvie encountered a band of Han on the North Fork of the Tatonduk River. He described their winter dress as:

made of deer [i.e., caribou] skins dressed with the hair on and worn with the hair inside. The pants and boots are made in one piece, and the coat is made in the manner of a shirt. In putting it on it is simply pulled over the head, and the arms passed down the sleeves, so that, when it is on, there is no opening for any wind to pass through, and no part of the body, except the face, is exposed to the atmosphere. In the case of children, sometimes the end of the sleeve is sewed up so that the hand cannot get out, but this is done only when the child is going out.[34]

Another photograph of Chief Charley (again clearly a different man) taken about 1891 (Figure 39), illustrates how these one-piece skin pants and boots were worn with a row of beads running down the pant seam and around the ankles. Charley's mittens are gauntlet style and attached to each other with a cord that runs across the back of the collar. In this way, the mittens could be removed without dropping them into the snow. Charley's parka appears to be made from corduroy cloth decorated on the upper sleeves with strips of beaded moosehide.

By 1891, however, some younger Han men had begun to wear manufactured brimmed caps resembling those worn by crew members on steamboats (Figures 7 and 21). These caps contrast sharply with what appear to be hand-made brimless embroidered cloth caps worn by boys and older men. By this time all of the people in David's band were wearing some form of western-style clothing, but the caps, vests, neckerchiefs, and double-breasted shirts worn by these younger men must have carried a considerable amount of prestige.

Rev. Richard Bowen, who visited the Han at Fort Reliance in 1895, observed that the caribou skins for women's clothing were not smoked and were of a much lighter color than the skins for men's clothing. Without describing other gender differences in clothing, Bowen said he asked why the men were more ornately dressed than the women. "The reply was brief and to the point: because the male bird and animal carry the brightest feathers, furs, and horns."[35]

Clothing styles changed rapidly during the gold rush. With an ethnographer's eye, the intrepid journalist Tappan Adney observed a difference between the dress of younger men and older men, saying the younger men wore bright wool blanket coats in the colors of red, green, and yellow. With these they wore blanket trousers tucked into the tops of their moccasins. Meanwhile, the older men continued to wear the one-piece caribou-skin trousers and moccasins. Their mittens were made

Figure 40. Indians [probably Han] standing by sleds loaded with trade goods on Front Street, Dawson, 1898. The man on the left with the Stetson hat and light-colored coat is identified by Percy Henry as Sam Smith, the first Indian constable at Moosehide.

of caribou skin with the hair inside, although one old man wore a pair made of hare skin. An old shaman named John carried a single-barreled shotgun in a caribou-skin case embroidered with beads and red cloth, and a richly beaded bullet pouch made of black cloth. By this time, Han women were wearing light cloth dresses when they were indoors, and when traveling they put on a blanket coat over a short blanket skirt, or "a voluminous overdress of caribou skin having a hood."[36]

Adney went to some length to describe the clothing of Chief Isaac, saying that he was dressed in "a black fur cap of peculiar design, a coat of gorgeous 'upholstery' patterned Mackinaw blanket, 'store' trousers further encased in leggings of the same material as the coat, moose-hide moccasins with pointed toes and bright scarlet tops." He also had "a pair of large caribou-skin mittens" hanging from his neck by "a thick plaited green and white worsted cord" and had around his neck "a knit yarn scarf."[37]

After the gold rush began in the 1880s, Han clothing styles continued to change quite radically. Skin clothes, except for moosehide slippers and mittens, soon gave way to the "Sunday styles" worn by well-to-do

Figure 41. Chief Isaac with his son in a caribou skin parka, 1899.

white prospectors and businessmen. One of the Peel River Gwich'in, a member of the "Dawson Boys" who arrived in the Klondike during the gold rush, recalled buying a black suit with a white shirt and tie, a watch chain, and a Stetson hat, "as every boy in Moosehide did."[38] By 1898 broad-brimmed Stetson hats and fancy three-piece suits with neckties and bow ties were all the rage (Figures 40 and 41), while fur clothes were still made for children. Stetsons were even worn by women.

Figure 42. Indian family at Fortymile City, 1899.

A photo taken of an Indian family at Fortymile (Figure 42) in 1899 shows the father wearing a formal three-piece dress suit and necktie while the mother wears a cloth dress under a distinctive two-layered cloak trimmed with what appears to be tanned moosehide. She and the three girls are all wearing scarves tied around the neck. This well-dressed family was still living in a canvas tent, although there is a log cabin in the background.

A 1904 portrait of a Han woman carrying her baby along the river-bank in Eagle (Figure 43) illustrates again how clothing styles changed after prolonged contact with white settlers. This woman is wearing an ankle-length cloth dress and has a long-fringed plaid wool blanket draped over her shoulders. She also wears a cloth scarf over her head, something we see some Han women still wearing today.

A couple of years later we see a beautiful Han woman, Sarah Juneby, wearing an ulu-shaped earring and posing with her two children, both of whom are wearing skin parkas (Figure 44). It would seem that children still wore traditional dress well after adults made the switch to western styles. The boy in this photo is wearing moose-skin pants and knitted wool socks underneath moose-skin boots, and the hoods of the parkas of both children appear to be embroidered. The older child's parka, judg-

Figure 43. Han woman walking on riverbank with baby, Eagle, 1904.

ing from its color and texture, may be sheep or wolf, while the baby's parka appears to be made of caribou. A plaid woolen blanket rests on Sarah's lap, and a braided baby strap or sash is draped on the ground.

The Eagle Village potlatch photo from 1907 (Figure 33) illustrates yet another convergence of traditional and western-style dress. Each man in the front row of the photo has a calico cloth tunic that extends to just below the waist, but each tunic is totally unique in the way it is trimmed. The striped one in the center appears to be made of mattress ticking. The most striking objects, nevertheless, are the men's pointed tasseled caps. Han outfits of this kind have never been photographed since, so it is not known how long they stayed in fashion. Perhaps the biggest mystery of the photo is the wolf-head mask and cape worn by the young man crouched in front of the group, perhaps associated with some kind of shamanic

Figure 44. Sarah Juneby with baby Jacob and son (probably Bob Jim) at Eagle, 1906.

dance. Certainly these calico cloth tunics do not represent the everyday dress of the Han in 1907. Many of the men are wearing dance tunics and fancy head regalia while, juxtaposed against them, several other men in the background are wearing suits and ties and caps of the style worn by riverboat captains and deck hands. The men may have acquired these caps in the course of working on steamboats. Another 1907 photo (Figure 34) shows about half of the men wearing suspenders.

By 1919, formal coats and ties had converged with with traditional winter dress such as marten hats and moosehide mittens (Figure 30). Schmitter observed that "most of the clothing now worn is that cast off by the white people. Although the skin parka and breeches are still frequently seen, they have been mostly replaced by canvas parkas and other white men's clothing" (Schmitter 1910: 4–5).

Figure 45. Chief Isaac of the Moosehide Indians in ceremonial garb for a Discovery Day celebration near Dawson. August 15, 1924.

Chief Isaac, photographed in Dawson on August 15, 1924 (Figure 45), illustrates another striking blend of Indian and western dress styles. Here Isaac sports a white shirt, dress suit, and bow tie under a wool Tlingit-style button blanket. He has a bowler hat with two eagle feathers sticking out, the beaded bandolier draped over his shoulder, and dentalium shell earrings. The button blanket and the dentalium shells (called *ch'inthin* in Hän) probably came from the coast via Tlingit traders. To complete the stylistic juxtaposition, Isaac's shoes are laced leather with stiff soles, and in his left hand is a half-smoked cigar. An automobile in the background of this photo helps to contextualize it within the roaring twenties.

It would be a mistake to assume that the photographs we have selected here are indicative of Han everyday dress. Photographs of chiefs tend to distort reality because they represent the richest and most powerful people and not the average Indian family. Chief Charley with his relatively plain functional clothes presents an antithesis to Chief Isaac in his fancy, formal garb. More Indians probably dressed like Chief Charley than like Chief Isaac, at least before the gold rush.

The paucity of historic photographs from Eagle and Moosehide for the years 1924 to 1973 makes it difficult to describe changes in Han dress styles for this period. Village styles probably mirrored the changes in factory-produced, non-Native fashions. A good example comes from the photograph of Elisha Lyman, Andy Stevens, and Arthur Stevens (Figure 31), taken about 1922. Two things that grab our attention are Elisha's striped pullover sweater and Arthur Stevens's fancy button shoes and string tie.

Elizabeth Hayes Goddard, who visited Eagle Village in the mid-1930s, observed the dress styles of those attending a Sunday church service: "The Indian women were wearing bright full skirts flounced with lace ruffles. Their heads were tied with gay colored handkerchiefs. The men were uniformly dressed in blue overalls and blue shirts. All were wearing beaded moccasins."[39]

From the 1970s through the 1990s, Han dress styles were quite casual and almost indistinguishable from those of non-Natives living in the bush. Today only a few of the older women still wear skirts and dresses. Slacks and jeans, cotton shirts, T-shirts, and sweatshirts are commonplace on both men and women. Virtually all of the everyday clothing now worn by the Han, except for the occasional pair of beaded moosehide slippers, is mass-marketed and purchased from stores.

A few of the younger men still wear long hair and red or blue folded kerchief headbands of the style often seen among the Navajo and Apache in the American Southwest. At the opposite end of the spectrum, Percy Henry (Plate 10) now makes occasional appearances in his formal Anglican deacon's collar.

While Han handmade clothing has all but disappeared, some rare and beautiful examples of transitional dress were worn by Benny Juneby and his niece Jody Potts (Plate 11) at the Fourth of July parade held in Eagle City in 1997. Both of their beaded moosehide outfits, the beaded vest and the fringed dress, were sewn by Jody's mother and Benny's sister, Adeline Juneby Potts. The wide beaded moosehide headband seems to be a fairly recent development.

Han Folk Art

The early styles of Han clothing in themselves constitute folk art.[40] Beadwork, one component of traditional clothing, continues to be popular among the Han, although most of the items produced are for sale to tourists and are not often worn by the Han themselves. Schmitter mentioned that the commercial trade in beadwork and porcupine quill embroidery was already very strong during the time of his visit in 1906. In an area where wage employment has always been scarce, handmade items have provided women with a steady source of supplemental cash income. Although quill embroidery has since disappeared, some women occasionally make porcupine quill necklaces.

Han beadwork is characterized by couched beads, a sewing technique in which seed beads are strung on one needle and thread and then stitched down to the backing two at a time with another needle and thread. Han pieces all display six or more colors and radial symmetry. Most pieces have flower motifs, with leaves and curling stems embroidered against a tanned moose-skin background.[41]

Items being made today by Han beadworkers include slippers (see Figure 26), barrettes (Plate 12), and eyeglass cases (Plate 13). Apparently one item no longer being produced is the fringed moosehide pillow cover, which seems to have gone out of fashion. The most prominent Han bead sewers in Alaska today are Adeline Juneby Potts, Bertha Ulvi, Ruth Ridley, Angela Harper, Ellen Rada, Rebecca Malcolm, Caroline Fee, Martha Malcolm, and Adeline Gallen.

Perhaps the penultimate Han expressive art is basketry, and the foremost basket artist of the mid to late-twentieth century was the late Sarah Malcolm. Sarah was also a highly competent beader, and her beaded moosehide dress, an exquisite piece of work, remains on permanent exhibit in the Han room at the Wickersham Courthouse in Eagle City. But her artistic reputation was derived primarily from making birchbark baskets, which she began at age twelve, and it was from her many baskets that she received publicity and acclaim all across Alaska.[42]

A willow-root and birchbark basket (Plate 14) made by Martha Malcolm and a birchbark wastebasket made by Sarah (Plate 15) were acquired by the Alaska State Museum in Juneau in the early 1980s. Another taller cylindrical birchbark knitting basket with moosehide fringe and plastic trade beads was purchased from Sarah by Craig Mishler in the late 1970s (Plate 16). Sarah called this latter style of basketry "coffee cans."

Raw birchbark is harvested by Han women and men in spring or early summer from select traditional areas along the banks of the Yukon River at a time when the bark is full of sap. The white outer layer of bark is removed from the tree in two-foot lengths with a sharp knife, tied with willow bark or string, and stored in cylindrical rolls in a dark place to prevent it from getting dry and brittle (Plate 17).

In the process of basket making, the birchbark is reinforced on the edges with red willow bark and lashed together with spruce roots. The spruce roots are dug up with a willow stick. There is a knack for finding just the right kind of tree, one that will produce long straight red roots about one-quarter inch in diameter.

Schmitter said that "birch bark baskets are used, but since they break easily, are of little service except for cooking and drinking utensils on a hunting trip."[43] Nevertheless, birchbark was an important practical item in the Han camping assemblage, and it could be made into cups, plates, cooking containers, baby carrying seats, and storage containers for berries, fish, and meat. One trick for keeping ripened berries fresh over several months is to sew a birchbark lid over the top of the filled basket. Birchbark baskets with folded bottoms are waterproof and can be used for cooking meat or fish when they are filled with water and have hot rocks inserted into them. One of their foremost uses was and is for berry picking (see Chapter 3, Figure 20).

A fresh piece of birchbark can be used like a cast to set a broken arm or leg, and it is also used to make a moose call. For this purpose, a large piece of bark is rolled up into a conical shape like a megaphone, and the hunter hollers into it to amplify his voice. Elisha Lyman once said: "You make a sound like a moose, Oooah! Oooaoah! And the moose hears it, and the moose answers it, and he will come closer, too. He will come over and then you can kill him."[44]

Sarah Malcolm was a versatile artist, having once made a birchbark canoe for the *Dinjii Zhuu Enjit* Museum in Fort Yukon. Some people in Dawson believe that, because she made this canoe without instructions from anyone, she had learned to do it in a former life and was reincarnated. She was also an expert in the manufacture of caribou-skin mukluks, or *etrather kwantrun*. In Sarah's later years, Han birchbark baskets were considered to be more decorative than functional, and most of them were sold for gifts to non-Natives. Thankfully, many ended up in museum collections. In addition to the Alaska State Museum in Juneau, the University of Alaska Museum in Fairbanks and the Field Museum of Natural History in Chicago also hold excellent examples of her work, as do both authors of this book.

Since Sarah's passing, we are fortunate that Sarah's daughter Angela Harper carries on the tradition of birchbark basket making in her mother's way. Sarah's youngest son, Micah Malcolm, has become very skilled at wood carving, making miniatures of such things as log cabins with moss-covered roofs, log caches, fishwheels, toboggans, dog teams pulling sleds, and tiny snowshoes that can be worn as earrings (Figure 46). Micah's miniatures are the continuation of a tradition that goes back at least a hundred years.[45] Rich in nostalgia, Micah's work encapsulates the Han material culture he grew up with in the 1940s and 1950s. At the same time it should be observed that the wood worker is a traditional Han man's occupation, identified in the language as *atsan hohtséi*.

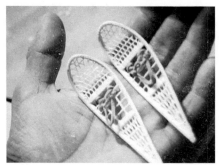

Figure 46. Miniature snowshoes carved by Micah Malcolm.

In recent years Micah has taken to carving small model bush planes of the kind that served Eagle and other parts of rural Alaska during his childhood. His detailed replicas of various airplanes that flew out of Weeks Field in Fairbanks between 1945 and 1952 were formerly on exhibit inside a glass case at the Fairbanks International Airport. They are hand carved from local spruce and birch.[46]

With the opening of the *Tr'ondëk Hwëch'in* Cultural Centre in Dawson in July 1998, a small but growing collection of Han art and material culture has been assembled for public display to tourists. Another small art collection is on exhibit in the downstairs part of the Wickersham Courthouse in Eagle City. The continuous making of fine baskets, moosehide beadwork embroidery, and wood carvings illustrates the many artistic ways in which the Han maintain close spiritual and economic ties to the land and its wild natural resources. By teaching these traditional arts at youth culture camps, the Han are maintaining and strengthening their identity. They are reversing the devastating influence of the gold rush, when assimilation into white culture seemed to be their only option.

Notes

1. Alexander Hunter Murray, *Journal of the Yukon, 1847–1848*. Edited by J. J. Burpee (Ottawa: Publications of the Public Archives of Canada, No. 4, 1910), 1–125.

2. Robert McDonald, Journal, 3 July 1863. David Salmon, a Gwich'in elder and Episcopal priest from Chalkyitsik, thinks the French name *Gens du fous* or *Gens des fous* probably derives from the Han penchant for making up funny stories and teasing people. David Salmon, personal communication to Craig Mishler in Fairbanks, 24 March 2001.

3. Schmitter, *Upper Yukon Native Customs and Folk-Lore*, 16.

4. Ibid.

5. Rooth, *The Alaska Expedition 1966*.

6. Ibid., 287.

7. Mary McLeod quoted in Richard Slobodin, "Notes on the Han," Appendix II to Preliminary Report on Ethnographic Work, 1962. Unpublished Manuscript. Ottawa: National Museum of Man, Ethnology Division, 1963, 17–18.

8. Martha Kates, personal communication to Craig Mishler, 22 August 2000.

9. Primary source materials on Han song and dance are scarce indeed. What little there is can be found in Alexander Hunter Murray's 1847 journal and Schmitter's 1910 monograph. Among the few sources on Han dances are the accounts published in the *Dawson Daily News*, 5 and 7 January 1924, following the 1923 Christmas holidays.

10. Kenneth Thomas Sr., interviewed by Craig Mishler at Tanacross, 8 September 2000; also 30 October 2000. Videotapes and transcripts. Private collection.

11. Doris Adair quoted in Heather Pringle, "People of the Klondike." *Canadian Geographic* 116, No. 6 (November–December 1996): 36–46.

12. Frederick Schwatka's chance encounter with David and Peter took place on the Yukon River at Fort Selkirk, while they were traveling in the company of a young American prospector named Frank Bowker. Schwatka's account of the 1891 expedition and his observations of the tunes being sung or hummed by the Han has recently been reprinted. See Arland S. Harris, ed. *Schwatka's Last Search: The New York Ledger Expedition Through Unknown Alaska and British America* (Fairbanks: University of Alaska Press, 1996), 138.

13. The account of the "squaw dance" at Fortymile that was written by Josiah Spurr is quoted at length in Osgood's ethnography, *The Han Indians*, 135–136). For the original see Spurr's *Through the Yukon Gold Diggings* (Boston: Eastern Publishing Company, 1900), 116–119. In this description the only dance style mentioned is the waltz, but it seems clear that during the gold rush quadrilles or running sets were also introduced. The latter dances take as long as 30 minutes to complete. The only available source on Athabaskan fiddle music and dance is Craig Mishler's *The Crooked Stovepipe: Athapaskan Fiddle Music and Square Dancing in Northeast Alaska and Northwest Canada* (Urbana & Chicago: University of Illinois Press, 1993), a monograph which concentrates primarily on the Gwich'in tradition in Alaska and

northwest Canada. Since the Han intermarried with Gwich'in from Peel River and the Chandalar and traded with the Hudson's Bay Company posts in Fort Yukon and Rampart House, they inevitably acquired many of the same tunes and dances associated with the "upriver style."

14. *Dawson Daily News*, 5 and 7 January 1924.

15. Some documentation of this fiddling has occurred. On December 23, 1973, Craig Mishler recorded Willie Juneby playing his fiddle at home with son Archie on guitar, and one day later, made two tapes of Willie Juneby playing at a Christmas eve dance in Eagle Village. In August 1982, Mishler made an audiotape of Tim Malcolm playing his fiddle with brother Micah on guitar, and in July 1997, he made a videotape of Tim Malcolm performing outdoors on his fiddle with Edward David on guitar. A portion of this tape was broadcast statewide on the televised program, *Heartbeat Alaska*, hosted by Jeanie Green.

16. Gerald Isaac's speech was transcribed with his assistance from a video on the 1994 *Han Gathering, Han Gathering at Moosehide, 1994*. 15 mins. Whitehorse: Northern Native Broadcasting Yukon.

17. For insights into the Han musical revival and play, *Beat of the Drum*, we are indebted to Dan Davidson whose vivid description, "Returning to the Beat of the Drum," appeared in *The Klondike Sun* on 12 July 1996.

18. In July 1997, Craig Mishler videotaped a youth song and drum workshop held at Moosehide Village. The video contains performances of these songs. See "Film and Videotape Sources" in the bibliography.

19. See Leroy McQuesten, *Recollections of Leroy N. McQuesten: Life in the Yukon 1871– 1885* (Dawson City: Yukon Order of Pioneers Dawson City, 1952), 11.

20. Schmitter, *Upper Yukon Native Customs and Folk-Lore*.

21. Ibid., 17–18. For an account of the Dogrib hand game, see June Helm and Nancie Lurie, *The Dogrib Hand Game*. Bulletin No. 205, A.S. No. 71 (Ottawa: National Museum of Canada, 1966).

22. The caribou toe-bone game *ts'ik'e ootth'an* was described to Gordon Marsh by Charlie Stevens in Marsh's unpublished Han Language Field Notes, August 1956, at the University of Alaska Native Language Center Library. A description of this game appears under the English name "Ring and Pin" in the compilation by Michael Heine, Ruth Carroll, and Harvey Scott, *Traditional Dene Games: A Resourcebook* (Yellowknife: Northwest Territories Municipal and Community Affairs, 1996), 42–43. The game is also played by the Gwich'in, Chipewyan, Dogrib, and Slavey. *Traditional Dene Games* describes games played by the Chipewyan, Dogrib, Gwich'in, Hare (Sahtu), and Slavey, but the Han are not directly represented. McKennan's discussion of the Gwich'in willow hoop game *neehilak* is another useful reference. See Robert McKennan, *The Chandalar Kutchin* (Montreal: Arctic Institute of North America, 1965), 48–50.

23. A beautifully illustrated volume on northern Athabaskan dress styles is Judy Thompson's *From the Land: Two Hundred Years of Dene Clothing* (Ottawa: Canadian Museum of Civilization, 1994), although we are sad to say that no examples from the Han are included. Traditional clothing (tunics, mittens, moccasins) along with

baskets, babiche bags, and tools presumed to be Han have been photographed and published on compact disc in the Royal Ontario Museum's *D. A. Cameron Collection: Dawson City, Yukon, 1901–1908* (Toronto: Royal Ontario Museum, 2001).

A more general reference on Han artistry and material culture is the museum exhibition catalog called *The Athapaskans: Strangers of the North* (Ottawa: National Museums of Canada 1974), which contains photographs of two Han items from Moosehide—a wooden hunting bow and a bag made from the leg skins of a bird, ornamented with folded and sewn color-dyed porcupine quills. Cornelius Osgood, in *The Han Indians*, published a photograph of a Han chief's collar made out of moose skin and decorated with red, white, and blue porcupine quills (1971: Plate 3). The collar was collected by Ferdinand Schmitter and donated to the Smithsonian Institution in Washington, D.C.

24. Major sources of information on Han traditional dress and body ornamentation are Murray, *Journal of the Yukon, 1847–1848*; Strachan Jones's report, "The Kutchin Tribes," in *Annual Report of the Smithsonian Institution for 1866*, 320–327 (Washington, D.C.: Government Printing Office, 1872); William Ogilvie's *Exploratory Survey of Part of the Lewes, Tat-on-duc, Porcupine, Bell, Trout, Peel, and Mackenzie Rivers, 1887–88* (Annual Report for the Department of the Interior 1889, Part VIII, Section 3 [Ottawa: B. Chamberlin, 1890]; and Tappan Adney's descriptive essays "Moose Hunting with the Tro-chu-tin" (*Harper's New Monthly Magazine* 100, No. 598 [1900] 494–507); and "The Indian Hunter of the Far Northwest on the Trail to the Klondike" (*Outing* 39 [1902] 623–633).

25. Murray, *Journal of the Yukon*, 94.

26. Ibid., 85.

27. Schmitter, *Upper Yukon Native Customs and Folk-Lore*, 5.

28. Catharine McClellan, "Feuding and Warfare among Northwestern Athapaskans." In *Proceedings: Northern Athapaskan Conference, 1971*, Vol. 1, edited by A. McFadyen Clark. Mercury Series, Canadian Ethnology Service Paper No. 57 (Ottawa: National Museum of Man, 1975), Part 1, 302.

29. The significance of the hawk claw, beaver's shoulder, bear claw, and weasel skin are all detailed in Robert McKennan's unpublished notes at the Rasmuson Library archives, University of Alaska Fairbanks (see McKennan Collection, Series 2 Box 14, Folder 62).

30. Murray, *Journal of the Yukon*, 56.

31. Ibid., 94.

32. William H. Dall, *Alaska and Its Resources* (Boston: Lee and Shepard, 1870), 101.

33. Some of the most telling information about Han dress comes from historic photographs, many of which are included throughout this volume. Richard Slobodin's essay, "The Dawson Boys: Peel River Indians and the Klondike Gold Rush," *Polar Notes*, No. 5 (1963): 24–36, offers insights into the formal dress standards adopted by the Indians at Moosehide during the years 1900–1910.

34. Ogilvie, *Exploratory Survey*, 53.

35. Richard Bowen, *Incidents in the Life*, 92.

36. Adney, *The Klondike Stampede*, 501, 505.

37. Adney, "Moose Hunting with the Tro-chu-tin," 496.

38. Slobodin, "The Dawson Boys," 30.

39. Elizabeth Hayes Goddard, "Yukon and Koyukuk Rivers Alaska—Summer 1934." Typescript, 36. Alaska and Polar Regions Department, Rasmuson Library, University of Alaska Fairbanks.

40. Sources drawn upon in this section are Kate Duncan's *Some Warmer Tone: Alaska Athabaskan Bead Embroidery* (Fairbanks: University of Alaska Museum, 1984) and her more technical doctoral dissertation, *Bead Embroidery of the Northern Athapaskans: Style, Design Evolution, and Transfer* (Ann Arbor: University Microfilms, 1982), which has a brief discussion of Han style markers.

41. Thirteen elegant examples of what appear to be Han beadwork and handicrafts made during the gold rush era now reside at the California Academy of Sciences (CAS), Department of Anthropology, in San Francisco. The collection, which came from Fort Egbert at Eagle City in 1901–1903, includes three pairs of gauntlet-style mittens, three pairs of moccasins (Plate 19), a highly decorated dog sled or toboggan pouch (Plate 20), a rifle case, two pairs of ochre-stained snowshoes, two miniature toboggans, and a powder horn. These objects were donated to the Academy by Mrs. Elizabeth Trueholtz in 1954. Mrs. Trueholtz was apparently the wife or daughter of Clarence Trueholtz, the U.S. Army post surgeon at Fort Egbert from January 5, 1901 until June 16, 1903. Two necklaces or chokers which would seem to be from a Native American culture other than Han (probably Apache) are also identified as being from Fort Egbert, probably mistakenly. Most of the items may be seen online through the CAS Anthropology database by searching for "Han" in the Culture field, checking the "Images" box, and entering "Alaska" in the State/Prov./Dist. field at www.calacademy.org/research/anthropology/collections/Search.htm

42. The collection of essays *From Skins, Trees, Quills, and Beads: The Work of Nine Athabascans* (Anchorage: Institute of Alaska Native Arts, 1984), edited by Jan Steinbright, features a photographic essay and many details on exactly how Sarah Malcolm made her birchbark baskets. Three of Sarah's baskets are illustrated in William Simeone and James Vanstone's monograph on contemporary Athabaskan material culture, *"And He Was Beautiful": Contemporary Athapaskan Material Culture in the Collections of the Field Museum of Natural History*. Fieldiana Anthropology New Series No. 10 (Chicago: Field Museum of Natural History, 1986), 63–64, representing collections at the Field Museum of Natural History in Chicago. For more on Sarah Malcolm it is useful to consult Diana Greene's short essay, "Mukluks, Maklaks, Etrather Kray." *The Alaska Journal* 8, No. 3 (1978), 370. A short biography of Sarah's remarkable life appears in Elva Scott's *Jewel on the Yukon: Eagle City* (Eagle City: Eagle Historical Society and Museums, 1997), 151–155.

43. Schmitter, *Upper Yukon Native Customs and Folk-Lore*, 10.

44. Rooth, *The Alaska Expedition 1966*, 282.

45. Miniature toboggans similar to Micah's are represented in the California Academy of Sciences collection dating to 1901–1902. See note 41 above.

46. Lynn Watson, a newspaper columnist based in Eagle City, provides a solid discussion of Micah Malcolm's expertise as a wood carver and describes his tool kit, all of which fits neatly into a shoebox. See Watson's "Micah Malcolm Carves Mighty Into Micro," *The Northland News* (June 1987): 16.

Chapter Eight

The Han People Today

We are people of the river; we cannot fade away. The Yukon is our lifeline for subsistence and survival.
　　—*William Silas,* The Northland News, *April 1988*

This chapter first presents a narrative history of the Han from World War II to the present. Our narrative, like a churning fishwheel, catches major events and contemporary issues of importance to the Han, even though it allows a lot of smaller fish to escape upriver. After finding an eddy, however, we abandon the broad sweep of Han history and grab our long-handled dip nets to touch the bottom of the river, to reach more deeply into the ethnographic past and present. In the second part of this chapter, we retrieve a single evening in Eagle Village in 1973 and a single day in the same community again in 1997. These ethnographic snapshots allow us to reveal something personal, intangible, and detailed about the Han that cannot be caught by conventional historiography.

Part I. Han History Since World War II

World War II
The coming of the Second World War in 1941 had a profound impact on the lives of the Han. In Eagle Village at least twelve men served in

the U.S. military, most of them trained at the Fort Richardson Army base near Anchorage. Those who served their country during the war include Bob Stacey (Figure 47), Jacob Malcolm, Pete Malcolm, Matthew Malcolm (Plate 7), Charlie Silas, Silas Stevens (Plate 4), David Andrew, and Jim Juneby (Figure 50). Later on, Peter Silas served in Korea, and Harry David Jr. went to Vietnam.[1]

Altogether, this group comprised most of the adult men in the village, and the women and children were left to fend for themselves. Only two of these veterans, Silas Stevens and Matthew Malcolm, are still alive at this writing. Silas told us part of his story. He was drafted right out of high school at Eklutna in 1941 and served on Shemya Island in the Aleutians, along with Charlie Silas, until his discharge in 1946. Silas recalled:

Figure 47. Bob Stacey and Charlie Stevens, 1960.

They [the Japanese] bombed us. I was in a quonset hut. It was wrong side of the runway, at Shemya. They call it "Two-by-Four Island." When I first got there it was just knee-deep mud, that's all it was. No way to get around, even in a big semi-truck. So they finally got the road built, so a couple times they came over us and bombed us, but most of the time before they got to Shemya, they turned them away, you know.[2]

With the war effort underway, the federal government quickly closed down the gold dredges at Coal Creek and Woodchopper Creek. This put a number of Han men out of work, and many of them went into the service. At the same time, construction crews were being hired to work on the Alaska Highway, a road that connected Alaska with Canada and the Lower 48 states. This project provided many new jobs with good wages. Steamboats and barges were also used to carry military vehicles up the Yukon River to Canada (Figure 48), and some of these barged vehicles were apparently used to build the new highway.

Figure 48. The steamboat Klondike *at Eagle City, pushing a barge with World War II military vehicles.*

The Post-War Years

> *It can hardly be overstated that the collapse of the fur*
> *market in 1947 and 1948, coming as it did on the*
> *heels of dramatic social changes brought by the Alaska*
> *Highway, brought complete economic dislocation on the*
> *scale of a disaster to the Yukon Indian people.*
> —Robert McCandless, 1985

Figure 49. Group photo taken in Eagle Village, circa late 1940s. Left to right Dorothy Juneby, Clara Stevens, Angus Alex (wearing Matthew Malcolm's army uniform), Lillian Malcolm, and Martha Stevens.

After the war, the gold mines at Coal Creek and Woodchopper re-opened, and the Bureau of Indian Affairs school in Eagle Village closed. As a result, most of the families in Eagle Village, including the Junebys, the Davids, and the Pauls, moved downriver to work on the dredges.[3] In 1953, when the school in Eagle Village reopened and construction of the Taylor Highway began, these three large families moved back up to Eagle. One photo taken right after the war shows Angus Alex comically wearing the army uniform of Matthew Malcolm (Figure 49). Another from 1949 shows several village families gathered in front of the Episcopal Church (Figure 50).

This was also the period when alcohol abuse started to become a serious community problem. Silas Stevens recalled that during the early

Figure 50. Group portrait taken at Eagle Village Episcopal church, 1949. As identified by Angela Harper and Joanne Beck, left to right: Hannah Stevens, Louise Paul, Annie Billy, Grace Stacey, Angela (Malcolm) Harper, Sarah Malcolm, Fred Stevens, Sophie Stevens, George Malcolm, Bella Biederman, Oliver Lyman, Walter Benjamin, Rev. Crosson, Eliza Malcolm, Mary Paul, Martha Stevens, Elisha Lyman, Jim Juneby, and Little Paul James (also known as Nahtryaa or Bo Tsav).

1940s, even before the war was over, liquor became readily available by air freight from Fairbanks. Before that, he added, "there was just a little homebrew floating around, here and there, now and then."[4]

Easy access to alcohol came in tandem with government welfare programs. Fur prices plummeted between 1947 and 1950 and welfare dependency expanded. Family trapping and hunting out on the land during the winter was largely abandoned as a traditional way of life. These developments put even more stress on Han families. In 1964 an Eagle Village school teacher succeeded in passing a moratorium on liquor sales in Eagle City, and the community has been officially "dry" ever since. Nevertheless, bootleggers have been quick to step in and fill the gap.[5]

Percy Henry complained about the way Canadian government welfare, beginning in about 1955, nearly destroyed his people's willingness to work and their skill in living off the country:

> I say, "We never bother government. Why bother us?" When I was young I never have to go to nobody. If I want money, or if I start to get hungry, I hitch up my dogs and go out in the bush, and there's lots to eat there. Or I can pick up my Swede saw and axe, go out there and cut wood. Money right there. That's how simple it is.[6]

The Taylor Highway

Completion of the Alaska Highway to Fairbanks in 1943 made it possible to build another single-lane highway connecting the Alaska Highway at Tetlin Junction to Eagle and Eagle Village. Construction of the 160-mile Taylor Highway began in 1953 and was completed in 1955. Within a few years, the Taylor was connected to the Top of the World Highway going across the border from Jack Wade to Dawson. As more freight began to be hauled into Eagle and Dawson by truck and airplane, the grand era of the Yukon River steamboats came to an end.

Construction of the Taylor Highway provided new job opportunities for the Han. Before his eyesight deteriorated, Matthew Malcolm drove a Caterpillar and worked for several years to build the Taylor Highway and then to maintain it. Since the Taylor Highway connected Eagle and Eagle Village with Chicken, where there were a lot of mining operations, some villagers such as Tim Malcolm were able to find summer work on the gold dredge there. Tim and his brothers, Matthew and Jacob, also found that the Taylor Highway, although closed in the winter months, provided a smooth and easy access trail for running dog teams up to American Summit and to Champion Creek, where caribou were abundant and the marten trapping was excellent.

Maintained initially by the Territory of Alaska and then by the State for six months each year, the Taylor Highway has greatly reduced the cost of bringing groceries into the village. However, it has also given residents relatively quick access to the liquor stores operating outside the city limits, first at O'Brien Creek and more recently at American Summit. Since its opening, the highway has tragically claimed the lives of several Eagle Village residents making "runs" up the road.

In retrospect, what Robert McCandless has said of the Alaska Highway also applies to the Taylor Highway: "The Alaska Highway's most important effect was an intangible one; it changed people's perception of the land....The highway opened new territory to easy hunting, and effectively closed the old hunting grounds because it was no longer as convenient to get to them...the land itself would seem to shrink as well."[7]

The Taylor Highway is a mixed blessing. It has made it easier for the Han to hunt caribou during their fall migration south through the high country of the Fortymile; it has also increased competition for the Fortymile herd by providing motorized access to non-local hunters.

Non-Natives from Fairbanks and elsewhere have been attracted to Eagle for its great natural beauty and bush lifestyle. As a partial result of the Taylor Highway then, the population of Eagle City has increased steadily since the mid-1960s while the population of Eagle Village has plummeted from sixty-four in 1966 to just twenty-four in 1997 and thirty in 2000 (see Table 1). This is especially significant in view of the relative stability of the David's Band/Eagle Village population between 1888 and 1966.

The Exodus from Moosehide Village

During the 1950s many of the men from Moosehide found jobs in Dawson and began to move their families into town. The resulting drain on the school population led the government, in 1957, to withdraw the village teacher. Reverend Martin, the last full-time resident of Moosehide, moved to Dawson in 1962. In the 1990s a few households have returned to reside at Moosehide year round. Today Moosehide is the site of a summer culture camp run by the *Tr'ondëk Hwëch'in*, and a biannual Han gathering there draws Athabaskan people from throughout the Yukon Territory and Alaska.

Game Laws

One major political difference created by the international border between Alaska and the Yukon is a sharp disparity in game management laws.[8] In the Yukon, First Nations people such as the Han who have negotiated a final land claims agreement with the territorial and federal governments may hunt freely for subsistence in their traditional territory and face no seasons or bag limits except those set by their own First Nation governing council. They may hunt any species and take either cows or bulls. They do not need a license but must have written consent from another First Nation if they are hunting on lands outside their traditional territory.

The Alaskan Han, however, must cope with a tangled web of hunting restrictions created by the State of Alaska and the Federal Office of Subsistence Management. This is due at least in part to the relinquishment of aboriginal hunting and fishing rights by Alaska Natives in settling their land claims with the federal government following the Alaska Native Claims Settlement Act of 1971 (ANCSA).

Hungwich'in Village Corporation lands, being privately owned, are subject to state regulations set by the Alaska Board of Game, and all hunters, Native and non-Native, must now have a state hunting license. Since the mid-1990s, hunting on federal lands, which adjoin most Han village corporation lands, has been regulated by the Federal Subsistence Management Board. The Alaska National Interest Lands Conservation Act (ANILCA), enacted by Congress in 1980, provides a subsistence priority to rural Alaskan residents hunting on federal lands, but this priority is not reserved exclusively for Alaska Natives.

In the upper Yukon and Fortymile River area, state and federal seasons for large game are restricted to the last two weeks of August and the month of September. State bag limits allow just one bull moose to be taken annually in Game Management Unit 20E, the area surrounding Eagle Village. Hunters are limited to bulls with spike-fork antlers for the first part of the season (in late August), and all hunters must enter a drawing in order to hunt antlerless moose.

Caribou hunters in Game Management Unit 20E must obtain a permit by registration, and hunting is limited to Alaska residents with a bag limit of one animal per year. A second resident registration hunt for caribou, designed to serve the needs of local residents, is also available between December 1 and February 28, but the combined bag limit is still only one caribou per year for both seasons. Federal law also prohibits the use of motorized off-road vehicles from August 5 through September 20 in the Glacier Mountain Controlled Use Area north of the Taylor Highway.

The Fortymile Herd

As noted in Chapter 3, the Han have historically depended on caribou for much of their subsistence. They have adapted most closely to the Fortymile herd, although some use of the Porcupine herd is also evident, particularly on the Canadian side. The Fortymile herd winters in the Yukon, migrates northwest into Alaska in the spring, and heads southeast into the Yukon again in the fall, sometimes crossing the Yukon River. A good part of its range lies in the heart of the Han homeland, and the Han have historically benefited from intercepting the herd's annual migration.

Although no records were ever kept, the gold rush to the Fortymile River and the Klondike certainly took a toll on the herd's population between 1896 and 1900. However, by 1920 the Fortymile herd had rebounded to somewhere between 350,000 and 568,000 animals. At that time the herd's range was estimated to extend all the way from Whitehorse to the White Mountains north of Fairbanks.

In the 1930s, for reasons that remain rather mysterious, the Fortymile herd's population crashed to 10,000 to 20,000. By the 1950s it recovered to an estimated 60,000 animals but then nearly vanished in the late 1960s and early 1970s due to overharvesting, heavy predation, and harsh winters. The animals became easy prey for hunters driving up the Taylor Highway during the fall, especially when scouted ahead of time with small planes.

The herd's size remained flat or grew very slowly from the 1980s through the 1990s. Today its former range is greatly diminished. It extends only a few miles into the Yukon Territory and no longer crosses the Steese Highway. In 1994, due to widespread concerns, the Fortymile Caribou Herd Planning Team was organized. This group of Alaskan and Yukon residents and representatives from state, federal, and territorial wildlife management agencies developed a set of recommendations for the Fortymile herd to recover its former range and population. The Han and Tanacross people were included as part of this planning team. Ed Kormendy of Dawson was a key member representing the *Trondëk Hwëch'in*, while Isaac Juneby represented the Han at Eagle Village.

The Fortymile Caribou Management Plan was implemented in 1995, when the herd's population was estimated at 22,000.[9] To aid in the recovery, the Yukon Territorial Government passed regulations banning all sport hunting of the Fortymile caribou. The *Tr'ondëk Hwëch'in* volunteered to give up their subsistence harvest of the herd, directing all of their hunting effort toward the Porcupine herd to the north, accessible via the Dempster Highway. Meanwhile, Alaskans agreed to hunt only 150 bulls per year for subsistence for the duration of the plan (until 2001).

Another key element of the plan was the nonlethal control of wolves. Amid much political controversy, some Alaskan wolves in the Fortymile area were sterilized and others were relocated to other habitats. The commercial trapping of wolves in the area of the herd's calving grounds was encouraged to improve calf survival. By March, 2000, the plan seemed to be working to the advantage of hunters. At that time the herd's population had increased to an estimated 33,000 animals, high enough for the Alaska Board of Game to authorize an increased harvest of 860 animals starting in 2001.

Han Land Claims

The traditional lifestyle still lives in me.
—Howard David, 2001

The American Side

Since the passage of ANCSA, nearly every village in Alaska has been incorporated with an elected President and Board of Directors. With the restoration of at least some of their ancestral lands, the Han now have hope for improving their economic and social well-being. Each person originally enrolled in the village corporation is now a voting shareholder. Under the provisions of ANCSA, the Han in Eagle Village are also shareholders in Doyon Limited, a regional corporation based in Fairbanks and representing many interior Dene villages.

The purpose of these corporations is to select and acquire lands from the federal government, make business investments, and manage their assets for a profit. At this writing the president of the Hungwich'in Corporation is Howard David. To date about 80,000 acres of village lands have been conveyed to the Corporation from the federal government, with another 12,160 selected but still pending transfer (see Map 4). Some of the conveyed lands are actually located within the

Map 4
Hungwitchin Corporation
Conveyed and Selected Lands

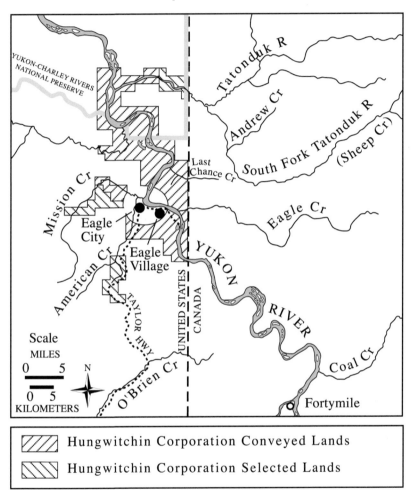

	Hungwitchin Corporation Conveyed Lands
	Hungwitchin Corporation Selected Lands

Yukon-Charley Rivers National Preserve and were selected because of their importance to subsistence. For this reason, the Han have a special interest in the long-term management of the preserve.

In addition to the corporation lands, the Han have selected and acquired individual land parcels called "Native allotments" through the Bureau of Indian Affairs. Most of these Native allotments are based on evidence of a past history of family use for residency and subsistence, and most of the parcels are located within a few miles of the village. A number of Native allotments in and around Eagle Village have been sold to non-Natives for cash, and this trend continued into the late 1990s.

Chief Joanne Beck announced plans in 2000 to move the entire village upriver to a large parcel of land belonging to the the Hungwich'in Corporation. In trying to acquire new federal housing to replace aging log cabins at the village site, she discovered that the Department of Housing and Urban Development was resistant to building there because it is located on a forty-year flood plain. The new site farther upriver is road accessible and offers a high bank and good protection against Yukon River spring flooding.

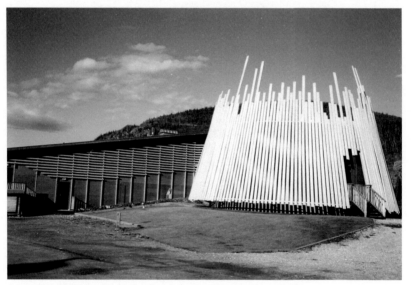

Figure 51. Tr'ondëk Hwëch'in Cultural Centre, Dawson City, July, 2000.

The Canadian Side

In the summer of 1997, after twenty-three years of negotiations with the Canadian federal government, the *Tr'ondëk Hwëch'in* at Dawson reached a framework for settlement of its First Nation land claims.[10] The Han will receive 2,598.5 square kilometers of land and approximately $30 million in cash over the next fifteen years, of which $9 million must be reimbursed to the Canadian government.

Most importantly, the *Tr'ondëk Hwëch'in* will retain aboriginal hunting rights throughout their traditional territory. They will have strong representation on boards and committees assuming responsibility for the management of natural resources in their area, including the Dawson Renewable Resource Council, the Yukon Fish & Wildlife Management Board, the Regional Land Use Planning Commission, the Water Board, the Surface Rights Board, and the Development Assessment Board.

This settlement includes the transfer of the Moosehide and Fort Reliance Reserves to the *Tr'ondëk Hwëch'in*. It also creates the *Tr'oojuu Hwëch'in* Heritage Site at the old village site of "Lousetown," located at the place where the Klondike River empties into the Yukon. The Lousetown or *Tr'ochëk* site will be developed and interpreted under a joint management plan with Parks Canada and the Yukon Territorial Government in such a manner as to provide economic opportunities for the band, possibly through tourism.

A large tract of land—Tombstone Territorial Park west of the Dempster Highway—will be withdrawn from mining and set aside. Percy Henry, one of those who pushed for the withdrawal, described the area as "my university," saying that during tough times the Han could always count on the abundance of the fish and game on the Tombstone and Blackstone River drainages.

The *Tr'ondëk Hwëch'in* will also assert self-government on all their lands. This includes the administration of justice, law-making powers, and the ability to tax. The agreement also makes special provisions for the protection of Moosehide Village and Twelvemile (Chandindu) River.

This settlement was ratified by a 72 percent majority of the *Tr'ondëk Hwëch'in* on June 12, 1998, and signed off on July 16. The agreement has a far-reaching impact on the Alaska Han as well, since anyone with at least one Canadian Han ancestor is entitled to share in the settlement. During the summer of 1997, Joe Joseph of Dawson, one of the land claims negotiators, made an extended visit to Eagle Village to enroll individuals and families in the settlement. This enrollment effort has helped bring the Han nation back together, giving the people a sense of their common heritage through kinship.

Repatriation Efforts

Under the provisions of the U.S. Native American Graves Protection and Repatriation Act of 1990 (NAGPRA), Alaska Native tribes have been reclaiming human remains, funerary objects, sacred objects, and other artifacts taken from their homelands by archaeologists and deposited in museums and federal agencies. The Han at Eagle Village have been among those demanding the return of such items taken from grave sites in their homeland.[11] The *Tr'ondëk Hwëch'in* Final Agreement also contains provisions for repatriation.

At a conference held in Fairbanks in the fall of 1999, Karma Ulvi, a member of the Eagle Village tribal council, announced plans to recover the human remains and artifacts now curated in the collections of the University of Alaska Museum in Fairbanks.

"Our ancestors don't need to be sitting in a museum," she said. "They need to be brought home and reburied on their Native land." The remains in question consist of one partial skeleton, beads, and birchbark excavated on BLM land near the National Park Service visitor center in downtown Eagle City. The discovery of these remains provides additional evidence that the Han were displaced from their original village and forced to move upriver when Fort Egbert was built.

The Yukon Quest International Sled Dog Race

Every February since 1984, the one-thousand-mile Yukon Quest International Sled Dog Race is run between Whitehorse, Yukon, and Fairbanks, Alaska. This long-distance race brings out the most determined and physically fit dog mushers in the North and is extremely popular with Alaska and Yukon Indians. The Yukon Quest is more rugged than its more publicized rival, the Iditarod Trail Sled Dog Race, because it has fewer checkpoints and goes through much colder country with fewer hours of daylight. On even-numbered years, the race starts in Fairbanks, and on odd-numbered years, it starts in Whitehorse.

Eagle Village lies approximately half-way through the Yukon Quest race course, which runs along the Yukon River between Circle and Dawson. The race requires many volunteers as well as corporate sponsors, and the Han eagerly volunteer to staff the checkpoints and provide logistical support. Even though there are no dog mushers in Eagle Village and no Han competing in the race, virtually everyone comes out to watch and cheer on the mushers as they zoom into the village. The race reminds the Han of their own storied past when dog teams pulling toboggans were the only way to get around the Interior from late fall through spring. After the Christmas holidays, this race is the high point of winter.

Han Gatherings

Semi-annual Han "gatherings" have replaced the elaborate memorial potlatches of old as venues for social solidarity. These popular gatherings feature hundreds of people camping outdoors, singing, dancing, making speeches, and feasting. In contrast to funeral and memorial potlatches, they are organized more around friendship than kinship obligations and are open to Dene groups other than the Han. Still, they provide an opportunity for the Alaska Han and the Canadian Han to strengthen social ties and jointly celebrate Han culture.

Han gatherings were perhaps prompted by the success of the modern Gwich'in gatherings, which began in Arctic Village in 1989. The first was held at Moosehide in the summer of 1993, and subsequent ones have taken place in 1994, 1996, 1998, and 2000. Due to the enormous amount of planning and work they entail, Han gatherings are held every other year. The Han people always look forward to them with great excitement.

Moosehide is located in a beautiful natural setting, on a grassy hillside overlooking the majestic Yukon River. The 2000 Moosehide Gathering, held July 27–30, attracted more than five hundred people, including many tourists. It featured workshops, crafts sales and demonstrations, games, and musical performances by diverse Native groups. Those attending were able to ride back and forth from Dawson to Moosehide on small skiffs operated by Han river drivers approximately every ten minutes between 9 A.M. and 9 P.M. Every evening the Han provided a free feast featuring Native foods such as bannock, salmon, moose meat, and moosehead soup, along with western foods.

The theme of the 2000 Gathering was *Ch'onk'ä Ts'än Jëje'in* ("Spirit of Our People"), and a major highlight was the unveiling of a large memorial plaque with the names of everyone known from historic records to have been buried in the Moosehide cemetery. With many people gathered, prayers were offered by Native clergy Percy Henry, Edith Josie, and Effie Linklater, as well as by Father John Terrell of the Anglican Church in Dawson.

Another important Han ceremony at this gathering was the distribution of "first fish," caught by young Han boys from ages nine to twelve at a fish camp downriver from Moosehide. Each boy, having learned how to catch and process fish, was required to give away his first salmon to an elder.

Although the Han performed three songs and dances several times over the four days of the Gathering, the spotlight was really on the many

Figure 52. Han Gathering gift giveaway, July 30, 2000, at Moosehide.

visiting dance groups and musicians who supplied a rich multicultural and intertribal experience. One group consisted of a mix of Navajo and Apache. Another group was the Sleeping Lady Singers from Anchorage, who performed pow-wow style drumming and singing. One of the biggest crowd pleasers was the Miracle Drummers group from St. Mary's and Wasilla, Alaska. This Yup'ik ensemble featured the comical dancer Cornelius Paukan and song composer James Afcan. Sarah and Susie, two fictional Native elders played by Jackie Bear and Sharon Shorty of Whitehorse, performed comic skits in which they flirted shamelessly with the Navajo men.

In the evenings Ben Charlie of Old Crow and Whitehorse played jigs and an assortment of two-steps, schottisches, and waltzes on the fiddle. Old Crow youth dancers demonstrated Gwich'in contras and reels. Other groups that performed were the Naa Luu Disk Gwai Dancers (a mixed Tlingit and non-Tlingit group based in Anchorage), the Northway Dancers, and the Dakwakada Dancers (a Southern Tutchone group from Haines Junction). Winston Wuttunee and his son Stephan of Vancouver Island, British Columbia, led several dance and drum workshops.

On the final day, just before the closing ceremonies, there was a big giveaway by the Han. Since it was preceded by a feast, the giveaway was reminiscent of contemporary potlatches among the Upper Tanana except for these differences: (1) only visitors from other communities (rather than persons of the opposite moiety) received gifts, (2) the gifts consisted almost entirely of household goods with only a few blankets and no rifles, and (3) very little ceremony was involved and very few speeches were given. The most expensive items, which included beaded moosehide moccasins and a large patchwork quilt, were raffled off in a drawing just prior to the giveaway. The 2000 Moosehide Gathering was supported in part by a $20,000 grant from the Community Development Fund of the Yukon Territorial Government.

The Han are working to bring back many of their traditional ways through these gatherings and culture camps, where youth and elders not only talk about but also demonstrate their rich heritage.

The Move into Tourism
The Han have taken two major steps toward capturing tourist dollars while also preserving their culture. The first step was the construction of the Heritage Centre and museum in downtown Dawson in 1998,

and the second is the River of Culture tour started in 2001.[12] River of Culture is a riverboat tour run by Han Natural Products, a subsidiary of Chief Isaac. This business, owned and operated by the First Nation, employs about eleven people, including a boat crew, a cooking and serving crew, and ticketing and reservations staff. The boat, named the *Łuk Cho* (King Salmon), carries up to forty-seven passengers. It is a retrofitted barge that once accompanied the sternwheeler *Brainstorm* when it pushed freight to Old Crow and back during the 1950s and 1960s, and it resembles a miniature steamboat without the paddle wheel. The tour starts with a visit to *Tr'ochëk* (also known as *Tr'oojuu Ech'in*, the former Han fish camp and heritage site) and then proceeds downriver to Moosehide Island, where tourists are served a meal of salmon, bannock, salad, and baked potatoes. Freda Roberts acted as the first on-board Han interpreter and guide.

Part II: Ethnographic Snapshots

Not only is the past recalled in what we see; it is incarnate in what we create.
—David Lowenthal, The Past Is A Foreign Country, 1985

An Evening in Eagle Village

It is Christmas eve, 1973.[13] The air is very cold and dry, and daylight lasts only about four hours. The Yukon is a broad streak of snow, and the line of old log cabins facing the river are all weathered and gray. But the lights are bright at the Eagle Village community hall, where the entire village has gathered to celebrate Christmas, Indian-style. Presents for everyone are piled up under the decorated spruce tree.

At 7:45 P.M. Louise Juneby and Louise Paul lead the singing of hymns and carols. They start with "Silent Night," move on to "It Came Upon a Midnight Clear," and finish with "Hark the Herald Angels Sing."

Santa Claus enters the hall at 8:05 P.M., dressed in a bright red suit and carrying his pack. Everyone recognizes him as Junior Biederman. Santa calls out the names of all of the children, and the presents are distributed to each of them. Then the adults pull the other presents from under the tree and distribute them to one another. They do not open the gifts immediately, but everyone gets something from everyone else, even if it is only a comb or a bar of soap. It is a relaxed informal happy atmosphere, and there are refreshments donated by the store managers in Eagle City, Jess and Kathryn Knight.

At 8:40 P.M. Chief Tony Paul announces that the dance will start after people take their presents home. After the announcement people mill about and trickle out the door. It is almost an hour later when Willie Juneby begins to tune up his fiddle (Plate 8). Willie's silver gray hair is cut into a distinctive brush cut, and he wears black cotton pants,

Figure 53. Eliza Malcolm, August 1973.

a red and gray plaid wool shirt, and blue Sorel boots. He is accompanied on guitar by his son Archie and a young white visitor, Dave Young. The lead-off tune is "Jingle Bells." Hearing the music, people begin to wander back into the hall.

After the musicians have warmed up with "Jingle Bells" the dance begins with "The Red River Jig," a popular step dance performed with one couple on the floor at a time. The lead-off couple is eighty-nine-year-old Grandma Eliza Malcolm (Figure 53) and Santa Claus. Many cheers go up. After about a minute they are spelled by another couple, and then another, until everyone has had a chance. The second dance is a slow waltz, "Over the Waves," followed by "Silver Bells," a two-step played two or three times. The next tune is a schottische and then "Red Wing," another two-step. As Willie plays, he rocks up and down on his toes to keep time, lifting and dropping his heels together to make a steady thump on the wooden floor.

At 10:45 there is a "square dance" with eighteen couples. It is not the kind of four-couple square dance usually done by non-Natives but an old-fashioned "running set" or quadrille, and the tune is "Turkey In the Straw." Tony Paul is the caller. The dance starts with a bow to your partner and a bow to your corner. Then everyone joins hands and circles right. Suddenly they reverse direction, circling left. The "running" begins as the lead-off couple joins hands with the couple to its right, forming a small circle. Now the lead couple breaks off and goes to the couple on its right. They join hands with the man, but the woman from the second couple stands in the center while the other three circle her right and circle her left. Then the man from the second couple stands in the center as the other three circle right and left around him. This step sequence is called "birdie in the cage." After a full revolution these two couples move again to join hands with the third couple, and then on to the fourth. With each couple the circle progressively gets larger and larger until all eighteen couples are engaged.

When the first "birdie in the cage" figure is completed, the first couple advances to the third couple and repeats the figure with them. When the first couple advances to the fourth couple, the second couple advances to the third couple. This time there are two "birdies" and two "cages." The progression continues until the first couple has done the figure with every couple on the floor. The birdies and the cages multiply. One by one the couples drop out of the progression. When the last couple has completed its progression around the floor, everyone swings their partner and promenades home.

Everyone is exhausted, but Willie and the band play on, doing more waltzes, jigs, schottisches, and two-steps. People finally begin to tire. At 12:30 A.M. the dancing ends and everyone gathers around the two Louises to sing a few more carols. Walking back to the cabin in the dark, we hear the crunch of our footsteps in the snow and suddenly realize it is Christmas morning.

A Day in Eagle Village

It is July 8, 1997, early in the morning. The sun has already been up for several hours, but the air is still cool as Oliver Lyman walks from his house down to the riverbank and sits for a few minutes on the wooden bench overlooking the river. He sits on the same bench where his father sat for many years. It is a very small and simple bench, made from two short posts and a board, but it provides an essential reference point for the Han view of the world. It is the seat of the universe.

Oliver's eyes scan the river. As the calm muddy currents of the Yukon swirl by, he observes how the ravens and peregrine falcons nest on the high white rocky bluffs across the river. He is intrigued with the way swallows swoop and dive into their nests in the bank just beneath him. Between the birds and the water, the universe is in motion.

Oliver's attention turns to the fishwheel he and Benny Juneby and some of the other men built just a few weeks ago (Figure 54). The wheel is a sturdy invention that catches salmon as they migrate up the silty Yukon River to their spawning streams. It is handmade from

Figure 54. Community fishwheel at Eagle Village, July 1997.

peeled spruce poles and chicken wire, and it has two baskets or scoops on a center shaft turned by the current.

Oliver quickly notices that the wheel is silent and not turning. He stands up, walks down the bank to the water, and steps out onto the wheel to dislodge a large stick which has drifted down and jammed underneath. The wheel begins turning again, its center shaft creaking as the current pushes heavily against its blades. Before he leaves the wheel, Oliver looks in the box next to the wheel. Inside is a twenty-pound king salmon, which he deftly grabs through the gills and carries to shore.

He takes the fish up to his house and slips it into a clean plastic garbage bag in the storm entrance to his house. Frosty, Oliver's white Samoyed puppy, is gnawing on a bloody salmon head, thrown to him yesterday by his master. The mosquitoes are attracted to the salmon head and swarm in a cloud around the puppy's head. As Oliver enters the house the telephone rings. It is his neighbor, Angela Harper, complaining that her house is cold. She asks Oliver if he could come up and build a fire in her wood stove.

Oliver drops the bag holding the fresh salmon into his white Ford truck and drives downriver about a hundred yards to Angela's place. Normally Angela would not call Oliver, but she has a house guest, Katherine Peter, visiting from Fairbanks, and she is concerned for Katherine's comfort. When Oliver comes in, Angela and her grand-daughter are still half asleep under the covers, but Angela opens her eyes and smiles. Oliver presents her with the fish, and she nods and tells him to set it on the kitchen counter. He builds a fire in the stove and leaves.

It is now 8:00 A.M. and seventy-one-year-old Matthew Malcolm (Plate 7) emerges from his house. Using a rope walkway, he gropes his way down to the gravel road and proceeds across the road to the riverbank. Completely blind, Matthew relies on his walking stick to find his way to his bench. He sits down carefully next to me and pulls out a can of Copenhagen snuff and tucks a pinch into his cheek. "If I run out, I go wild," he says. Within ten minutes a small white pickup truck pulls up in a cloud of dust, and a young white woman, Scarlet Hall, jumps out.

Scarlet greets us and offers Matthew her arm, and they banter amiably as they walk down the trail to Matthew's boat, tied up on the bank. Matthew gets in, and Scarlet lowers the kicker and yanks on the starting rope. In a few seconds the motor is idling, and Scarlet announces that she is ready. Matthew grabs a peeled spruce pole, stands up, and shoves the boat off. I go along for the ride, taking a video camera.

The boat is headed downriver about two miles to Matthew's gill net site, located on the far shore by a small eddy. When we arrive, they drop me off on the rocks where I will be out of the way. The net is anchored to a steel bar driven into the bedrock. Scarlet positions the boat near the shore, and the two begin working the net, untangling the salmon from the webbing. They work steadily, talking excitedly as they pull in a dozen king salmon caught somctime during the night or early morning. Matthew, though blind, does the same thing as Scarlett, relying on his years of experience. Although it is still early in the season, his hands are cut and bruised from handling so many fish.

With the net picked and reset, Scarlet starts the motor and points the boat back upriver. In ten minutes we are back at Matthew's fish camp. One by one, they carry the fish up the beach to the cleaning table. Matthew, relying on his sense of touch, announces which ones are females and which ones are males. He can tell their gender by the texture and touch of their bellies. Full of eggs, the females' bellies are soft and squishy. The males' bellies are firm.

Figure 55. Benny Juneby hanging a king salmon by the riverbank, Eagle Village, July 1997.

223

As Matthew and Scarlet clean the fish, they toss the viscera and some of the heads into a washtub. Scarlet and her husband are fur trappers, and these fish scraps are dried and saved to feed their dog team over the winter. "Nothing is wasted," says Matthew, as he cuts into the bellies. When each fish is cleaned, Matthew carries it down to the river and washes it. When he brings it back up, Scarlet asks Matthew to hold it steady while she attaches a loop of braided cotton rope around the tail. Once it is secure, she hoists the fish and hangs it from a pole under a tarp.

Matthew needles Scarlet, saying, "If I was rich like you I wouldn't be doing this." Scarlet says, "Rich? Me? Are you kidding?" Then she asks Matthew how many whole fish she can take out of the catch. Matthew asks how many they caught. When she says twelve, he tells her to take four.

The Han hang fish in the shade under a structure of spruce poles covered with a large tarp (Figures 14 and 17). Here they may stay for a few hours or overnight until someone else comes down to cut them or build a fire to smoke them. But for now, Matthew and Scarlet have done their share of the work. Scarlet sloshes the cleaning table with a bucket of fresh water, and together she and Matthew carry Scarlet's four fish and the scraps up the trail to her truck.

Matthew finds his way back to his bench and takes a little rest. "Everything is easy now," he says, referring to boats with outboard motors. "We used to take three dogs in the boat with us. We would float down and then after we pick the net we would use those dogs to line the boat back up to the village. Whenever we come up to a bluff we have to paddle across and line up the other side, then paddle back across again. That's how we got our fish home in early days."

It is now 10:00, and Richard Silas and Benny Juneby, two bachelors, are visiting Angela. Angela tells them she needs some birchbark and some spruce roots for her baskets. Would they get her some? The young men go off into the woods and return a few hours later with the desired items. Immediately Angela begins cutting the bark and punching it with an awl so that she can start sewing the pieces. She does this sitting on the front steps of her house in the heat of mid-day. As she works we look up and see the *Yukon Queen* headed upriver. This is the fancy white tourist boat that runs between Dawson City and Eagle. Seven days a week it passes the village, arriving in Eagle City at 11 A.M. and departing at 1:45 P.M. Joanne Beck's teenage son, Jonathan, works as a deckhand on the *Queen*, continuing a long tradition of Han men working on the riverboats.

Plate 10. Mabel and Percy Henry at the Han Gathering, Moosehide, July 29, 2000.

Plate 11. Jody Potts and Benny Juneby in transitional dress, Eagle City parade, July 4, 1997.

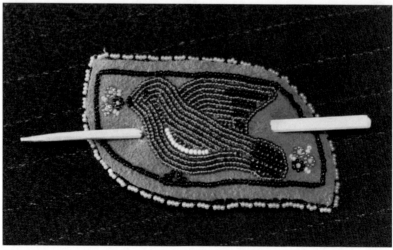

Plate 12. Woman's barrette with beaded bluebird; made by Bertha Ulvi, Eagle, 1997.

Plate 13. Moosehide eyeglass case with beaded flowers; made by Ruth Ridley, Eagle, 1997.

Plate 14. Willow root and birchbark basket; made by Martha Malcolm. Alaska State Museum, Juneau, ASM IIC-270.

Plate 15. Birchbark wastebasket made by Sarah Malcolm. Alaska State Museum, Juneau, ASM IIC-268.

Plate 16. Birchbark knitting basket made by Sarah Malcolm, Eagle, 1975.

Plate 17. Sarah Malcolm rolling up birchbark for basket making, early 1980s.

Plate 18. Elisha "Bugs" Lyman, Eagle Village, August 1973.

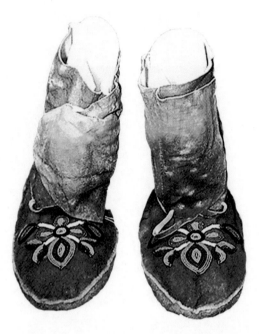

Plate 19. Ankle-wrap moccasins with teardrop bead motif; Fort Egbert, 1901–1902.

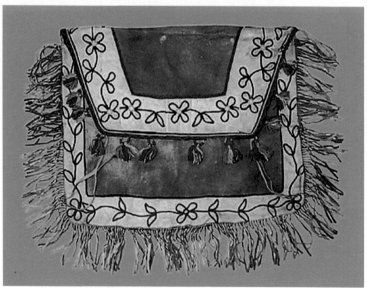

Plate 20. Beaded dog sled or toboggan bag; Fort Egbert, 1901–1902.

Chapter Eight

As the afternoon progresses, the heat drives people from their houses onto their shady front steps. As I drive along the road upriver to Joanne Beck's house, I don't see anyone moving. I'm told that Ruth Ridley is still sleeping, but she doesn't seem to mind being awakened, and before long she brings out a Mason jar full of cold lemonade for me. We sit in the shade and talk for about an hour. A middle-aged Indian man walks up with a can of Budweiser in his hand and sits down on a metal folding chair. He is intoxicated and chats amiably for a few minutes but then passes out in the chair.

At 3:00 Joanne, the village chief, comes home from the clinic where she works as the community health aide and shows me a wild brown baby hare which she found on the side of the highway after someone hit and killed its mother. She has had the "rabbit" now for about four days and feeds it milk with an eye dropper. This adopted "rabbit" will soon fit right in with her hutch operation, where she and her son are raising about fifty domestic rabbits.

Before I know it, Ruth has offered me some dinner, "Have some potatoes and backbone," she says. This means boiled potatoes and king salmon backbone, which are quite tasty. There is very little flesh on the backbone, and it is a part of the salmon that white people throw out, but as Matthew says, for the Han "nothing is wasted."

Back at Matthew's fish camp, Matthew's wife Martha is cutting the morning catch into fillets. Her method of cutting fish is different from that of other Athabaskan women I have seen. She makes a number of one-inch "square" cuts in the flesh, but leaves the skin intact. I help Martha carry a big washpan full of fillets up the bank. She takes the fillets to the smokehouse behind her house and hangs them up to dry. In the smokehouse she gathers a few sticks of green cottonwood and starts a little fire in a cut-down fifty-five-gallon drum. She covers the drum with a piece of tin so it will not get hot, and lets the smoke go to work on the fish. Already there are several skeins of salmon roe hanging next to the cut fillets. Some of the roe will be boiled with rice and onions for tonight's dinner. The rest will be sealed in plastic bags and frozen for winter. Later on I talk to Tim Malcolm, Matthew's younger brother. Tim says he cooks the roe by boiling it with macaroni and adding tomato sauce until it gets good and thick.

Joe Joseph, a Han man from Dawson, stops by and says that he needs to go uptown to the store but doesn't have a ride. Since I want to get to know him a little better, I offer to take him down. Joe is staying in a little camper trailer that sits in front of Oliver's house. He is in the village doing family genealogies to determine which village members have roots on the Canadian side. This is important because of the recent settlement of Canadian Han land claims. Anyone who has Canadian Han blood is entitled to enroll and share in the settlement. This includes most of the Junebys, all of the Davids, all of the Pauls, and possibly some others.

In Eagle City we stop at the Eagle Trading Company store to pick up a few groceries. On our way back we see Ethel Beck doing her wash at the coin-operated laundromat. On the left we pass by the village cemetery and the fresh grave of Louise Paul, who died only ten days ago. Her grave is elaborately decorated with flowers, and the words "Mother to All" are written on the white cross.

At 4:00 a late-model Ford truck arrives in the village. It is Matthew and Martha's daughter Adeline Gallen, who now lives with her family in Northway, an Athabaskan village on the upper Tanana River. On the upper Tanana there are no salmon runs, so Adeline has driven up with two friends to get some salmon from her father's net. She will stay for two days and go out with her father morning and night to pick and process fish, giving Scarlet a couple of days off. Adeline's two friends will also process the salmon, and they will distribute it to many of the households in Northway. These are the rights and privileges conferred by kinship.

In the late afternoon, about 5:00, some dark clouds roll in from the north. Suddenly there is thunder and lightning and a rush of wind. A heavy rain falls for about an hour, and everyone in the village retreats indoors. By 7:00 P.M. the sky is miraculously clear and sunny again.

Ruth Ridley observes the passing rain. She says Han women can change the route of a thunderstorm by making an arrow on the ground out of sticks or rocks and pointing the arrow in the direction they want the storm to go. They often do this while they are out berry picking. In Moosehide they "cut the sky with a knife" to make the sun come out.

By early evening, people are visiting in small groups at various places along the riverbank. Angela and Ruth are trying to get enough people together to play the Indian card game *Bizhur*, and I am eager to play but we can't find a fourth. Martha is lying down and Ruth's sister, Bertha Ulvi, is not to be found. At 8:00 we see Scarlet's truck drive up. She and Matthew go out to check the net and come back in half an hour with ten more salmon. They always go out twice a day, morning and evening, to bring the fish in before they get soft.

Eventually we find Joe Joseph, who agrees to be our fourth, and the card game begins in earnest. *Bizhur* is a lively trump game with no real stakes, and it is made more enjoyable by the old-time country music being played on Angela's tape deck. For two hours it is all George Jones, Loretta Lynn, and Hank Williams, Sr. singing "cry-in-my-beer" classics from the 1950s and 1960s with lots of fiddle and steel pedal guitar. Angela's granddaughter Abigail is in and out of the house, watching the game for a moment but distracted by Geraldine Malcolm's children next door (Figure 56). We sit in the kitchen, and I play partners with Ruth while Angela teams up with Joe Joseph. We have fun.

Angela and Joe win the first game. We play about four or five hands of the second game when Joe and Ruth both announce they are tired and want to quit, so we do. It is still light outside.

I walk down to the riverbank and sit in Matthew's metal folding chair on the gravel bar by his smoking fish. Things are quiet now. The late evening sun, shining low in the northwest, casts a pale light on the wet silvery skins of the hanging salmon. It is a little after midnight when I climb into the truck and drive back down to my canvas tent frame.

Figure 56. Geraldine Malcolm's children, Andrew (left) and Kenneth David, July 1997.

Notes

1. Material about the Han during World War II and the early post-war period is largely derived from interviews and follow-up telephone conversations with Silas Stevens (audiotapes 1–3, 1997).

2. Ibid., audiotape 1.

3. Information about the period when the Eagle Village families worked on the gold dredges at Coal Creek and Woodchopper comes from Louise Paul (audiotape H91-22-43, 1991). Data on the opening and closing of the Bureau of Indian Affairs School in Eagle Village and the Territorial Public School in Eagle City comes from A. F. Gavin's *Walking among Tall Trees*. n.p., c. 1989.

4. Silas Stevens, audiotape 2, 1997.

5. The sad story of alcohol abuse in Eagle Village has been chronicled in considerable detail by local historian Elva Scott in Chapters 5 and 13 of her book, *Health History of the Upper Yukon* (Eagle City, 1983). Serious drinking problems in the community were reported by village teachers as early as 1917–1918. Conditions improved for a while during Prohibition, which ended in 1933, but worsened again in the late 1940s and became acute starting in the early 1960s. See also Robert Jarvenpa's sadly comical experiences with the Han as a young anthropologist working in Dawson and Eagle Village in 1970 in his book, *Northern Passage: Ethnography and Apprenticeship among the Subarctic Dene* (Prospect Heights: Waveland Press, 1999).

6. Percy Henry, audiotape 1, 1999.

7. Robert G. McCandless, *Yukon Wildlife: A Social History* (Edmonton: University of Alberta Press, 1985), 87.

8. Game regulations in the Yukon Territory are published in a booklet, *Hunting Regulations Summary: 2000–2001* (2000), by the Government of the Yukon Department of Renewable Resources. These regulations may be viewed online at: http://www.renres.gov.yk.ca/hunting/.

   Alaskan hunting laws are summarized in *Alaska Hunting Regulations No. 41, July 1, 2000–June 30, 2001*, published by the Alaska Department of Fish and Game and updated annually. They may be downloaded from the Internet at: http://www.state.ak.us/local/akpages/FISH.GAME/wildlife/geninfo/regs/huntregs.htm.

   Federal subsistence hunting regulations for Alaska's Game Management Unit 20 are available for downloading at: http://www.r7.fws.gov/asm/regs00/regs00.html.

9. Source materials for the history of the Fortymile caribou herd and management plan can be found online at the web pages of the U.S. Bureau of Land Management at: http://aurora.ak.blm.gov/40milecaribou/default.htm and at the Alaska Department of Fish and Game website located at: www.state.ak.us/adfg/wildlife/geninfo/game/40-facts.htm.

10. Details of the *Tr'ondëk Hwëch'in* land claims settlement have been published in the *Klondike Sun* for June 13, 1997, June 26, 1998, and July 24, 1998. These issues and others going back to 1996 are available online at the *Sun's* web page: www.yukonweb.com/community/dawson/klondike_sun/.

    Percy Henry's remarks on the Tombstone Park withdrawal appear in *The Klondike Sun*, 4 August 2000.

11. Our summary of repatriation efforts at Eagle Village is drawn from a short article taken from the Associated Press entitled "Villages Go After Remains," appearing in the *Anchorage Daily News* on 18 November 1999.

12. See Heather Robb,"River of Culture Tours," *The Klondike Sun,* 17 August 2001.

13. Events portrayed in "A Night in Eagle Village" are taken directly and literally from Mishler's 1973 field notes. The events portrayed in "A Day in Eagle Village," however, transpired over the course of two weeks while we were working with the Han in Eagle Village in the summer of 1997. I have written about these events as if they all happened on a single day to produce a sustained narrative. All of the events did occur, and the names of the people and dogs are real. The only fictional element lies in their combination and sequence.

Appendix A

Methodology

T HE AUTHORS used multiple methods to write this ethnography. We benefited, first of all, from having visited the Han intermittently for several days at a time over a twenty-four-year period beginning in 1973. Mishler worked in Eagle Village in August and December 1973, in August 1975, and again in July 1982. This gave us some longitudinal comparisons and a few slices of personal experience embedded in recent Han history.

Mishler received permission to work in Eagle Village from Joanne Beck, Chief of the Eagle Village Tribal Council, and in Dawson and Moosehide from Debbie Nagano of the *Tr'ondëk Hwëch'in* First Nation. In March and April 1997, he began doing fieldwork with some of the Han living in Fairbanks, visiting Louise Paul and her daughters Bertha Ulvi and Ruth Ridley, along with Micah Malcolm, Angela Harper, and Silas Stevens. At this time Louise Paul was on kidney dialysis and greatly weakened by illness.

After these initial contacts with elders, we also benefited greatly from an intensive three-week period of field study in July 1997, when we lived only about a mile from the village and visited there as often as three or four times a day. In this residency phase of our fieldwork, we stayed in a rather comfortable furnished tent frame provided for us by the National Park Service at the Eagle airport, located halfway between Eagle City and Eagle Village. Using a state-owned blue Chevrolet pickup truck with a camper shell, we drove back and forth from our living quarters to the village. We also made one trip over the Top of the World Highway to Dawson City. These roads allowed us to traverse some of the traditional upland hunting areas used by the Han today and in the past.

At Dawson we took skiffs back and forth to Moosehide, the elegant old village three miles downriver from Dawson. We spent two days at the Moosehide culture camp, which was attended by Han teenagers living in Dawson. Although the camp lasted two weeks, we were there for only the very last part of it. At Moosehide, an alcohol-free community, we also attended a workshop on Han songs, played an evening of Indian bingo, and took an invigorating boat ride downriver to "Twelve-Mile" (the mouth of the Chandindu) in the cheerful company of Gwich'in elder Victor Henry.

While we were in Eagle Village, we made it a habit to visit the community several times a day just to see who was out and about, although sometimes we were following up on appointments. We sought formal structured interviews, but the Han seemed to be much more comfortable talking informally, so only a few new audiotapes were recorded (see bibliography).

Our village visits were fairly random, starting as early as 8 A.M. and ending as late as midnight. Inevitably, we saw people engaged in a wide variety of work and leisure pursuits, and we often ended up giving people rides to Eagle City, helping to run errands for those without motor vehicles. On numerous occasions we became participant-observers by cutting fish, repairing the fishwheel, shopping for groceries, and playing cards.

After visits to the village, it was our usual practice to return to camp and write up our observations as field notes. For this task we benefited from a portable laptop computer, but we also jotted down numerous particulars in notebooks. We found good additional material at the Eagle Public Library and at the Eagle Historical Society Archives.

One focus of our 1997 field research was to determine the significance of the Han memorial potlatch, now a lost tradition. Why and when was the potlatch, once a central feature of Han social life, discontinued? What happened to all the songs and dances that were an integral part of the potlatch?

Another primary thrust of our fieldwork was the elicitation of family trees. We made this a focus of our research with the hope that we could identify the Han and establish connections between Han living in Alaska and those living in the Yukon Territory. But in this task we were only partially successful. Joe Joseph of Dawson, who was visiting in Eagle Village, shared with us just enough to show how his own family's roots reached across the international border.

Although we interviewed representatives of every family in Eagle Village, we were limited to only five days in Canada in 1997 and did not have an opportunity to interview elders about their family history. By sheer good luck, however, we ran into Percy Henry at the annual meeting of the Oral History Association held in Anchorage in October 1999, and thanks to an introduction by Linda Johnson of the Yukon Archives, we had a chance to interview him at some length.

One final foray into the field came when Mishler attended the large Han Gathering in Moosehide from July 28–30, 2000. This visit led to a friendship and e-mail correspondence with elder Martha Kates, now of Edmonton, Alberta. If we could do anything over again, we would spend more time working with elders in Dawson and Moosehide.

While in the field, we audiotaped a few interviews and documented a few others with written notes, according to the expressed desire of those being interviewed. Additional time in the field was not possible, although more in-depth discussions could have occurred. In both Eagle Village and Moosehide, we took a rather large number of 35 mm color photographs and made three digital videotapes. Those who participated in ethnographic interviews were asked to sign release forms so their words could be used in this book and the tape recordings could be permanently deposited in the Oral History Collection of the Rasmuson Library at the University of Alaska Fairbanks.

It was our mindful practice to pay all of our key respondents, both those participating in ethnographic interviews and those who provided genealogical data. This was not done through direct cash payments while we were in the field but via checks mailed out a couple of weeks after our departure.

Although our practice as co-authors was to collaborate on the contents of each chapter, the division of labor was largely as follows: Mishler wrote most of the Introduction and most of Chapters 4, 6, 7, and 8; Simeone wrote most of Chapters 1, 2, 3, and 5. Mishler sketched out the Methodology in Appendix A, outlined the Han card game rules in Appendix C, and compiled the Han Family Trees in Appendix D; Simeone assembled the bibliography. The historical chronology in Appendix B was largely compiled by Terry Haynes.

Chronology of Major Events in Han History, 1847–1997

A profound process in the history of the upper Yukon for the entire period is the great loss of life from disease. In 1847 there were perhaps eight hundred Han. By 1871, only twenty-four years later, diseases such as smallpox and scarlet fever reduced the population to less than two hundred.

1847: Alexander Hunter Murray opens a trading post for the Hudson's Bay Company at Fort Yukon. For the first time the Han have direct access to European trade goods.

1862: Reverend Robert McDonald, Anglican Church missionary, is assigned to Fort Yukon and travels frequently to nearby Native communities. Some Han learn about Christianity by reading McDonald's translations of the Bible and Anglican prayer book into the Gwich'in language.

1867: The United States purchases Alaska from Russia.

1869: The Hudson's Bay Company is forced to relocate its post from Fort Yukon to Rampart House on the Porcupine River. This diverts Han trading routes.

1871: Robert McDonald travels upriver from Fort Yukon and visits four Han summer camps. He meets Chief Charley at one of them.

1874: Leroy "Jack" McQuesten and Frank Bonfield establish Fort Reliance, the first trading post within Han territory. The Han village of Nuklako is located on an island directly across from the fort.

1875: Reverend Kenneth McDonald, brother of Robert McDonald, makes a missionary visit to Chief Charley's winter camp on the Yukon River and provides the first detailed account of Han subsistence.

1877: Because of competition and problems with the Han, Arthur Harper and Alfred Mayo abandon the post at Fort Reliance.

1879: McQuesten decides to reopen Fort Reliance and heads upriver from Fort Yukon on the sternwheeler Yukon, the first steamboat to enter Han Territory. The elder Han chief Catseah is on board. Enroute to Fort Reliance, they stop at Charley's Village at the mouth of the Kandik River and learn that three Han have died after eating arsenic left behind at the fort to kill off the mouse population.

1880: François Mercier opens a small trading post for the Western Fur and Trading Company near present-day Eagle City at David's Village, a Han community, to compete with the Alaska Commercial Company post at Fort Reliance.

1882: Mercier builds a new single-cabin trading post for the Alaska Commercial Company at David's Village, near the site of the abandoned Western Fur and Trading Company post. He names the new post Fort Bell and it later becomes known as Belle Isle. Stiff competition between the two posts works to the advantage of the Han.

1883: Reverend Vincent Sim of the Anglican Church travels into Han territory and visits David's Village. Sim also preaches to the Han at Fort Reliance.

1883: Gold is discovered on Birch Creek.

1886: The first rich coarse gold placer in the Alaskan interior is discovered near Han Territory. A party led by Howard Franklin, Mickey O'Brien, and Harry Madison stakes a claim thirty miles up the Fortymile River in September, at a site they called Franklin's Bar on Franklin Creek.

1886: Responding to the discovery of gold on the Stewart and Fortymile rivers, Harper and McQuesten abandon Fort Reliance and open a post named Fort Nelson on the Stewart River. Within a year they move their operation to the mouth of the Fortymile River, where a new town springs up. The fur trade becomes secondary to the business of supplying goods to the mining industry as steamboats become more common.

1887: Robert McDonald makes a summer trip upriver from Fort Yukon to visit Han camps, meeting Chief Charley and Chief David. Bishop William Bompas establishes the first Christian mission in Canadian Han territory at Fortymile and remains there until 1901. The site, located on an island, is called Buxton Mission.

1894: Leroy McQuesten founds Circle City, and another boom town is built at the lower limits of the Han homeland.

1896: Two Tagish Indians, Skookum Jim and Dawson Charlie, and non-Native George Carmack discover gold on Bonanza Creek, a tributary of the Klondike River. The mining camps at Fortymile and Circle City empty out almost overnight.

1897: Dawson City is established. In the midst of the gold stampede, the Klondike Han at Tr'ochëk are relocated by Anglican missionaries to the new community of Moosehide, three miles downriver from Dawson.

1898: The overflow of Klondike prospectors, many of whom are disgruntled with Canadian mining laws and customs duties, move west into Alaska and establish Eagle City.

1899: A permanent military district is established on the Yukon River. The U.S. Army establishes the Fort Egbert military reservation at Eagle City, forcing the Han to relocate from the mouth of Mission Creek to present-day Eagle Village.

1899: Congress amends the Customs Acts of 1868 and 1879 to allow the trapping of furbearers by non-Natives. This results in increased competition with Native trappers.

1901: Chief Isaac, along with Walter Benjamin and Little Paul, travel downriver on a steamboat to St. Michael and then on to Seattle and San Francisco as guests of the Alaska Commercial Company. Chief Isaac's return to Dawson is celebrated with much hoopla.

1902: Reverend Charles F. Ensign and his wife replace the Kirks to head the Presbyterian Mission in Eagle, whose population shrinks to less than one hundred people. Reverend A. R. Hoare establishes an Episcopal Church in Eagle Village; for the first time, the Native population has its own church.

1902: Chief David's funeral potlatch is held at Fortymile. David is succeeded as chief by his son Peter.

1906: Ferdinand Schmitter, M.D., is assigned to Fort Egbert. As a result of the good relationship he establishes with the Han at Eagle

Village during his tenure, Schmitter records ethnographic information and traditional stories. His are the first "scientific" investigations among the Han.

1909: Following the death of the Han chief in Eagle Village in 1905, Schmitter reports that invitations to his potlatch were sent "east to the Moosehide Indians up the river, west to the Charley Creek Indians down the river, and south over the hills to the Kechumstuk Indians."

1909: Smallpox breaks out in Eagle Village in February. The Interior Department and the Secretary of War instruct the Fort Egbert post surgeon to take all steps necessary to check the disease and prevent its spread.

1913: Porcupine Paul Josie begins working as a deckhand on the steamboat Yukon, opening the way for many other Han men.

1932: Chief Isaac of Moosehide dies of pneumonia. Cornelius Osgood of Yale University, the first cultural anthropologist to visit the Han, does fieldwork in Moosehide, Eagle Village, and Nation.

1935: In a petition to the Alaska Road Commission, Eagle City residents indicate that residents of Eagle Village had cut brush and trees to make a rough road connecting the two communities in 1934. Because the road is used six months each year for the Eagle-to-Dawson mail run, the petitioners request funding to grade the road. They ask that village residents be hired to do the work under supervision.

1936: Willie Juneby begins working at Heinie Miller's Camp at Sheep Creek (the Tatonduk River), driving a Cat and hauling firewood for the steamboats. The Stevens family also moves there.

1937: The Yukon River floods Eagle Village, forcing everyone to evacuate their homes.

1938: The Biederman family loses the contract it has held for twenty years to deliver the mail by dog team between Eagle and Circle. The mail is now delivered by airplane.

1941–1945: Twelve men from Eagle Village join the military and serve their country in World War II.

1945–1950: The Juneby, David, and Paul families leave Eagle Village and move down the Yukon River to Coal Creek and Woodchopper to work on the gold dredges.

1952–1953: The Eagle Village school reopens and Han families begin moving back upriver from Coal Creek and Woodchopper. Construction work begins on the Taylor Highway.

1954: The S.S. Nenana, the last steamboat operating on the Yukon River, is taken out of service.

1955: Construction of the Taylor Highway is completed, although Eagle Village becomes accessible by road during construction beginning in the summer of 1953. The 152-mile gravel road extends southward from Eagle City to the Alaska Highway.

1957: The school is closed at Moosehide Village, marking a general exodus of families to Dawson City.

1971: The Alaska Native Claims Settlement Act is passed by Congress. Eagle Village becomes part of the regional corporation Doyon, Ltd., and the Tanana Chiefs Conference and launches its own Hungwich'in Village Corporation. Each Han becomes a stockholder in Doyon and Hungwich'in.

1980: U.S. Congress passes the Alaska National Interest Lands Conservation Act (ANILCA), creating the Yukon-Charley Rivers National Preserve.

1993: The first Han Gathering is held at Moosehide Village. It is followed by additional gatherings in 1994, 1996, 1998, 2000, and 2002.

1997: *Tr'ondëk Hwëch'in* land claims agreement is reached with the Canadian federal government.

Appendix C

Han Card Games

C ARD GAMES remain an important part of Han social life. These performance-based descriptions of *Bizhur* and Indian Bingo come from our own participant observation. Card games closely related to *Bizhur*, such as Euchre, are described in *The New Complete Hoyle* (Morehead et al. 1956).

Bizhur ♣♦♥♠
(As played in Angela Harper's kitchen in Eagle Village on July 10, 1997.)

Bizhur is a trump game for four adult players; neither more nor less will suffice. The game is also popular with the Gwich'in, who know it as *Mazhur*, but Ruth Ridley identifies it as a "Yukon River card game," rather than a Gwich'in game. Because of its metaphorical references to "The Company," it seems to be associated with the Hudson's Bay Company and was most likely introduced to the Gwich'in and the Han trading at Fort Yukon in the mid-nineteenth century. The four players sit opposite from one another to form two partnerships or sides, as in

Bridge or Pinochle. Like Bridge and Pinochle, *Bizhur* is organized into hands and tricks, but judging from the rules, the deck, and the course of play, *Bizhur's* closest structural relative seems to be four-handed Euchre.

The Deck

A full pack of fifty-two cards is used but only thirty-six are dealt or drawn. The rank of cards in each suit is A, 10, K, Q, J, 9, 8, 7, 6. One suit, more powerful than all the others, is drawn from the pack and designated as trump or *shriidin* (lit. "knife lying motionless"). In terms of taking tricks, the most powerful card in the deck is the King of Hearts ("Big *Bizhur*" also known as "Heart King"), followed immediately by the Jack of Clubs ("Little *Bizhur*" also known as "Club Jack"). The smallest cards in the deck—the 5, 4, 3, and deuce—form a kitty, which is known as "the Company." When these cards are drawn out of the Company two at a time (two cards are equal to "one dollar") to award the winners of a hand, they are referred to as *laraa* (< French *l'argent*, money). Unlike poker chips, however, these cards have no cash value at the end of the game. Real money is not used, so these cards simply provide a handy means of keeping score without resorting to pen and paper.

Object of the Game

The winner of the game is the side that captures all the "money" and ends up "owning the Company." The winner of each hand receives two cards from the Company, and since there is a total of sixteen cards in "the Company" at the start of the game, a full game nearly always requires a minimum of eight hands.

After all the dollars are paid out of the Company, the two sides or partnerships must begin paying one another "a dollar" (two cards) at a time. This continues until one side goes completely broke, which ends the game. The odds are that the "dollars" will see-saw back and forth between the two sides for a considerable length of time, and this occasionally results in a game lasting eight or nine hours. When Bizhur games become prolonged this way, it is quite common for substitute players to enter. Generally there are other people drifting in and out of the house, either members of the host family, or visitors stopping by to talk and watch the game. This free substitution of players allows a long game to proceed without exhaustion or tedium. Sometimes, however, one or two players make up an excuse to quit, and the game may end before total victory is achieved.

The immediate object of each hand of *Bizhur* is to capture tricks containing "pointers." A point is earned by a side when it captures either an ace or a 10 or when it captures the final trick of the hand. A side that manages to capture the final trick of the hand with a 10 is awarded two extra points. Normally, there are nine points in a hand, and the side that gains at least five of these points will earn "one dollar."

Preliminaries and the Deal
Players arrange themselves around a flat playing surface, which may range from a large kitchen table to the corner of someone's bed. It is customary, however, to cover the playing surface with a folded tablecloth or towel. One person arbitrarily takes it upon himself to shuffle the cards and deal out three cards face down to the other players. The deal begins with the player immediately to the left of the dealer receiving the first card, and so on in a clockwise manner, one card at a time, until all players have three cards.

The Hand Play
When all players have three cards, the two players to the left of the dealer play one card face up. This card is supposed to be a pointer, either an ace or a 10, if such a card has been dealt. Then the dealer turns up trump, and the other two players get an opportunity to play and take the trick. Surprise! This usually gives one side three or four points right away, and the action heats up because the side that wins these three or four points will really be trying to "make bread" on the very next trick. Whoever wins the first hand of a game gets two dollars, which means four cards from the kitty.

The person directly to the left of the dealer leads first. He or she may play any card, and his opponents, as well as his or her partner, may also play any card, for following suit is entirely optional. Nevertheless, the highest card in the suit led takes the trick unless it is trumped or unless either Big *Bizhur* or Little *Bizhur* is played. Play proceeds rapidly clockwise, and the person who takes the trick initiates play on the next trick. All players draw a new card off the top of the deck after each trick, with the person who captured the trick being the first to draw, and the other players drawing in clockwise order.

If someone draws or is dealt the 6 of trump, that person may at any time substitute the 6 for the higher upturned trump beneath the deck. The game continues at a very fast tempo until all the cards have been drawn and those remaining in each player's hand have been played. The Han play their cards without hesitation, almost never taking more than a split second to deliberate which card they will play. In the final draw, the upturned trump goes to the player who draws last. Altogether, there are nine tricks to a hand.

At the end of the hand, the person collecting tricks for each partnership flips over the trick cards face side up in a broad fanfold and verbally counts the pointers. If successful, this person collects "money" from the Company or from the other team.

Strategy

The end-game is usually the most exciting part of the play. After all the draw cards have been taken, there are just three tricks left to be played, and these are usually the highest point-getters. Consequently, most players try to save their "pointers" and their highest trump for these final tricks. Of course, partners try to help each other out by tossing on "pointers" when it becomes obvious or highly likely that a trick will be taken by the first partner to play. In fact, such a strategy is fundamental to a side attempting to "make bread" in the early going.

If the "heart king" (Big *Bizhur*) is played on the last trick, it is worth one point, but if played earlier in the hand, it counts for nothing even though it automatically captures all the other cards. If a player has both the "Heart King" (Big *Bizhur*) and the "Club Jack" (Little *Bizhur*) at the end of a hand, he or she may just toss them both down face up, knowing that no other cards in the deck can challenge these two.

Making Bread

When one side manages to capture all of the first five pointers played in a given hand, it is said to "make bread" or "make bannock." In Gwich'in, bread is called *łuchy'aa*, and a side that "makes bread" is entitled to two dollars (four cards) at the end of the hand instead of the usual one dollar. However, for partners to "make bread," they must capture five points exactly. If someone from the opposing side throws off an extra pointer on the trick that produces the fifth point, thereby making six points instead of the desired five, the result is called "burned bread." The side earning six points will still win the hand but will not be awarded more than the usual "one dollar" and will usually receive a big laugh from the opposing side.

Cheating

A player may warn an opponent that he or she cannot turn all the cards from captured tricks upside down on the table. This is perceived as unfair because players are supposed to remember in their heads how many pointers they need to make "bread" or "bannock." Knowing how many pointers you have taken helps to prevent "burned bread."

A player may not tell his or her partner verbally what card to play and when to play it. This raises complaints of cheating, but it still happens. It is acceptable, however, if you wink at your partner or kick his or her foot under the table to signal that there is a pointer or two waiting to be taken in that trick.

Indian Bingo ♣♦♥♠
(As played in Angie Joseph's cabin at Moosehide on July 16, 1997.)

This card game is not uniquely Han but was introduced by some people living at Ross River at the 1996 Han summer gathering. As noted above, Ross River was also the source of a dance the Han were doing in 1924. In contrast to *Bizhur*, Indian Bingo is a gambling game, although the stakes are pretty limited and no bets are placed. Angie Joseph considers it more fun than gambling at Diamond Tooth Gertie's Casino in Dawson. It is now played by Indians all over the Yukon Territory and is especially well-suited for small groups.

There is no apparent limit to the number of players, but a minimum of four is desirable if only to increase the size of the pots. The more players there are, the harder it is to win, and the bigger the pots become. When we played, there were seven players. Each player needs about ten dollars in quarters to get into the game. There is usually a way to trade currency for quarters when a player runs out of quarters.

The Deck
A full deck of fifty two cards is used.

The Pots
There are three pots of money and thus three ways to win: one is for the dealer's "call card," one is for anyone who hits "bingo," and the third and biggest is placed in the middle for anyone who is dealt two red deuces. This third pot generally grows to be quite large and can be worth at least sixty to seventy dollars. Each "pot" consists of a ceramic soup or cereal bowl containing a large or small stockpile of Canadian quarters.

The Ante
Each player must ante up a quarter into each of the three pots before each hand begins. This amounts to 75 cents per player per hand ($2.25).

As the ante is tossed into the bowl, it creates a ring or jingle according to the size and shape of the bowl.

The Deal

The dealer is the person who last hit bingo, but the game can start with any player. The dealer calls a hot card and deals out five cards to each player one card at a time. Anyone who has the hot card wins the "call card" pot. For example, "Heart four" might be the call card. Players often ask to have this repeated as the deal continues. If someone has the 4 of hearts, he reaches over and cleans out the pot. The call card is restored to the lucky person's hand and play continues.

The dealer starts laying down cards and calling out whatever card it is, regardless of suit. As the dealer lays down the cards, the cards are stacked face up five across. When the fifth card is dropped and announced, the dealer goes back and lays the sixth card down on top of the first, the seventh on top of the second, and so on.

As the cards are called, the players discard their hand face up. If an ace is announced, then any player holding an Ace drops it down on the table face up. If a player has two or three of a kind, the player is allowed to drop both or all three at once. When a player gets down to his or her last card, he or she announces to the group, "Last card!" and the anticipation builds. The excitement is especially high when more than one person announces "Last card!"

A player who can dispose of his or her last card shouts "Bingo!" and claims the pot of money specifically set aside for "Bingo." If no one can make bingo before the dealer lays down and announces all of the cards, everyone has to ante up another quarter into each pot.

Cheating

There is no way to cheat unless a player hides the cards he or she throws on the table and piles them all on top of one another. No one ever inspects the winning bingo hand to see whether a self-proclaimed winner actually won. Bingo is recognized by self-ascription and mutual trust, but the person who is dealt the dealer's call card always turns it face up for everyone to see, as does anyone lucky enough to win the big middle pot with the two red deuces.

Han Family Trees

THERE ARE at least ten distinct Han families whose ancestry we have been able to trace back as many as five or six generations, to the early nineteenth century. Almost all of these are now located primarily in Eagle Village, even though they originally may have come from Charley Village, Moosehide, Fortymile, or other settlements. Many more families exist on the Canadian side that we have not documented.

We have attempted to be reasonably comprehensive for the Alaska Han. Regrettably, however, we have not been able to include some Han families that appear in early censuses but, to our knowledge, have no living descendants. In Chapter 4 we noted that there was a Chief Phillip or Felix at Charley River. However, the only families with the Felix surname we could locate were in Fort Yukon and the abandoned village of Kechumstuk, and it is uncertain whether they are indeed Han.

The Johnson family, which originated at Charley River, moved to Fort Yukon and intermarried with Gwich'in families very early in the twentieth century. There are others, such as the Nukons and the Josies,

who do not appear in the official censuses but were raised in Eagle
Village, speak Hän, and now reside in Old Crow. According to elder
Dick Nukon, his father John Nukon was raised in Fort McPherson but
moved to Dawson and then to Eagle in 1898 where he met and married
his Han wife Miria (see Darbyshire 1989: 43–45; Sherry and Vuntut
Gwitchin First Nation 1999; Livingstone 1999). In 1927 they moved
to Whitestone Village, on the upper Porcupine River, and to Johnson
Creek. They also spent time on the Miner River before settling in Old
Crow in 1950. The Malcolms were also from the Miner River area.
Edith Josie was born in Eagle Village in 1921 and raised there before
moving with her parents and siblings to Whitestone Village in 1940 and
then to Old Crow in 1942, where she still lives. Although her parents
were Peel River Gwich'in, Edith speaks Hän and thinks of herself as
both Han and Gwich'in.

Our sources for these family trees are oral interviews with Han
families, official U.S. censuses from 1900, 1910, and 1920, Episcopal
Church records at the University of Alaska Fairbanks Rasmuson Library,
Anglican Church Records at the Yukon Archives in Whitehorse, and
Bureau of Indian Affairs village census records in the National Archives,
Anchorage. A special thanks goes out to Virginia Joseph of Dawson and
Martha Roberts Kates, now living in Edmonton, Alberta, for assisting
us with Moosehide family trees.

Wherever possible, we have tried to highlight families that have demonstrated intermarriage across the Alaska–Yukon border or between
tribal groups. Due to time and space limitations we have not been able
to trace some of these families down to the present day. The roots are
there but some of the branches are missing. The software database in
which we compiled these genealogies is Personal Ancestral File. As of
this writing there are approximately 388 individuals in the database,
spanning up to seven generations. From Personal Ancestral File, we
were able to export most of the data to our word processor. However,
Personal Ancestral File allows us to keep notes on each individual to
indicate sources and biographical information. None of that personal
data are included here. The compilation date for all of these family trees
is October 7, 2000.

In these family trees each individual name has a number listed to the
left that indicates which generation that individual is in relation to his
or her most distant known family ancestor. In other words, the oldest
known ancestors of each family are considered the first generation and
designated with a 1— next to their names. The second generation from

those ancestors are designated with a 2——, and so on. Spouses, whether by marriage or by cohabitation, are labeled Sp. If there are multiple spouses, they are shown as Sp1 for the first spouse and Sp2 for the second. In parentheses to the right of many individuals is the year of their birth and the year of their death, if known.

When going back to the first generation in each family, it is tempting to try to make connections between them. Old David K'ay, for example, has the same Han name as Old Peter K'ay, ancestor of the Peter and Juneby families. We do know that Chief David had one son named David (Robert McDonald, Journal 17 July 1891) and another son named Peter (*Yukon Sun*, 18 April 1903). So if Old Peter K'ay and Old David K'ay (spelled *Kkaih* in the U.S. Census records) were both sons of Chief David and Eliza, as they seem to be, then the Juneby and David families have a common ancestor.

Although we have not been able to retrieve very many Han personal names, it is clear that many Han still have Hän nicknames, which are an important part of their identity. Individuals in the Joseph family and the Paul family trees are easy to confuse because of the strong admixture of given names and surnames. Thus we encounter a Susie Paul, a Joe Susie Joseph, and a Paul Josie (pronounced Joe–zee). There is a Peter Silas and a Silas Stevens. Even more disturbing is the fact that there appear to be two Chief Charleys.

Many of the first English names adopted by the Han were undoubtedly bestowed on them out of the Bible by early Christian missionaries. We also have a hunch that some came from the names of steamboats such as the three sister ships *The Susie, The Sarah*, and *The Hannah*, which were among the largest and most elegant boats running on the Yukon.

Appendix D

CHIEF CHARLEY FAMILY TREE

1—Chief Charley Nootle (Nootł'ee)* (b. circa 1832) (from the
Old Crow area)
Sp—Sarah (from the Old Crow area)
  2—Grace Charley (b. 1867)
  Sp—William Stacey (1864–1925)
    3—Benjamin Stacey (b. 1892)
    3—Robert "Bob" Stacey (b. 1904)
    Sp—Eva Moffit (from Salcha)
    3—Henry Stacey (1904–1905)
    3—Anna Stacey (b. 1908)
    3—Laura Stacey (1917–1939)
    Sp—Elisha "Bugs" Lyman (1901–1978) †
      4—Jimmy Stacey (b. 1934)
      4—Oliver "Naasa" Lyman (1936–2002)
      4—Arthur William Lyman (b. 1938)
    3—William Hunt Stacey (b. 1913)
  2—Dolphus "Cap" Charley (1884–1945)
  Sp—Victoria (b. 1886)
  2—Myra Charley (adopted) (b. 1892)

*Nootle, *Nootł'ee*, *Nootł'ah*, *Nootł'ët*, and *Nooglit* are variant spellings and pronunciations of the Han word for 'white man.'

†Elisha's father, Old Lyman (Gusuu͟x TÒ'inikit, b. 1861), was a Chilkat Tlingit (see Figure 57).

Figure 57. Old Lyman (originally from Chilkat), c. 1935–1945.

256

CHIEF CHARLEY NOOTLAH AND ROBERTS FAMILY TREE

1—Chief Charley Nootlah (aka Chief Charles) ‡
Sp—Charlotte ✚
 2—Robert Nootlah (aka Chief Robert Charles) (1877–1911)
Sp—Sarah Jane James
  3—Mary Roberts
   4—Fred Harper
  Sp—Charles Rivers
    4—Charles Rivers Jr.
    4—Stanley Rivers
    4—Sarah Rivers
    4—Frank Rivers
    4—Unknown daughter
  3—Gladys Roberts
  Sp—Johnny John
    4—Ada John
  3—Sarah Roberts
  Sp—Dan Curry
  3—Stanley Roberts
    4—Mary Halon
  3—David Charles Roberts
  Sp—Magdalene May Wood
    4—David Esau Roberts
    4—Arthur "Archie" Roberts (1926–1997)
    4—Ada Martha Roberts
    4—Sarah Grace Roberts
    4—Mary Elizabeth Roberts
    4—John Daniel Roberts
    4—Edward Wilfred Roberts
    4—Doris Margery Roberts
    4—Herbert Charlie Roberts
    4—Martha Rose Roberts
    4—Freddy Albert Roberts (1946–1970)
    4—Delores Magdalene Roberts
    4—Marion Laurena Roberts
  3—Bertha Harper (Robert's stepdaughter)
  Sp—Curly Russell
    4—Mary Russell

Note: This chart shows a marriage across the border between a Han man from Fortymile ‡ and a Han woman ✚ from Eagle Village. This family tree has not been extended beyond the fourth generation. It is not known for certain whether Chief Charley Nootlah was a different man than Chief Charley (Charley NootÒ'ee) from the Old Crow area, but several photos lead us to that conclusion, and family members say Charles Nootlah had some Russian blood in him. It is possible, nevertheless, that Charles Roberts was a sibling of Grace and Dolphus Charley and that the two families are indeed one. For reasons unknown, the surname of Roberts rather than Charley or Charles was adopted.

DAVID FAMILY TREE

Myra (1890–1935)
Sp1—David *K'ay* (also known as Old David) (1859–1919)
    2—Elisha David (1911–1923)
    2—Harry David Sr. (1913–1980) † (Figure 58)
    Sp—Bessie Grace Simon (1925–1983) ✚
        3—Shirley Ann David (b. 1944)
        3—Daniel "Danny" David (b. 1946)
        3—Harry David Jr. (b. 1948)
            4—Mary Ann David
            4—Wendell David
        3—Michael John David (1951–1981)
        Sp—Arlene Grant
            4—Ernest Ryan David (b. 1980)
        3—Jimmy Wayne David (b. 1953)
        3—Mary Rose David (b. 1956)
            4—Rita David
        3—Roger David (b. 1959)
        3—Edward James David (b. 1960)
        3—Norman Eldred David (b. 1962)
        3—Howard Eugene David (b. 1966)
        Sp—Deborah Stevens
            4—Michael Eugene Stevens (b. 1984)
    2—Andrew David aka "David Andrew" (b. 1919)
    2—Ellen David ✚
    Sp—Abel Tritt (b. 1912) ✱
        3—Franklin Tritt (b. 1944)
        3—Fannie Tritt (b. 1946)
        3—Daniel Tritt (b. 1949)
        3—Raymond Tritt (b. 1951)
        3—Mary Rose Tritt (b. 1953)
        3—Joel Tritt (b. 1955)—twin of Joseph
        3—Joseph Tritt (b. 1955)—twin of Joel
        3—Jessie Bertha Tritt (b. 1956)
        3—Faith Tritt (b. 1960)
Sp2—Joe Adam
    2—Daniel Adam (b. 1922)
    2—Neil Adam (b. 1924)

Note: This chart shows a marriage across the border between a Han man from Charley Village † and a Han woman from Moosehide ✚, and another between a Gwich'in man ✱ from Arctic Village and a Han woman ✚ from Eagle Village. There are numerous descendants from the third generation of Tritts who are not listed here. Most of them live in Arctic Village and Venetie. It is unclear whether David's Indian name was pronounced *K'ay* ("willow") or GhÅy ("skinny").

Figure 58. Harry David Sr. hauling water with yoke and axe, Eagle Village, December 1973.

JOSEPH FAMILY TREE

1—Old Susie Joseph (1860–1925)
Sp—Selina (b. 1861)
    2—Joe Susie Joseph (1905–1985) †
    Sp—Susan Elsie Simon (1912–1992) ✚
        3—Angie Joseph
        3—Virginia Joseph
        3—Joe Joseph
    2—Martha Joseph (b. 1912)

Note: This family tree has not been extended beyond the third generation. This chart and that of the Isaac, Wood and Simon families (page 260) are designed to show the intermarriage of two Charley Village Han men † to two Han sisters from Moosehide ✚. They do not show all the descendants to the present generation on the Canadian side. See also the Peter and Juneby and the Silas and James family trees.

Appendix D

ISAAC, WOOD, AND SIMON FAMILY TREE

1—Unknown parents
  2—Chief Isaac (from the Eagle Village area), (d. 1932)
  Sp—Eliza Harper (daughter of Catseah)
    3—Agnes Isaac
    3—Edward Isaac
    3—Pat Isaac
    3—Angela Isaac
    3—Fred Isaac
    3—Charlie Isaac
  2—Jonathon "Johnson" Wood (1854–1938) (Eagle Village area)
  Sp–Ellen (d. 1948)
    3—Mary Wood
    Sp—Old Martin Simon
      4—Bessie Grace Simon (1925–1983) ✙
      Sp—Harry David Sr. (1913–1980) †
        (for descendants see David family tree, p. 258)
      4—Susan Elsie Simon (1912–1992) ✙
      Sp—Joe Susie Joseph (1905–1985) †
        (for descendants see Joseph family tree, p. 259)
      4—Eva Simon
      4—Agnes Simon
      4—Martha Simon
      4—Daniel Simon
    3—Magdalene May Wood
    (for descendants see Charley Nootlah family tree)
    3—Michael Wood
    3—James "Jimmy" Wood
    Sp—Lucy James
      4—Irene Silas (adopted)
      4—William Adams Wood (adopted)
    3—Martha Wood
    3—Moses Wood
    3—Edward Wood
  2—Walter Benjamin (1872–1951) (Eagle Village area)
  Sp–Sarah (1884–1943)
    3—Yukon Benjamin (adopted, b. 1906)

Note: This family is not shown past the fourth generation. According to Robert Jarvenpa (1998:46), Chief Isaac's father was the brother of Chief Charley Nootlah of Fortymile.

Figure 59. Chief Isaac's cabin at Moosehide.

JOHNSON FAMILY TREE

1—Johnson ChatÒ'at (b. 1865) (from Charley River)
Sp—Emma (b. 1870) (from Charley River)
    2—Charlie Johnson (b. 1888)
    Sp—Mary (b. 1893)
        3—Lena Johnson
        3—Fred Johnson (b. 1927)
        3—Madeline Johnson (adopted) (b. 1931)
    2—Eva Johnson (b. 1890)
    2—John Johnson (b. 1892)
    2—Joseph Johnson (b. 1893)
    2—David Johnson (b. 1894)
    2—Martha Johnson (b. 1897)
    2—Frances Johnson (b. 1899)
    2—Peter Johnson (b. 1903)
    2—Elliot Johnson Sr. (b. 1908)
    Sp—Lucy Alexander (b. 1911)
        3—Mary Johnson (b. 1931)
        3—Elliot Johnson Jr. (b. 1932)
        3—Edward Johnson (b. 1937)
        3—Christopher Johnson (b. 1939)
        3—Johnny Johnson (b. 1940)
        3—Amos Johnson (b. 1943)
        3—Marian Johnson (b. 1945)
        3—Christy Johnson
        3—Rose Johnson

Note: The chart of the Johnson family tree has not been extended beyond the third generation. It gets extremely large with the fourth generation.

Appendix D

PETER AND JUNEBY FAMILY TREE

1—Chief David (d. circa 1902)
  2—Old Peter *K'ay* (1849–1922)
  Sp—Laura
    3—Sam Peter (1870–1957) †
    (from Charley Village)
    Sp1—Martha (b. 1875)
      4—Charlie Peter (b. 1896)
      4—Elisha Peter (b. 1899)
    Sp2—Myra Sam (b. 1886) ✪ (from Circle)
      4—Edna Peter (b. 1919)
      4—Lois Peter (b. 1921)
      Sp—John Alexander
        5—Nancy Alexander
        5—John Alexander
    3—Paul Peter (1879–1915)
    3—Sarah Peter (1884–1936) ✚
    Sp2—Tom Young (1872–1937) ‡
    Sp1—Big Jim Juneby (1869–1915)
      4—Bob Jim Juneby (b. 1902)
      Sp1—Sarah
      Sp2—Mary
        5—Levi Juneby (1923–1941)
        5—Gladys Juneby (1924–1935)
        5—Jim Juneby (b. 1926)
        Sp1—Dorothy Clara Stevens (b. 1933)
          6—Bob Jim Juneby (b. 1951) †
          (from Eagle Village)
          Sp—Patty Herbert (from Chalkytsik)
            7—Deborah Juneby
            7—Michael Juneby
          6—Lawrence Juneby (b. 1952)
          6—Ivan Steven Juneby (b. 1954)
          6—Lorraine Juneby
          Sp—Ron Fabian
            7—Audrey Fabian
            Sp—James Degrote
              8—Wynter Degrote
              8—Raquelle Degrote
            7—Alicia Fabian
            7—Arlette Fabian
          6—Sarah "Tootsie" Juneby (b. 1960)
          Sp—Tom Evans
            7—Dorothy Juneby
              8—Terrell Juneby
              8—Shania Juneby
              8—another daughter

Appendix D

Sp2—Mary Elizabeth Paul
    6—Paul Juneby (adopted out)
  5—Agnes Alice Juneby (b. 1929)
4—Jacob Juneby (b. 1905)
4—Gladys Juneby (1908–1909)
4—Charlotte Juneby (b. 1909)
4—Willie Jim Juneby (1912–1981) †
(from Charley Village)
Sp—Louise Silas (1917–1986) ✚ (from Moosehide)
  5—Mary Ann Juneby (1935–1960)
  Sp—Silas Stevens (b. 1926) (see Stevens family tree)
  5—Charlie Peter Juneby (b. 1939)
  5—John Juneby
  5—Isaac Juneby (b. 1941)
  Sp—Sandi Leider
    6—Sky Louise "Christy" Juneby (adopted)
  5—Sara Rose Juneby (b. 1944)
  Sp—Horace "Junior" Biederman
    6—Maureen Biederman (b. 1967)
    6—Willard Biederman
    6—Corrine Biederman
    Sp1—Larry Weize
      7—Azia Bree
    Sp2—Leon Toller
    6—David Biederman
    Sp—Corrine
      7—unknown son
  5—Adeline Juneby (b. 1946) ✚
  Sp1—Ray Foster ☆
    6—Patrick "Sonny" Foster
  Sp2—Mike Potts ☆
    6—Jody Ann Potts
      7—Isaiah Potts
      7—Quannah Rose Potts
  5—William Jim Juneby Jr. (b. 1947)
  5—Margaret Carol Juneby
  5—Arthur "Archie" Juneby (b. 1950)
  5—Ellen Juneby (b. 1954)
    6—Arthur Rada
  Sp1—James Frazier Jr.
    6—James Frazier III
  Sp2—Mel Rada
  5—Benjamin "Benny" Juneby (b. 1956)
  Sp—Arlene Pitka
    6—Kenneth Juneby
    6—Mary Ann Juneby
    6—Vivian Juneby

Appendix D

Note: The chart of the Peter and Juneby family tree (pp. 262–263) shows across-the-border marriages between a Han man from Eagle Village † and a Han woman from Moosehide ✖, along with a Han man from Moosehide ‡ and a Han woman from Eagle Village ✖. It also shows marriages between Han men † and Gwich'in women ◉, and between Han women from Eagle Village ✖ and non–Native men ☆.

NUKON, JOSIE, AND PAUL FAMILY TREE

1—Albert Nukon (aka "Old Nukon")
Sp—Jane Nukon
   2—John Nukon (d. 1942)
   Sp—Miria (b. 1902; prounounced like "Mariah")
      3—Jessie Nukon
      Sp—Charlie Thomas
      3—Sarah Nukon
      3—Rachel Nukon
      3—Kenneth Nukon
      Sp—Annie
         4—Doris Nukon
         4—Rachel Nukon
         4—John Nukon
         4—Henry Nukon
      3—Dick Nukon (b. 1927)
      Sp—Marian Abel
         4—Sally Nukon
         4—Gloria Nukon
         4—Christine Nukon
         4—George Nukon
         4—Ken Nukon
         4—Leonard Nukon
   2—Elizabeth (1889–1964) (from Peel River area)
   Sp—"Porcupine" Paul Josie (1884–1963; aka "Paul Porcupine" or Paul Josie) (from the Porcupine River area, Yukon Territory)
      3—Susie Paul (b. 1908; aka "Josie Paul")
      Sp—Louise Malcolm (1921–1997)
         4—Mary Elizabeth Paul (b. 1938)
            5—Harold Paul
         Sp1—Howard Edmunds
            5—Margaret (Maggie) Edmunds
            Sp—Victor Joseph
               6—three unknown children
            5—Barbara Edmunds
         Sp2—Jim Juneby (b. 1926)

4——Paul Juneby (adopted out)
4——Matthew John Paul (b. 1939)
4——Sarah Ann Paul
4——Ethel Margaret Paul (b. 1942)
    5——Joanne Beck
       6——Jonathan Beck
Sp1——Silas Stevens (b. 1926)
Sp2——Max Beck
    5——Tony Beck
    Sp——Twila Christiansen
4——Bertha Sally Paul (b. 1944) ✠
    5——Peter Paul
Sp——Dana Ulvi ☆
    5——Karma Ulvi
4——Anthony "Tony" Paul ◆
Sp——Hannah Wallis ✪ (from Ft. Yukon)
    5——John Robert Paul
    Sp——Ruth Bessett
       6——Darlene Paul
       6——George Anthony Paul
4——Ruth Sharon Paul (b. 1950) ✠
Sp——Mike Ridley ☆
    5——April Ridley
    Sp——David Frank
       6——Victoria Frank
          7——Michael Douglas Frank
          7——Valerie Frank
          7——John Frank
    5——Brian Ridley
3——William Paul (b. 1915)
3——Albert Paul (b. 1917)
3——Amos Paul (b. 1919)
3——Edith Josie (b. 1921)
    4——William Josie
    Sp——Vicki
       5——Tammy Josie
       5——Paul Josie
    4——Jane Josie
    Sp——Jim Montgomery
       5——Charles Montgomery

This chart depicts marriages between an Eagle Village Han man ◆ and a Gwich'in woman ✪ and between two Eagle Village Han women ✠ and non-Native men ☆. The first three generations of this family tree were provided orally by Edith Josie, whos assistance is gratefuly acknowledged.

Appendix D

Figure 60. Edith Josie at Old Crow, April, 2003. Edith is a member of the Order of Canada and the author of Here Are the News, *a collection of columns about Old Crow published in the* Whitehorse Star.

MALCOLM FAMILY TREE

1—Carolyn Malcolm (1865–1935) (from Canada)
  2—Joseph Malcolm (1890–1972) (from Miner River area, YT)
  Sp—Eliza (b. 1884) (from Canada)
    3—Mary Malcolm (1913–1930)
    3—William Malcolm (b. 1920)
    3—Louise Malcolm (1921–1997)
    Sp—Susie Paul (b. 1908) (from Canada) (see Paul family tree)
  2—Edward Malcolm (1899–1948) (came from Canada in 1911) †
  Sp—Sarah Stevens (1904–1991) ✠
    3—Pete Malcolm (1920–1960)
    3—John Malcolm (b. 1922)
    3—Jacob Malcolm (b. 1924)
    3—Matthew Malcolm (b. 1926)
    Sp—Martha Stevens (b. 1933)
      4—Adeline Malcolm (b. 1952) ✠
      Sp—Norman Gallen (from Northway) ‡
        5—Ramona Gallen
          6—2 or 3 children
        5—Matthew Gallen
        5—Norman Gallen Jr.
      4—Rebecca Malcolm (b. 1954)
        5—Diane Malcolm

Sp—Dennis Volkheimer
    6—Kiana Volkheimer
    6—Shoshawna Volkheimer
  5—Richard Malcolm
4—Vernon Malcolm (b. 1956)
  5—3 daughters
4—Edwin Malcolm (b. 1961)
Sp—Astrid
  5—Degan Malcolm
4—Marlene Malcolm (b. 1963)
  5—Alfred
  5—Jessica
4—Geraldine Malcolm (b. 1964) ✚
Sp—Bill Gary David Sr. (from Tetlin) ‡
  5—Gary "J.R." David
  5—Carl David
  5—Alberta David
  5—Andrew David
  5—Kenneth David
3—Nancy Mary Malcolm (b. 1928)
Sp—Charlie John Silas (b. 1921)
(see descendants under Silas family tree)
3—Lillian Malcolm (b. 1931)
3—Mark Malcolm (b. 1933)
3—Timothy Malcolm (b. 1936) ✠
Sp—Annie Flett ✾
  4—Steven Flett
3—Angela Rose Malcolm (b. 1939)
Sp—Art Harper
  4—Edward Arthur Harper
  Sp—Fanny
    5—Abigail Harper
    5—Samantha Harper
  4—Joyce Harper
  Sp—Mickey Roberts
    5—Artisha Roberts
  4—Ron Harper
  Sp—Rachel Gimel
    5—Kimberly Harper
3—Micah James Malcolm (b. 1943)
3—George Edward Malcolm (b. 1945)
Sp—Florida "Flo"
  4—Mark Malcolm

This chart shows the intermarriage of two Han women from Eagle Village ✚ with Upper Tanana men ‡; of a Han man ✠ with a Gwich'in woman ✾; and of a Gwich'in man † with a Han woman from Eagle Village ✚.

STEVENS FAMILY TREE

1—Simon
Sp—Susan (b. 1834)
   2—Big Stephen Simon (b. 1853)
   Sp—Louisa
      3—Mary Stevens (b. 1884)
      3—Charlie Stevens (b. 1889)
      Sp—Hannah Peter (b. 1904)
         4—Louise Stevens
         4—Mary Margaret Stevens (b. 1930)
         4—Dorothy Clara Stevens (b. 1933)
         Sp—Jim Juneby (b. 1926)
         (see descendants under Peter and Juneby family tree)
      3—Martha Stevens (b. 1892)
      3—Sarah Stevens (adopted) (b. 1898)
      3—Elijah Stevens (b. 1899)
      3—Helen Mary Stevens (b. 1904)
      3—Arthur Stevens (b. 1904)
      Sp—Sophie Andrews (1904–1982)
         4—Andrew Peter Stevens (1924–1989)
         4—Silas Stevens (b. 1926)
         Sp1—Mary Ann Juneby (1935–1960)
            5—Walter Silas Stevens (b. 1952)
            Sp—Alice John
               6—Arthur Silas Stevens
            5—Regina Marie Stevens (b. 1953)
            Sp1—Dennis Beatty
               6—Shyanne Beatty
            Sp2—William Goebel
               6—Conan Goebel
               6—Shawna Goebel
            5—Sophie Clara Stevens (b. 1956)
            Sp—James Rustad
               6—Brendan Rustad
            5—William Arthur Stevens (b. 1957)
            Sp—Ula
            5—Deborah Stevens
            Sp—Howard Eugene David (b. 1966)
               6—Michael Eugene Stevens (b. 1984)
         Sp2—Ethel Margaret Paul
         4—Walter Stevens (1929–1962)
         Sp—Elizabeth Whittaker
            5—James "Jimmy" Stevens
            Sp—Mary Ann
               6—Amy Stevens
               6—Jeanine Stevens

```
            6—Kristin Stevens
        5—Brian Stevens
        Sp—Barbara
            6—Dara Stevens
            6—Erika Stevens
        5—Becky Stevens
        Sp—Tim Waggoner
            6—Alissa Waggoner
            6—Joe Waggoner
            6—Ashley Waggoner
            6—John Waggoner
        5—Kathy Stevens
        Sp—Clyde Mayo Sr.
            6—Clyde Mayo Jr.
            6—Charlie Mayo
    4—Clara Stevens (b. 1929)
    Sp—Vern Hooker
        5—Vern Hooker Jr.
        5—Harold Hooker
    4—Martha Stevens (b. 1933)
    Sp—Matthew Malcolm (b. 1926)
    (see descendants under Malcolm family tree)
    4—Titus Stevens (b. 1936)
    4—Freddy Charlie Stevens (b. 1940)
    Sp—Sharon
        5—Joy Marie Stevens
            6—Shawn
            6—Michelle
2—Little Stephen Simon (b. 1872)
Sp—Phoebe
    3—Sarah Stevens (b. 1905)
    Sp—Edward Malcolm (1899–1948)
    (see descendants under Malcolm family tree)
    3—John Stevens
    3—Wilson Stevens
```

Appendix D

SILAS AND JAMES FAMILY TREE

1—Little Paul James aka "Nahtryaa" ("Wolverine") or "Bo Tsaw" ("Picks Up Junk")
Sp—Jane (d. 1932)
    2—Lyman James
    2—Ellen James (b. 1899)
    Sp—Andrew Silas (b. 1890) (son of Captain Silas and Catherine)
        3—Louise Silas (b. 1917) ✠
        Sp—Willie Jim Juneby (b. 1912) ‡
        (see descendants under the Peter and Juneby family tree)
        3—Charlie John Silas (b. 1921)
        Sp—Nancy Mary Malcolm (b. 1928)
            4—Charlie John Silas Jr. (b. 1949)
            4—William Silas (b. 1955)
            4—Richard Andrew Silas (b. 1957)
                5—Samantha Silas
                    6—Charles Silas
            4—Ricky Wayne Silas
            (adopted out—now Ricky Crofoot)
        3—Peter Andrew Silas
        Sp—Kay Green
            4—Patricia Silas
            4—Peter Andrew Silas
            4—Andrew Silas
        3—Caroline Silas (b. 1928)
        Sp1—Bill Jackson
            4—Gloria Jackson
            Sp—Ramsey
                5—Theresa Ramsey
                    6—Cheyenne Ramsey
                5—Eva Ramsey
        Sp2—Charles Fee

This chart shows an across-the-border marriage between an Han man from Eagle ‡ and a Han woman from Moosehide ✠.

Bibliography

Abel, Kerry. *Drum Songs*. Montreal & Kingston: McGill-Queens University Press, 1993.

Adney, Edwin Tappan. "Moose Hunting with the Tro-chu-tin." *Harper's New Monthly Magazine* 100, No. 598 (1900): 494–507.

———. *The Klondike Stampede*. New York: Harper and Brothers, 1900.

———. "The Sledge Dogs of the North." *Outing* 38 (1901): 129–137.

———. "The Indian Hunter of the Far Northwest on the Trail to the Klondike." *Outing* 39 (1902): 623–633.

———. "Yukon Bark Kaiaks." Manuscript, n.d. Box 73, Folder 1. Peabody Essex Museum, Salem, Massachusetts.

Andrews, Elizabeth F. "Report on the Cultural Resources of the Doyon Region, Central Alaska." *Cooperative Park Studies Unit Occasional Paper No. 5*. Fairbanks: University of Alaska, 1977.

———. "Archeological Perceptions of Early Contacts of Han Athabaskans at Eagle, Alaska." *Eagle Historical Symposium*, July 3, 1986.

———. "Archaeological Evidence of European Contact: The Han Athabaskans near Eagle, Alaska." *High Plains Applied Anthropologist* 7, No. 2 (1987): 51–63.

Anonymous. Note to a letter written by a Han man named Arthur. Manuscript 3704. Smithsonian Institution Archives, Washington, D.C., n.d.

———. "Moosehide—A Brief History." Dawson Band Land Claims Office. Dawson City, n.d.

Bibliography

————. "Yukon Yarns." *Alaska-Yukon Magazine* 3, No. 2 (March 1907): 84–87.

Associated Press. "Villages Go After Remains." *Anchorage Daily News*, 18 November 1999: B-4.

Barry, Mary J. "Eagle–U.S.A." *Alaska Northern Lights* 1, No. 3 (1967): 18–20.

Beck, Joanne. Interviewed by William E. Simeone in Eagle Village, 23 July 1997. Notes only.

Bland, Richard L. "Charley Village: Has It Finally Been Located?" Unpublished manuscript. Anchorage: National Park Service, 1994.

Bompas, Charlotte S. *A Heroine of the North: Memoirs of Charlotte Selina Bompas, 1830–1917.* Comp. by S. A. Archer. London: Society for Promoting Christian Knowledge, 1929.

Bowen, Richard John. *Incidents in the Life of the Reverend Richard John Bowen Among the Natives, Trappers, Prospectors, and Gold Miners in the Yukon Territory Before and After the Gold Rush of the Year 1898.* Manuscript in the National Archives of Canada, Ottawa, n.d.

Brooks, Alfred Hulse. "A Reconnaissance from Pyramid Harbor to Eagle City, Alaska, Including a Description of the Copper Deposits of the Upper White and Tanana Rivers." *21st Annual Report of the U.S. Geological Survey, 1899–1900*, Part II (1900): 331–391.

Bureau of the Census, Department of Commerce. *Twelfth U.S. Census, 1900.* Microfilm. National Archives and Records Service, Anchorage.

————. *Thirteenth U.S. Census, 1910.* Microfilm. National Archives and Records Service, Anchorage.

————. *Fourteenth U.S. Census, 1920.* Microfilm. National Archives and Records Service, Anchorage.

Bureau of Indian Affairs, Department of the Interior. *Village Census Rolls, 1940–1966.* RG 75. Microfilm. National Archives and Records Service, Anchorage.

Burgess, George. "St. Paul's Mission." *Alaska Churchman* 5 (August 1911): 24.

Caufield, Richard A. *Subsistence Use In and Around the Proposed Yukon-Charley National Rivers.* Cooperative Park Studies Unit Occasional Paper No. 20. Fairbanks: University of Alaska, 1979.

Chase, Will H. *Reminiscences of Captain Billie Moore.* Kansas City: Burton Publishing Co., 1947.

Clark, Donald. *Fort Reliance, Yukon: An Archaeological Assessment.* Mercury Series, Archaeological Survey of Canada Paper No. 150. Ottawa: Canadian Museum of Civilization, 1995.

Coates, Ken S. "Furs Along the Yukon: Hudson's Bay Company–Native Trade in the Yukon Basin, 1830–1893." *B.C. Studies* No. 55 (Autumn 1982): 50–78.

————. *Best Left Indians: Native-White Relations in the Yukon Territory, 1840–1973.* Montreal & Kingston: McGill-Queen's University Press, 1991.

Cody, Hiram Alfred. *An Apostle of the North: Memories of the Right Reverend William Carpenter Bompas.* New York: E. P. Dutton, 1908.

Cohen, Stan. *Yukon River Steamboats: A Pictorial History.* Missoula: Pictorial Histories Publishing Company, 1982.

Cole, Douglas, and Ira Chaikin. *An Iron Hand Upon the People: The Law Against the Potlatch on the Northwest Coast.* Seattle: University of Washington Press, 1990.

Bibliography

Council for Yukon Indians. *A Finding Aid for Oral History Resources of Yukon First Nations People*. Whitehorse, 1994.

Crow, John R., and Philip R. Obley. "Han." In *Handbook of North American Indians 6: The Subarctic*, edited by June Helm, 506–513. Washington, D.C.: Smithsonian Institution, 1981.

Cruikshank, Julie. *Their Own Yukon: A Photographic History by Yukon Indian People*. Whitehorse: Yukon Press Ltd., 1975.

————. *Athapaskan Women: Lives and Legends*. Mercury Series, Canadian Ethnology Service Paper No. 57. Ottawa: National Museums of Canada, 1979.

————. *Dän Dhá Ts'edeniitth'é: Oral and Written Interpretations of the Yukon Past*. Vancouver & Toronto: Douglas and McIntyre, 1991. Reprinted by University of Washington Press, Seattle, 1997.

Dall, William H. *Alaska and Its Resources*. Boston: Lee and Shepard, Boston, 1870.

Darbyshire, Earl. "Dick Nukon." In *In Their Honor*, 43–45. Whitehorse: Ye Sa To Communications Society, 1989.

Dawson Indian Band. *Han Indians: People of the River*. Dawson City, Yukon, 1988. Also available online at www.trondek.com/history.

Davidson, Dan. "Returning to the Beat of the Drum." *The Klondike Sun*, 12 July 1996.

de Laguna, Frederica. "Matrilineal Kin Groups in Northwestern North America." In *Proceedings: Northern Athapaskan Conference, 1971*, edited by A. McFayden Clark. Vol. 1, 17–145. Mercury Series, Canadian Ethnology Service Paper No. 27, Ottawa: National Museums of Canada, 1975.

Dobrowolsky, Helene. "Hammerstones: A History of Tr'ondek Village." *The Northern Review* 19 (Winter 1998), 226–237. Available online at www.trondek.com/history.

————. and T. J. Hammer. *Tr'ochëk: The Archaeology and History of a Hän Fish Camp*. Dawson City: Tr'ondëk Hwëch'in First Nation, 2001.

Drane, Frederick B. *A Circuit Rider on the Yukon*. Unpublished manuscript, 1925. Drane Collection, Box 7, Folder 15. Fairbanks: Alaska and Polar Regions Department, Rasmuson Library, University of Alaska.

Duncan, Kate. *Bead Embroidery of the Northern Athapaskans: Style, Design Evolution, and Transfer*. Ph.D. dissertation, University of Washington, 1982. Ann Arbor: University Microfilms, 1982.

————. *Some Warmer Tone: Alaska Athabaskan Bead Embroidery*. Fairbanks: University of Alaska Museum, 1984.

Easton, Norm. "Students Enjoy Moosehide Hospitality." *Yukon News* (30 July 1999).

Fisher, Robin. *Contact and Conflict: Indian-European Relations in British Columbia, 1774–1890*. Vancouver: University of British Columbia Press, 1977.

Fortuine, Robert. *Chills and Fever: Health and Disease in the Early History of Alaska*. Fairbanks: University of Alaska Press, 1989.

Gates, Michael. *Gold at Fortymile Creek: Early Days in the Yukon*. Vancouver: University of British Columbia Press, 1994.

Gavin, A. F. *Walking among Tall Trees*. n.p., 1989. Copy at the Eagle Public Library, Eagle and at Rasmuson Library, University of Alaska, Fairbanks.

Gillespie, Beryle. "Nahani." In *Handbook of North American Indians 6: The Subarctic*, edited by June Helm, 451–453. Washington, D.C.: Smithsonian Institution, 1981.

Bibliography

Goddard, Elizabeth Hayes. "Yukon and Koyukuk Rivers Alaska—Summer 1934." Typescript. Alaska and Polar Regions Department, Rasmuson Library, University of Alaska, Fairbanks.

Goodrich, Harold. "History and Conditions of Yukon Gold District in 1897." In *Geology of the Yukon Gold Districts, Alaska, Part III Economic Geology*. Eighteenth Annual Report of the United States Secretary of the Interior, 1896–1897. Washington: U.S. Government Printing Office, 1898), 161–162.

Grant, John Webster. *Moon of Wintertime: Missionaries and the Indians of Canada in Encounter since 1534.* Toronto: University of Toronto Press, 1984.

Greene, Diana. "The Birch Bark Basket: A Tradition of Design." *Alaska Magazine* (December 1977): A18–22.

———. "After the Klondike." *The Alaska Journal* 8, No. 3 (1978): 222–228.

———. "Mukluks, Maklaks, Etrather Kray." *The Alaska Journal* 8, No. 3 (1978): 370.

———. "The Myth of Isolation: Winter's coming and life is back to normal at Eagle." *Alaska Magazine* (October 1979): 6–8; 103–104.

———. *Raven Tales and Medicine Men—Folktales from Eagle Village.* Eagle Village (?): n.p., 1988(?). Copy at Eagle Public Library, Eagle and at Rasmuson Library, University of Alaska, Fairbanks.

Griffin, Kristen P., and E. Richard Chesmore. *An Overview and Assessment of Prehistoric Archaeological Resources, Yukon-Charley Rivers National Preserve, Alaska.* Report AR-15. Anchorage: National Park Service, 1988.

Gruening, Ernest. *The State of Alaska.* New York: Random House, 1954.

Guédon, Marie-Françoise. *People of Tetlin, Why Are You Singing?* Mercury Series, Ethnology Division Paper No. 9. Ottawa: National Museums of Canada, 1974.

Harris, Arland S., ed. *Schwatka's Last Search: The New York Ledger Expedition Through Unknown Alaska and British America.* Fairbanks: University of Alaska Press, 1996.

Haskell, William. *Two Years in the Klondike and Alaska Gold-Fields.* Hartford: Hartford Publishing Company, 1898.

Haynes, Terry L. *The Best Days are Gone: A Visit to Alaska's Fortymile.* Report prepared for the Bureau of Land Management. Boulder: Resource Development Internship Program, Western Interstate Commission for Higher Education, 1977.

Heine, Michael, Ruth Carroll, and Harvey Scott. *Traditional Dene Games: A Resourcebook.* Yellowknife: Northwest Territories Municipal and Community Affairs, 1996.

Heller, Herbert, L., ed. *Sourdough Sagas.* New York: Ballantine Books, 1972.

Helm, June, and Nancy Lurie. *The Dogrib Hand Game.* Bulletin No. 205, Anthropological Series No. 71. Ottawa: National Museum of Canada, 1966.

Henry, Percy, and Mabel Henry. *Han Language Lessons: Klondike-Moosehide Dialect.* Whitehorse: Yukon Native Language Center, 1994.

High School Students of Eagle, Alaska. *Land of the Midnight Sun.* Tok: Alaska Gateway School District, 1980.

Hurtado, Albert L. *Indian Survival on the California Frontier.* New Haven: Yale University Press, 1988.

Jarvenpa, Robert. *Northern Passage: Ethnography and Apprenticeship among the Subarctic Dene.* Prospect Heights: Waveland Press, 1998.

Bibliography

Jones, Strachan. "The Kutchin Tribes." In *Annual Report of the Smithsonian Institution for 1866*, 320–327. Washington, D.C.: Government Printing Office, 1872.

Juneby, Isaac. *Han Language Lessons: Dialect of Eagle, Alaska*. Whitehorse: Yukon Native Language Center, 1994.

———. *Han Language Listening Exercises*. Whitehorse: Yukon Native Language Center, 1995.

Juneby, Willie. Interviewed by Reggie Goebel on 9–10 December 1980. Typescript, Eagle Historical Society Archives, Eagle.

Kari, James. *Tatl'ahwt'aenn Nenn,' The Headwaters People's Country: Narratives of the Upper Ahtna Athabaskans*. Fairbanks: Alaska Native Language Center, University of Alaska, 1986.

Kennicott, Robert. "List of Kutchin Tribes." MS 203-b, circa 1869. Washington, D.C.: National Anthropological Archives.

Knutson, Arthur E. *Sternwheels on the Yukon*. Kirkland, WA: Knutson Enterprises, 1979.

Littlepage, Dean. *Gold Fever in the North: The Alaska-Yukon Gold Rush Era*. Anchorage: Anchorage Museum of History and Art, 1997.

Livingstone, Roxanne. "Whitestone Is Where His Heart Is." *The Yukon News*, 15 September 1999, 16ff.

Lowenthal, David. *The Past Is a Foreign Country*. Cambridge & New York: Cambridge University Press, 1985.

MacGowan, Michael. *The Hard Road to the Klondike*. Trans. V. Iremonger. London & Boston: Routledge and Kegan Paul, 1962.

Malcolm, Sarah. Interviewed by Jerry Dixon and Reggie Goebel on 6 September 1980. Typescript, Eagle Historical Society Archives, Eagle.

Matthews, Richard. *The Yukon*. New York: Holt, Rinehart, and Winston, 1968.

McCandless, Robert G. *Yukon Wildlife: A Social History*. Edmonton: University of Alberta Press, 1985.

McClellan, Catharine. "Feuding and Warfare among Northwestern Athapaskans." In *Proceedings: Northern Athapaskan Conference, 1971*, Vol. 1, edited by A. McFadyen Clark, 181–258. Mercury Series, Canadian Ethnology Service Paper No. 57. Ottawa: National Museum of Man, 1975.

———. *My Old People Say: An Ethnographic Survey of Southern Yukon Territory*. 2 Pts. Publications in Ethnology 6. Ottawa: National Museum of Man, 1975.

———. *Part of the Land, Part of the Water: A History of the Yukon Indians*. Vancouver & Toronto: Douglas and McIntyre, 1987.

McDiarmid, Joy. "Pat Lindgren, Daughter of Chief Isaac." *Yukon Indian News*, 25 October 25 1977, 9.

McDonald, Doyle. First Nations: Council Notes, 1921–1934. Vertical file, Dawson City Museum, Dawson.

McDonald, Kenneth. Journals 1873–1875. Microfilm. Letters and Papers of the Church Missionary Society, London. Winnipeg: Rupert's Land Provincial Archives.

McDonald, Robert. Journals, 1863–1891. Microfilm. Letters and Papers of the Church Missionary Society, London. Rupert's Land Provincial Archives, Winnipeg.

Bibliography

McKennan, Robert A. *The Upper Tanana Indians*. New Haven: Yale University Publications in Anthropology No. 55, 1959.

——. *The Chandalar Kutchin*. Technical Paper No. 17. Montreal: Arctic Institute of North America, 1965.

——. Collected Papers. Fairbanks: Alaska and Polar Regions Department, Rasmuson Library, University of Alaska, Series 2, Box 14, Folder 62, n.d.

McPhee, John. *Coming into the Country*. New York: Farrar, Strauss and Giroux, 1977.

McQuesten, Leroy N. *Recollections of Leroy N. McQuesten: Life in the Yukon 1871–1885*. Dawson City: Yukon Order of Pioneers Dawson City, 1952.

Mercier, François. *Recollections of the Youkon, Memoires for the Years 1868–1885*. Translated, edited, and annotated by L. Finn-Yarborough. Alaska Historical Commission Studies in History No. 188. Anchorage: The Alaska Historical Society, 1986.

Miller, Lloyd Benton. "Eagle Natives seek to exercise old powers." *Tundra Times*, 27 June 1984.

——. "Native Sovereignty Issue Calls for State Negotiation." *Anchorage Daily News*, 22 July 1984.

Mishler, Craig. Eagle Village Field Notes, 1973–1975, 1997. Unpublished.

——. *Born with the River: An Ethnographic History of Alaska's Goodpaster and Big Delta Indians*. Report of Investigations #86-14. Fairbanks: Alaska Division of Geological & Geophysical Surveys, 1986.

——. *The Crooked Stovepipe: Athapaskan Fiddle Music and Square Dancing in Northeast Alaska and Northwest Canada*. Urbana & Chicago: University of Illinois Press, 1993.

——, ed. *Neerihiinjìk: We Traveled From Place to Place: The Gwich'in Stories of Johnny and Sarah Frank*. 2nd ed. Fairbanks: Alaska Native Language Center, University of Alaska, 2001.

——. Sam Peter: Biographical Notes and Gwich'in Texts. Unpublished manuscript, n.d.

Mitchell, William L. *The Opening of Alaska*. Edited by Lyman Woodman. Anchorage: Cook Inlet Historical Society, 1982.

Moessner, Victoria Joan, and Joanne Gates, eds. *The Alaska-Klondike Diary of Elizabeth Robins, 1900*. Fairbanks: University of Alaska Press, 1999.

Montgomery, Jane, Angie Joseph-Rear, and John Ritter. *Han Literacy Lessons*. 3 vols. Whitehorse: Yukon Native Language Center, 1992–1994.

——. *Han Literacy Session: Dawson City, Yukon*. Whitehorse: Yukon Native Language Center, 1995.

Morehead, Albert H., Richard L. Frey, and Geoffrey Mott-Smith. *The New Complete Hoyle*. New York: Doubleday & Company, 1956.

Murie, Olaus J. *Alaska-Yukon Caribou*. North American Fauna No. 54. Washington, D.C.: U.S. Department of Agriculture, Bureau of Biological Survey, 1935.

Murray, Alexander Hunter. *Journal of the Yukon 1847–48*. Edited by J.J. Burpee. Ottawa: Publications of the Public Archives of Canada, No. 4 (1910): 1–125.

Murray, David W. "Self-Sufficiency and the Creation of Dependency: The Case of Chief Isaac, Inc." *American Indian Quarterly* 16, no. 2 (Spring 1992): 169–189.

Bibliography

National Museums of Canada. *The Athapaskans: Strangers of the North*. Ottawa: National Museum of Man, 1974.

Ogilvie, William. *Exploratory Survey of Part of the Lewes, Tat-on-duc, Porcupine, Bell, Trout, Peel, and Mackenzie Rivers, 1887–88*. Annual Report for the Department of Interior 1889, Part VIII, Section 3, Ottawa: B. Chamberlin, 1890.

————. *Information Respecting the Yukon District*. Ottawa: Department of the Interior, 1897.

————. *Early Days on the Yukon and the Story of Its Gold Finds*. London, New York, & Toronto: John Lane, 1913.

Osgood, Cornelius. *The Han Indians: A Compilation of Ethnographic and Historical Data on the Alaska-Yukon Boundary Area*. New Haven: Yale University Publications in Anthropology No. 74, 1971.

Paul, Gaither. Interviewed by William E. Simeone, 10 December 1986. Anchorage, Alaska. Tape and transcript.

Paul, Louise. *Proceedings, Historical Symposium*, 2–4 July 1986, 39–43. Eagle: Eagle Historical Society, 1986.

Pitka, Mike. "First potlatch in over 85 years held by Eagle Village." *The Council* 18, No. 6 (July/August 1993): 3.

Potts, Adeline Juneby. *Walk by the Spirit*. Laramie, Wyoming: Jelm Mountain Press, 1993.

Pringle, Heather. "People of the Klondike." *Canadian Geographic* 116, No. 6 (November–December 1996): 36–46.

Pyle, Ernie. *Home Country*. New York: William Sloane Associates, 1947.

Quehrn, Patricia. *Nineteen Times Water: Entry to the Fortymile*. Report prepared for Bureau of Land Management Boulder, Colorado: Resource Development Internship Program, Western Interstate Commission for Higher Education, 1977.

Quirk, William A, III. *Historical Aspects of the Building of the Washington, D.C.–Alaska Military Cable and Telegraph System, with Special Emphasis on the Eagle-Valdez and Goodpaster Telegraph Lines 1902–1903*. Fairbanks: U.S. Department of the Interior, Bureau of Land Management, 1974.

Ray, Arthur J. "Periodic Shortages, Native Welfare, and the Hudson's Bay Company 1670–1930." In *The Subarctic Fur Trade: Native Social and Economic Adaptations*, 1–20. Edited by Shepard Krech III. Vancouver: University of British Columbia Press, 1984.

Reynolds, Georgeanne Lewis, and James Jordan. *Archeological Reconnaissance of the Yukon-Charley Rivers National Preserve*. Report AR-3. Anchorage: National Park Service, Alaska Region, 1983.

Reinicker, Juliette C., ed. *Klondike Letters: The Correspondence of a Gold Seeker in 1898*. Anchorage: Alaska Northwest Publishing Co., 1984 [published simultaneously in the *Alaska Journal* 14, No. 4, 1984].

Ridley, Ruth. "Moose Hunting on the Yukon." *Theata* 1, No. 1 (1973): 50–55.

————. *Eagle Han Huch'inn Hòdök: Stories in Eagle Huch'inn*. Fairbanks: Alaska Native Language Center, University of Alaska, 1983.

Roberts, Edward. *Han Language Listening Exercises: Trondëk Dialect*. Whitehorse: Yukon Native Language Center, 1996.

Robinson, Sally. The Han: A History of Change, 1847–1910. Unpublished manuscript COR 128 #79/119. Dawson City Museum and Historical Society. Whitehorse: Yukon Archives, 1978.

Rooth, Anna Birgitta. *The Alaska Expedition 1966: Myths, Customs, and Beliefs among the Athabascan Indians and the Eskimos of Northern Alaska.* Section 1, Theologica, Juridica, Humaniora, 14. Lund: Acta Universitatis Lundensis, 1971.

———. *The Importance of Storytelling.* Uppsala & Stockholm: Almquist and Wiskell, 1976.

———. *The Alaska Seminar.* Uppsala & Stockholm: Almquist and Wiskell, 1980.

Rowe, Peter Trimble. "Report of the Bishop of Alaska." In *Annual Report of the Board of Missions of the Protestant Episcopal Church in the United States of America 1910– 11.* Copy on file at Episcopal Church Archives, Austin, Texas.

Royal Ontario Museum, Department of Anthropology. *D. A. Cameron Collection, Dawson City, Yukon, 1901–1908.* Compact disc. Toronto: Royal Ontario Museum, 2001.

Salisbury, Richard F. "Affluence and Cultural Survival." In: *Affluence and Cultural Survival: 1981,* 1–11. Proceedings of the American Ethnological Society, edited by Richard Salisbury and Elisabeth Tooker. Washington, D.C.: American Ethnological Society, 1984.

Salmon, David. Interviewed by Craig Mishler in Fairbanks, 24 March 2001. Notes only.

Schmitter, Ferdinand. *Upper Yukon Native Customs and Folk-Lore.* Smithsonian Miscellaneous Collections, v. 56, no. 4. Washington, D.C.: The Smithsonian Institution, 1910. Reprinted by the Eagle Historical Society, Eagle City, and by the Alaska Historical Commission, Anchorage.

Schneider, William S. "On the Back Slough: Ethnohistory of Interior Alaska." In *Interior Alaska: A Journey Through Time,* 147–194. Edited by Jean S. Aigner et al. Anchorage: Alaska Geographic Society, 1986.

Schwatka, Frederick. *Along Alaska's Great River: A Popular Account of the Travels of the Alaska Exploring Expedition of 1883; Along the Great Yukon River from Its Source to Its Mouth, in British North-west Territory and in the Territory of Alaska.* New York: Cassell, 1885.

———. *Report of A Military Reconnaissance in Alaska Made in 1883.* Washington, D.C.: Government Printing Office, 1885.

———. *A Summer in Alaska.* St. Louis: J.W. Henry, 1893.

Scott, Elva. "Eagle Schools Eighty Years." Unpublished manuscript, 1981.

———. "Health History of the Upper Yukon." Eagle City, Alaska, 1983. Copy on file at ARLIS Library, Anchorage.

———. "Historic Eagle and Its People." Copy on file at Rasmuson Library, University of Alaska, Fairbanks, 1993.

———, ed. *Proceedings, Historical Symposium,* 2–4 July. Eagle City: Eagle Historical Society and Museums, 1986.

———. *Jewel on the Yukon: Eagle City.* Eagle City: Eagle Historical Society and Museums, 1997.

Sherry, Erin, and the Vuntut Gwitchin First Nation. *The Land Still Speaks.* Old Crow, YT: Vuntut Gwitchin First Nation Land and Resources Department, 1999.

Bibliography

Shinkwin, Anne. D., Elizabeth F. Andrews, Russell H. Sackett, and Mary V. Kroul. *Fort Egbert and the Eagle Historic District: Summer 1977.* Technical Report No. 2. Fortymile Resource Area, Tok: U.S. Department of Interior, Bureau of Land Management, 1978.

Silas, William. "Age of Progress Replaces Thinking." *Fairbanks Daily News-Miner*, 30 December 1987.

⸻. "In Eagle, Boundaries Are Only in the Mind." *The Northland News*, February 1988, 5.

⸻. "Yukon River a Force That Has Lots of Respect." *The Northland News*, March 1988, 4.

⸻. "Our Potlatches Give Villages Togetherness." *The Northland News*, April 1988, 8.

⸻. "Despite Change Eagle Still Abounds With Traditions." *The Northland News*, May 1988, 12.

Simeone, William E., and James W. VanStone. *"And He Was Beautiful": Contemporary Athapaskan Material Culture in the Collections of the Field Museum of Natural History.* Fieldiana Anthropology NS, No. 10. Chicago: Field Museum of Natural History, 1986.

Skoog, Ronald. *Ecology of the Caribou (Rangifer tarandus granti) in Alaska.* Ph.D. dissertation. Ann Arbor: University Microfilms, 1968.

Slobodin, Richard. *Band Organization of the Peel River Kutchin.* Ottawa: Department of Northern Affairs and National Resources, 1962.

⸻. "Notes on the Han." Appendix II to Preliminary Report on Ethnographic Work, 1962. Unpublished manuscript. Ottawa: National Museum of Man, Ethnology Division, 1963.

⸻. "The Dawson Boys: Peel River Indians and the Klondike Gold Rush." *Polar Notes*, No. 5 (1963): 24–36.

Schmitter, Ferdinand. *Upper Yukon Native Customs and Folk-Lore.* Washington, D.C.: The Smithsonian Institution, 1910.

Sniffen, Matthew, and Thomas Carrington. *The Indians of the Yukon and Tanana Valleys, Alaska.* Philadelphia: Indian Rights Association, 1914.

Spurr, Josiah. *Through the Yukon Gold Diggings: A Narrative to Personal Travel.* Boston: Eastern Publishing Company, 1900.

Steinbright, Jan, ed. *From Skins, Trees, Quills and Beads: The Work of Nine Athabascans.* Anchorage: Institute of Alaska Native Arts, 1984.

Stuck, Hudson. *Ten Thousand Miles with a Dog Sled: A Narrative of Winter Travel in Interior Alaska.* New York: Charles Scribner's Sons, 1914.

⸻. *Voyages on the Yukon and Its Tributaries: A Narrative of Summer Travel in the Interior of Alaska.* New York: Charles Scribner's Sons, 1917.

⸻. Diaries for 1905, 1911, & 1912. Records of the Protestant Episcopal Church in Alaska. Microfilm 91. Fairbanks: Alaska and Polar Regions Department, Rasmuson Library, University of Alaska.

Thomas, Kenneth Sr. Interviewed by Craig Mishler at Tanacross, 20 August 2000 and 30 October 2000. Videotapes and transcripts. Private collection.

Thomas, Lowell. *Woodfill of the Regulars: A True Story of Adventure from the Arctic to the Argonne.* New York: Doubleday, Doran & Company, 1929.

Bibliography

Thompson, Judy. *From the Land: Two Hundred Years of Dene Clothing*. Ottawa: Canadian Museum of Civilization, 1994.

VanStone, James W. *Athapaskan Adaptations: Hunters and Fishermen of the Subarctic Forests*. Chicago: Aldine Publishing Co., 1974.

Walden, Arthur. *A Dog-Puncher on the Yukon*. New York: Houghton-Mifflin, 1928.

Watson, Lynn. "Micah Malcolm Carves Mighty Into Micro." *The Northland News*, June 1987, 16.

———. "Alcoholic Tells of Her Pain and a Reunion." *The Northland News*, April 1988, 5ff.

Webb, Melody (Grauman). "Eagle: Focus on the Yukon." Unpublished manuscript, National Park Service, 1975. On file at the Rasmuson Library, University of Alaska, Fairbanks.

———. *Yukon Frontiers: Historic Resource Study of the Proposed Yukon-Charley National River*. University of Alaska Cooperative Parks Study Unit, Occasional Paper No. 8. Fairbanks: University of Alaska, 1977.

———. *The Last Frontier: A History of the Yukon Basin of Canada and Alaska*. Albuquerque: University of New Mexico Press, 1985. Reprinted by the University of Nebraska Press, 1993, under the title *Yukon: The Last Frontier*.

Wesbrook, Mary E. "A Venture into Ethnohistory: The Journals of Rev. V. C. Sim, Pioneer Missionary on the Yukon." *Polar Notes*, No. 9 (1969):34–45.

White, Richard. *The Middle Ground: Indians, Empires, and Republics in The Great Lakes Region, 1650–1815*. Cambridge: Cambridge University Press, 1991.

Wickersham, James. *Old Yukon: Tales, Trails, Trials*. St. Paul: West Publishing Co., 1938.

Wright, Allen A. *Prelude to Bonanza: The Discovery and Exploration of the Yukon*. Sydney, BC: Gray's Publishing, 1976.

Young, Stephen B., ed. *The Environment of the Yukon-Charley Rivers Area, Alaska*. Wolcott, VT: Center for Northern Studies, 1976.

Bibliography

EAGLE HAN AUDIOTAPES AT RASMUSON LIBRARY, UNIVERSITY OF ALASKA, FAIRBANKS ORAL HISTORY COLLECTION

H91-22-43 National Park Service
Collection-Yukon Charley
Narrator: Louise Paul with Ruth
Riddley
Interviewer: Bill Schneider
Date: 8/26/91
Restrictions: none
Language: English, Han Athabaskan
Audio quality: fair

H91-22-18 National Park Service
Collection-Yukon Charley
Narrator: Matthew Malcolm
Interviewer: Steve Ulvi and William
Schneider
Date: 8/27/91
Restrictions: None
Language: English
Audio quality: good to excellent

H95-69-06 National Park Service
Collection-Yukon Charley
Narrator: Matthew and Martha Malcolm
Interviewer: Steve Ulvi
Date: 7/26/89
Restrictions: release is required

H95-69-11 National Park Service
Collection-Yukon Charley
Narrator: Sarah Malcolm
Date: 6/16/86
Restrictions: none, release signed by
son Micah Malcolm
Audio quality: very poor, not useable

H95-69-05 Parts 1-3 National Park
Service Collection-Yukon Charley
Narrator: Charley Biederman
Date: 7/16/85; 7/25/86
Restrictions: release required

H91-12-317/320 Songs and Legends
Collection
Narrator: Willie Juneby
Date: 3/8/76
Restrictions: none
Language: Hän Athabascan, English

H91-12-317 Old Days and Ways.
Counting Months of the Year, Indian
New Year's Celebration

H91-12-318 Indian Wars

H91-12-319 Old Tribes and Chiefs
Audio Quality: very poor on H91-317
(not useable); good on 318 & 319

H95-14
Narrator Charley Biederman
Interviewer: Laurel Tyrell
Language: English
Date: 11/29/94
Restrictions: None
Audio quality: good

H91-22-63 National Park Service
Collection-Yukon Charley
Narrator: Louise Paul with Ruth Ridley
Interviewer: William Schneider in
Fairbanks
Date: 3/25/93
Language: English
Restrictions: none
Audio quality: good

H91-12-317
Narrator Willie Juneby
Interviewer: Mary Matthews (?)
Date: 3/8/73
Language: English
Restrictions: none

OTHER HAN AUDIOTAPES

Audio quality: good
Louise Paul #1
Interviewer: Craig Mishler
Craig Mishler private collection
Language: Hän Athabascan and English
Date: 12/7/73
Restrictions: None, but no release
Audio quality: excellent

Louise Paul #2, #3 (with Bertha Ulvi)
Interviewer: Craig Mishler
Alaska Depart of Fish and Game
    Collection
Language: English, Hän Athabascan
Date: 3/20/97; 3/21/97
Restrictions: none; release signed
Audio quality: excellent but on one
    channel only

Sarah Malcolm #1, #2
Interviewer: Craig Mishler
Craig Mishler private collection
Date: 8/15/75
Restrictions: none, but no release
    (deceased)
Audio quality: excellent

Silas Stevens #1
Interviewer: Craig Mishler
Alaska Department of Fish and Game
    Collection
Date: 4/7/97
Language: English
Restrictions: none, release signed
Audio quality: excellent, but on one
    channel only

Silas Stevens #2 and #3
Interviewer: Craig Mishler
Alaska Department of Fish and Game
Date: 11/11/97
Restrictions: none, release signed
Audio quality: excellent

Sarah Malcolm #1 and #2
Interviewer: Yvonne Howard
Yvonne Howard private collection,
    Eagle City
Date: 6/20/90; 6/21/90
Restrictions: none, but no release
    (deceased)
Audio quality: poor

Tim Malcolm
Interviewer: Craig Mishler
Alaska Dept of Fish and Game
Date: 7/11/97
Restrictions: none, release signed

Martha Malcolm
Interviewer: Craig Mishler
Alaska Dept of Fish and Game
Date: 7/20/97
Restrictions: none, release signed

Elisha Lyman #1 and #2
Interviewer: Craig Mishler
Craig Mishler Private Collection
Date: 8/30/73 and 12/22/73
Restrictions: none but no release
    (deceased)

Mike Potts (with Adeline Juneby Potts)
Interviewer: Craig Mishler
Alaska Depart of Fish and Game
Date: 11/14/97
Restrictions: none, release signed
Audio quality: excellent

Percy Henry #1 and #2
Interviewer: Craig Mishler
Craig Mishler Private Collection
Date: 10/11/99
Restrictions: none
Notes: audio quality good; some
    dropouts

Bibliography

FILM AND VIDEOTAPE SOURCES

Documentary footage on Yukon River near Eagle, with Chief Alec, Percy de Wolfe, and an Indian couple at Eagle Village, 1945–1950. Fred and Sara Machetanz Film Collection, Alaska Film Archives, Rasmuson Library, University of Alaska, Fairbanks.

Documentary footage from Eagle Village and Moosehide, 1997. 2 hours. Videography by Craig Mishler. Craig Mishler Private Collection.

Han Gathering at Moosehide, 1994. 15 mins. Whitehorse: Northern Native Broadcasting Yukon.

PERIODICALS

Alaska Weekly, 1932.
Dawson News, 1924, 1932.
Fairbanks Daily News-Miner, 1987–1988.
The Eagle Historical Society Newsletter, Eagle, 1985–present.

The Klondike Sun [available online at www.yukonweb.com/community/dawson/klondike_sun/], Dawson City, 1996–2000.
The Northland News, 1988.
Yukon Indian News, 1977.
Yukon Sun, 1903.

UNPUBLISHED WRITTEN AND PHOTOGRAPHIC ARCHIVAL SOURCES

Anglican Church Archives, Toronto, Ontario, Isaac O. Stringer Collection.

Alaska State Library, Juneau, Alaska, C. L. Andrews Photo Collection (microfiche); Wickersham Collection (photographs).

Bancroft Library, University of California, Berkeley, California George Davidson Collection of historical photographs. "Views of Camp Davidson and Alaska, presented to Professor George S. Davidson by D.M. Kingsbury."

California Academy of Sciences, San Francisco, Elizabeth Trueholz Collection (artifacts and photographs of artifacts from Fort Egbert).

Dawson City Museum, Klondike History Library, Dawson City Yukon Territory Vertical Files (microfilm periodicals).

Eagle Historical Society Archives, Eagle City, Alaska (Episcopal Church burial records, photographs, interview transcripts, and other documents).

Episcopal Church Archives, Austin, Texas RG62-30 (Rev. Augustus Hoare); RG62-7 (George Boulter); RG62-45 (Rev. Jules Prevost).

Glenbow Museum Archives, Calgary, Alberta, Alexander Hunter Murray Fonds.

Gonzaga University, Spokane, Washington, Society of Jesus Alaska Missions Collection (microfilm rolls 7 and 36; copies on file at the University of Alaska, Anchorage Archives, Consortium Library).

McGill University Libraries, Department of Rare Books and Special Collections, Montreal, Quebec (Tappan Adney, Klondike Negatives).

Peabody Essex Museum, Salem, Massachusetts (Tappan Adney papers and drawings).

Rupert's Land Provincial Archives, Winnipeg, Manitoba, Letters and Papers of the Church Missionary Society, London (microfilm).

University of Alaska, Anchorage, Archives, Consortium Library, United States Army, Adjutant General's Office. Post Returns, Fort Egbert (Alaska); 1899–1911 (microfilm).

University of Alaska, Alaska Native Language Center Library, Fairbanks, Alaska, Gordon Marsh, Hän Language Field Notes, August 1956. 128 pp.

University of Alaska, Fairbanks, Rasmuson Library, Alaska and Polar Regions Department, Fairbanks Mertie Baggen Papers 1964–67 Field Notes, Box 1; Frederick Drane Collection, Box 7; Charles S. Farnsworth Collection; Robert J. Farnsworth Collection; Elizabeth Hayes Goddard Collection; Robert A. McKennan Collection; Hudson Stuck Collection.

Washington State Historical Society, Special Collections Division, Tacoma, Washington, Asahel Curtis Collection.

Yukon Archives, Whitehore, Yukon Martha Kates Collection; Claude B. Tidd Collection; Bishop William A. Geddes Collection; Bishop Isaac O. Stringer Collection; Mary Davis Anderson Moody Collection; Tappan Adney Collection; Dr. Andrew S. Grant Collection; Walter Jonas Collection.

Index

Page numbers in *italics* refer to illustrations.

Index

Moosehide Village (Moosehide),
20–24, *21*, 44, *50*, 89, 215;
administration of, 213;
celebrations at, 136, 172,
173, 175, 176, 215; and Chief
Isaac, 109–110, 172, *261*;
ethnographic research in, 239–
241, 245; Han chiefs at, 93; as
home to Han elders, xxvii, xxx;
missionaries at, 9, 25; population
of, 37; salmon fishing at, 60;
settlement patterns in, 207,
246, 253; social organization
of, 91. *See also* Isaac, Chief and
Flewelling, Frederick
Murray, Alexander Hunter, 3–5, 12,
30, 36, 171, 179–180, 196, 198,
242
music: drum, 115, 172, 176; drum-
beating stick, 172; fiddle,
xxix, 136, 173–175, 196–197,
217, 235; guitar, xxix; revival,
176–177; songs, 123, 125, 133,
137, 171–173, 177, 215. *See also*
dancing
muskrat, 6, 54, 48, 74

Nagano, Debbie, xxv, xxvi, 115, 177,
239
Nathaniel, Johnny, 167
Nation River, xxxix, 44, 55–57, 69,
75, 78, 245
National Park Service (NPS), xix,
xxv, 113, 214, 240. *See also*
Yukon–Charley Rivers National
Preserve
Native allotments, 211–212
Native American Graves Protection
and Repatriation Act
(NAGPRA), 213
Nibaw Zhoh, xxii, 41, 43
Northern Commercial Company, 76,
107
Northway, 90, 177, 217, 234
Nuklako, 5, 39, 43; population of, 36;

potlatch at, 129. *See also* bands
Nukon, Dick, 254
Nukon, John, 254
O'Brien Creek, 207
Ogilvie Mountains, xxvii, xxxvi,
43–44, 56, 63, 70
Ogilvie, William, 10, 38, 46, 86, 102,
183
Old Crow, xxviii, 96, 217–218, 254,
266
Old Alec, 43
Old Henry, 43
Old Man (*Tsà'Wëzhaa*): rock, 35, 142;
story of, 143–157, 168–170
Old Peter, xxix
Old Woman (*Ts'àchin*): rock, 35,
142–143, 158; story of, 143,
157–160, 168–169
Osgood, Cornelius, xviii, 14, 46, 58,
71, 90, 92, 105, 116–117, 120,
126, 132–133, 137, 161, 172,
245

Parks Canada, 213
Patty, Ernest, xxx
Paukan, Cornelius, 217
Paul, Gaither, 133
Paul, Louise (née Malcolm), xxv,
xxxviii, 24, 35, 65, 71, 74,
105, 109, 120–121, 139, 167,
205, 218, 234, 236, 239; clan
affiliation, 92; life history of,
xxx–xxxi; stories of, 143–157
Paul, Mary Elizabeth, *205*
Paul, Susie, xxix, xxxi, 79, 112, 255
Paul, Tony, 113–114, 219
Peel River, xxviii, xxx, 19, 74, 92,
132, 137
personal adornment: beads, xxviii,
4, 82, 179–181, 183, 192–193,
226–227, 232; dentalium shells,
179–180, 191; earrings, 187,
190–191; face painting, 179;
feathers, 190–191; hair styles,
4, 179; ocher, 179; porcupine

293

About the Authors

Craig Mishler *(right) arrived in Alaska in 1968 as a VISTA volunteer, and received his doctorate in anthropology and folklore from the University of Texas at Austin in 1981. His first book,* The Crooked Stovepipe: Athapaskan Fiddling and Square Dancing in Northeast Alaska and Northwest Canada *(University of Illinois Press) was published in 1993. Now retired from the Alaska Department of Fish and Game, he is currently Affiliate Assistant Professor of Anthropology at the University of Alaska, Anchorage and heads a consulting firm, Vadzaih Unlimited.*

William E. Simeone *(left) has lived in Alaska for over thirty years. During that time he has been a VISTA volunteer, a paralegal for Alaska Legal Services, a laborer on the Trans-Alaska pipeline, a self-employed artist and an anthropologist working for the Alaska Department of Fish and Game, Division of Subsistence. In 1990 he received a Ph.D. in anthropology from McMaster University. He lives in Anchorage.*